INDIAN AFFAIRS ANNUAL 2007

INDIAN AFFAIRS

ANNUAL

2007

(In 9 Vols.)

Vol. 9

Chronology of Events

(March 2007)

Dr. Mahendra Gaur

PUBLICATIONS

KALPAZ PUBLICATIONS

DELHI - 110052

INDIAN AFFAIRS ANNUAL 2007

ISBN : 81-7835-529-9 (Set)
ISBN : 81-7835-630-9 (Vol. 9)

Published in 2007 in India by
Kalpaz Publications
C-30, Satyawati Nagar,
Delhi - 110052
e-mail : kalpaz @hotmail.com

Printed at : Salasar Imaging System, Delhi

To

SANDEEP and MANISHA

With Love

Government of India-Ministries

- Prime Minister of India
- Union Cabinet
- Agriculture
- Agro &Rural Industries
- Atomic Energy
- Chemicals
- Child Development
- Civil Aviation
- Coal
- Commerce
- Communications
- Company Affairs
- Consumer Affairs
- Culture
- Defence
- Development of North East Region
  Earth Science
- Employment
- Environment
- Fertilizers
- Finance
- Food Processing Industries
- Food and Public Distribution
- Forests
- Health and Family Welfare
- Heavy Industries
- Home Affairs
- Human Resource Development
- Industry
- Information and Broadcasting
- Information Technology
- Justice
- Labour
- Law
- Mines
- Non-conventional Energy Sources
- Ocean Development
- Overseas Indian Affairs
- Panchayti Raj
- Parliamentary Affairs
- Personnel

- Parliamentary Affairs
- Personnel
- Public Grievances and Pensions
- Petroleum and Natural Gas
- Power
- Public Enterprises
- Railways
- Rural Development
- Road Transport
- Science and Technology
- Shipping
- Small Scale Industries
- Social Justice and Empowerment
- Space
- Sports
- Statistics and Programme Implementation
- Steel
- Textiles
- Tourism
- Tribal Affairs
- Urban Development
- Urban Employment
- Water Resources
- Women Development
- Youth Affairs

Commissions and Councils

- CBI
- CVC
- CAG
- EC
- NCW
- NHRC
- Planning Commission
- UPSC
- Central Water Commission
- National Knowledge Commission
- National Development Council
- National Integration Council
- Inter-State Council
- Finance Commission
- Central Information Commission

INDIAN AFFAIRS ANNUAL 2007

Chronology of Events

(March 2007)

5402. (1-3-2007) NEW DELHI: Industry on Wednesday hailed the grant of infrastructure status to gas pipelines and waiver of excise duty on biodiesel by Finance Minister P. Chidambaram. This would be a big boost to achieving energy security and for promotion of eco-friendly fuel, the sector said.The industrial sector is also happy about the reduction of Central Sales Tax by one per cent as this measure will help in cost-effective inter-State movement of petroleum products. Gas Authority of India Limited said the tax relief, in the form of infrastructure status, would be directly reflected in lower tariffs in the pipeline system and would make the product more affordable to consumers. The new concession would also make additional funds available as such investments would qualify for tax benefits under the new regime, said a senior official. Mr. Chidambaram also provided infrastructure status to the cross-country natural gas distribution network, including pipeline and storage facilities integrated with it. The status, which gives a 10-year income-tax holiday, would help bring down gas transportation cost by 12-14 per cent. The tax break would mean a net saving of about Rs. 300 crore to fertilizer companies if they used pipelines. Integrated Research and Action for Development executive director Jyoti Parikh said the waiver of excise duty on biodiesel would benefit farmers and make its manufacture lucrative. She stressed the need to provide direct support to farmers by way of incentives including increasing the purchase price of biodiesel from Rs. 25 to 30 in view of the excise cuts. Petroleum and Natural Gas Minister Murli Deora hailed the budget that, he said, was well balanced with the focus on the common man. "When we reduced the prices of petrol and diesel on February 15, the Finance Minister committed himself to partly meeting the reduction through changes in duties. I am happy to note that he has fulfilled the assurance and met the long pending demand of the oil industry." The elimination of excise duty on biodiesel would give a boost to environment friendly fuels.

5403. (1-3-2007) UDHAGAMANDALAM: A two-day visit of the Defence Secretary, Shekhar Dutt, to the Defence Services Staff College (DSCC) at Wellington near here concluded on Wednesday. Mr. Dutt addressed the officers of the DSSC. He emphasised the need for a strong and well-equipped military. Efforts should be made to accelerate the economic development of the country.He also called on the ailing Field Marshal SHFJ Manekshaw at the Military Hospital at Wellington.

5404. (1-3-2007) NEW DELHI: Union Finance Minister P. Chidambaram on Wednesday announced an additional cess of one per cent on all taxes to fund secondary and higher education and expand capacity by 54 per cent in all Central educational institutions for extending reservation to Other Backward Classes (OBCs).This will be in addition to the two per cent cess that has been in place since the first year of the United Progressive Alliance Government to fund the effort to universalise elementary education. The additional cess has been proposed in a year which will see allocation for education go up by 34.2 per cent, arguably the highest in any sector in the 2007-08 budget. The budget proposals reflect the current concerns of the Union Human Resource Development (HRD) Ministry: increasing access to secondary education as more students complete upper primary classes - courtesy the Sarva Shiksha Abhiyan (SSA) to universalise elementary education - and providing for a 54 per cent increase in intake in all Central educational institutions over the next three years in keeping with the 93rd Constitutional Amendment to extend reservation of seats in higher educational institutions to the OBCs without affecting the general category. School education gets primacy and the Finance Minister has proposed to increase the allocation by about 35 per cent from Rs. 17,133 crore in the ongoing fiscal to Rs. 23,142 crore in 2007-08. Of this, the SSA will get the lion's share of Rs. 10,671 crore. In view of the shortage of good teachers, allocation for teachers' training institutions has been enhanced from Rs. 162 crore to Rs. 450 crore and there is a proposal to appoint 2,00,000 more teachers and construct 5,00,000 more classrooms in 2007-08. The Finance Minster has conceded a long-pending demand of the HRD Ministry for extending the Mid-Day Meal Scheme - already the largest school meal programme - to upper primary classes in 3,427 educationally backward blocks. Though schemes for increasing access to secondary education are still being planned, the Finance Minister has doubled the provision for secondary education in anticipation from Rs. 1,837 crore in 2006-07 to Rs. 3,794 crore in 2007-08. Similar doubling has been proposed for technical education in the Department of Higher Education from Rs. 1,736.34 crore to Rs. 3,870 crore as this is where OBC reservation-related expansion requires maximum funding.

5405. (1-3-2007) NEW DELHI: Bowing to intense political pressure, the Centre has banned further trading in wheat and rice in the futures market with immediate effect. Trading that has already been done would, however, allowed to be squared up. Speculation in the prices of essential commodities is said to be a reason for high domestic prices.Making this announcement in his budget proposals in Parliament,

Union Finance Minister P. Chidambaram said a Committee was being set up under Member (Agriculture) in the Planning Commission Abhijit Sen.The panel would look into the impact, if any, of forward trading on retail and wholesale prices of agriculture commodities. It would submit its report in two months. The report would suggest remedial measures, if necessary. It is understood that the last-minute addition to the budget speech of Mr. Chidambaram was made following the Prime Minister Manmohan Singh's informal meetings with some of the Cabinet colleagues on Tuesday. Among others, the Rashtriya Janata Dal had urged the Government to take concrete action to contain inflation. Most parties see trading in agricultural commodities as the main cause for high prices of essential commodities. The Left Parties and the Janata Dal (United) had also sought a ban on futures trading of farm commodities. As compared to 59 in January 2005, 94 commodities were traded in the commodities futures market till December 2006, generating a volume of trade equivalent to Rs. 27.39 lakh crore. On Tuesday, the Economic Survey, 2006-07, tabled in Parliament, noted that the futures market helps in efficient price discovery of the respective commodities and does not impair the long-term equilibrium price of commodities.

5406. (1-3-1007) NEW DELHI: The Opposition on Wednesday flayed Finance Minister P. Chidamabaram's budget proposals, saying they would do nothing to contain inflation or address the problems of farmers and the farm sector.The Bharatiya Janata Party said the "timid" budget would fuel inflation further and encourage hoarders. It protested against religion-based allocation for minorities."When everything was going right with the economy progressing at over nine per cent, [with] reserves at $90 billion and the revenue was growing by leaps and bounds, the Minister could have taken some bold steps to provide relief to the common man by way of personal income tax relaxations and reducing interest rates on housing loans and agriculture credit but he chose to lose the golden opportunity," the former Union Finance Minister Yashwant Sinha said.There was hardly anything for farmers. Addressing rural indebtedness, main reason for rural distress and suicide, was postponed with the appointment of a committee to study the issue. Similarly, on fertilizer subsidy, there was only a promise of further study without providing any relief to farmers.The Janata Dal (United) president Sharad Yadav said the budget failed to address the issue of food, farmers' problems and price rise, and warned that the entry of big corporate houses into the retail sector would result in suicides even in urban areas.The Telugu Desam said Mr. Chidambaram neglected the rural poor and there was no relief for the working class too. "No concrete steps were announced to control the rising prices and no relief was incorporated for the middle class," said party leaders K. Yerannaidu and R. Chandrasekar Reddy. Calling the budget unfocussed, Janata Dal (Secular) leader M.P. Veerendra Kumar said it disappointed ordinary citizens and farmers. Samajwadi Party leader Amar Singh said the budget was "full of rhetoric and hollow, with nothing for the poor and farmers, who were committing suicide." It did not address the pressing issue of inflation.Raj Babbar of the Jan Morcha said it was a "strange budget," more like a balance sheet. It gave benefits to industry but not to the poor and farmers. "There is nothing in it to curb inflation."

5407. (1-3-2006) NEW DELHI: Finance Minister P. Chidambaram on Wednesday refuted the charge that his budget proposals for the new fiscal have put an extra tax burden on India Inc.Replying to a specific query at the post-budget press conference here, Mr. Chidambaram said, "There will be no additional burden on corporates," while pointing out that the entire focus of the budget was to benefit the common man for attaining "inclusive growth."The objective, he said, was to contain inflation at about four to five per cent. "Nothing is being done to hurt the growth story which remains intact," he said and noted that the overall growth during the next fiscal was likely to be 9 per cent compared to an expected growth of 9.2 per cent during 2006-07. On the issue of putting ESOPs (employee's stock options) under Fringe Benefit Tax (FBT), Mr. Chidambaram said that ESOPs were also fringe benefits extended mostly to top officials and a tax would have to be paid on such perquisites. Explaining the impact of the hike in education cess on personal income tax, he said taxpayers in the lowest income slab would get a minimum relief of Rs.980, even after accounting for the additional levy. On Minimum Alternate Tax (MAT), Mr. Chidambaram said the tax proposals, which was more like an advance tax, would not impose any additional burden on the corporate as they can take credit for the levy. Turning to the dividend distribution tax (DDT), he said that the tax is to be paid by companies and a 2.5 per cent hike in the levy would not put any major burden on taxpayers, as most investors receiving dividend income are in the higher tax bracket. On the effect of the excise duty cut in petrol and diesel, Mr. Chidambaram noted that it was done as part of the package agreed to with the Petroleum Ministry at the time of cut in oil prices earlier this month. As for cement prices, the impact of the excise changes was to reward those who sell cement up to Rs.190 per 50 kg bag by reducing duty from Rs.400 per tonne to Rs.350.

5408. (1-3-2007) NEW DELHI: Defence spending continued to inch towards the one lakh crore-mark with the Union budget allocating Rs. 96,000 crore for the next fiscal as against this year's outlay for defence of Rs. 89,000 crore and actual spending of Rs. 86,000 crore.Referring to Union Finance Minister P. Chidambaram's statement during his budget speech - "Needless to say, any additional requirement for the security of the nation will be provided" - Defence Minister A. K. Antony said, "with this commitment, we are satisfied."Capital outlay on defence services (purchase of major military equipment) has been proposed at a record high of about Rs. 42,000 crore and accounts for just over 40 per cent of the budget indicating that the Government's desire for a 50:50 ratio between capital equipment and revenue expenditure remains unfulfilled.Of the three armed forces, the highest outlay at about Rs. 16,500 crore was for the Indian Air Force (IAF) followed by Rs. 11,374 crore for the Army and just over Rs. 10,000 crore for the Navy. This does not take into account Rs. 2,700 crore earmarked for research & development, a euphemism for missiles and other strategic systems, Rs. 320 crore for the joint staff, Rs. 168 crore for special projects and smaller amounts for the Rashtriya Rifles (RR) and purchase of rolling stock, mainly specially designed railway wagons for carrying missiles. The specialised counter-insurgency force for the Army would also get better equipment with the budget allocating Rs. 73 crore for the purpose as against a modest Rs. 15 crore last year of which it was able to spend just over Rs. 6 crores. On the revenue side, which accounts for Rs. 54,000 crore, stores (mainly renewals and replacements) for the three services account for over Rs. 21,000 crore. The Army gets over Rs. 14,000 crore for salaries for its 11-lakh force. This is about Rs. 750 crore more than the expenditure during this fiscal and accounts for nearly one-seventh of the total defence budget. The Army has also been allocated Rs. 772 crore more for stores and Rs. 3,300 crore for RR. The emphasis on the work being done by the Defence Research & Development Organisation (DRDO) continues with the budget allocating Rs. 3,186.47 crore as against this year's spending of just over Rs. 3,000 crore. The allocation under most of the eight accounting heads remain undisturbed with research getting about Rs. 100 crore more compared to this year's Rs. 510 crore and stores accounting for over one-third of the R & D outlay. This is besides the Rs. 2,700 crore allocated in the budget of the armed forces for R & D.

5409. (1-3-2007) NEW DELHI: In a highly calibrated budgetary exercise, Finance Minister P. Chidambaram on Wednesday announced a comprehensive package for agriculture and related activities with the objective of easing supply-side bottlenecks in future. He meanwhile put in place a slew of "anti-inflationary" measures along with the much-needed push to certain other sectors of the industry to sustain the high-growth momentum of the economy.In doing this, Mr. Chidambaram sought to ensure marginal relief to the "aam aadmi" and all other taxpayers by way of a small hike in the exemption limit. But he appeared to displease many other sections, mainly the corporates, by increasing the dividend distribution tax and including the Employees' Stock Option Plan, or ESOPs, under the Fringe Benefit Tax (FBT) regime.Although Prime Minister Manmohan Singh as well as Mr. Chidambaram sought to explain the seemingly "harsh" budget proposals as measures to contain inflation and sustain the high-growth trajectory of the economy while trying to ensure more "inclusive" growth, not many seemed to buy that logic.

5410. (1-3-2007) LUCKNOW: The Opposition parties on Wednesday urged the Election Commission to ensure that officers loyal to the ruling Samajwadi Party and politicians with criminal antecedents and mafiosi are prevented from influencing the coming Assembly elections in Uttar Pradesh. The seven-phase polls begin on April 7 next.This was the outcome of Chief Election Commissioner N. Gopalaswamy's meeting with the political parties at Raj Bhawan here on Wednesday. Mr. Gopalaswamy began a two-day election review meeting on Wednesday.On its part, the Samajwadi Party delegation of national general secretary, Ram Gopal Yadav and Transport Minister, Naresh Agarwal, dismissed the allegation of misuse of official machinery. They urged the CEC to lift the Commission's bar on the ongoing development projects as huge funds had been invested in them. Mr. Gopalaswamy received separate delegations of the Bharatiya Janata Party, the Congress and the Bahujan Samaj Party. In its representation, the BJP expressed apprehension at the violation of the model code of conduct by Ministers and ruling party functionaries. The BJP delegation led by State unit president Kesari Nath Tripathi and Leader of the Opposition in the Vidhan Sabha Lalji Tandon told Mr. Gopalaswamy and the Election Commissioners that all transfers and postings in the last three months should be reviewed. The poll panel was also apprised of the need to keep a close watch on the administrative and police officials considered close to the ruling establishments. A similar demand was made by the Congress. Addressing a press conference, the leader of the delegation and UP Congress president Salman Khurshid said that a website containing the details of the arms licences issued should be created. Mr. Khurshid said the poll panel was told to tighten the noose around 70 political leaders with alleged criminal antecedents. The BSP delegation led by the party general secretary Satish Chandra Mishra urged the Commission to ensure free and fair polls by checking violations of the Model Code by SP leaders.

5411. (1-3-2007) BANGALORE: Banking unions have opposed the budgetary proposal to acquire the Reserve Bank of India (RBI)'s equity holding in the State Bank of India (SBI). This is another way of saying that they will acquire ownership of the SBI.Joint General Secretary of All India Bank Officers Confederation G.D. Nadaf told The Hindu that this move, for which Rs. 40,000 crore has been allocated in the Budget, would adversely affect the banking sector.The RBI had 59.73 per cent share in the SBI. This should not be disturbed, he said. He suspected that the Union Government might later disinvest the shares acquired from the RBI. "This is not necessary at all," he said. Mr. Nadaf said the All India State Banks Officers Federation, of which he is the general secretary, and the All India State Bank of India Staff Federation had written to the Finance Minister opposing the move. Though the proposal to open regional rural banks (RRBs) in areas that had no banks was good, the Government should give priority to open regular banks in such places. The proposal to allow non-resident external accounts and foreign currencies would benefit the rural banks. The budgetary proposal raising the ceiling on withdrawal of money from banks from Rs. 25,000 to Rs. 50,000 per day for individuals and Hindu Undivided Families would help financial institutions. This would encourage people to save money with banks. Another good measure was the announcement of reverse mortgage scheme in the housing finance sector. Reverse mortgage was an innovative option being given by banks to the aged, he added.

5412. (1-3-2007) BANGALORE: Delivering the 11th Sir C.V. Raman Memorial Lecture, hosted by the Institution of Electronics and Telecommunication Engineers (IETE), G. Madhavan Nair, Chairman, Indian Space Research Organisation (ISRO), spoke on social applications of space technology.ISRO had come a long way from its goals of achieving self-reliance to "an era now when satellite communication is being used to meet societal needs," he said.EduSat was one such application, Dr. Nair said. "It has reached education to 10,000 classrooms in the country, and the number could soon rise to 1,00,000 classrooms, with a little cooperation from the educational institutions," Dr. Nair said.By 2012, India was predicted to be the country with the largest population of youth aged below 25. "Young students must be equipped with scientific and exploratory skills so that they are encouraged to dream and convert those dreams into products and services for the global community." Speaking of the need for "scientific humility", Dr. Nair said that "failure, in particular, is a part of any scientific endeavour, and must be seen as an opportunity for learning and growth." The failure of ASLV's first two flights was a case in point, he said. "It took us two flights to learn our lesson. We thought we had everything in place for ASLV-2, and yet, it deviated from its path and scattered into pieces during the launch. But I believe we owe our recent successes to events such as these." Among ISRO's forthcoming ventures, Dr. Nair said, was the Indian Regional Navigation System, which promised to be more effective than the Global Positioning System. This advanced satellite system would ensure landing and take-off in aircraft with a precision of three metres, he added. The Institution of Electronics and Telecommunication Engineers (IETE), with 52 centres across India might now be receiving a channel from ISRO's Education Satellite (EduSat) programme, according to S. Narayana, President, IETE.

5413.(1-3-2007) NEW DELHI: Prime Minister Manmohan Singh on Wednesday sought to defend the Budget proposals for the new fiscal saying that they were anti-inflationary as their objective was to check the price spiral through cuts in excise duty and import tariff on a number of commodities. Speaking to newspersons here, Dr. Singh said the UPA Government had taken another step forward in its ongoing exercise of fiscal consolidation and deficit reduction. "The budget certainly has the anti-inflationary effect... Inflation will not be allowed to get out of hand. We are moving in that direction," he said. Noting that the Government had set a target of nine per cent GDP (gross domestic product) growth during the Eleventh Plan for speedy development, the Prime Minister said that it would not hesitate to import certain essential commodities in the wake of constraints in domestic supplies. For instance, apart from edible oils, the Government imported 55 lakh tonnes of wheat this year. In keeping with the Government's commitment on increased spending on social infrastructure, Dr. Singh said health and education, especially at the secondary level, received special focus. The budget proposed greater emphasis on improving access to social services and a safety net. "Education and healthcare are the primary imperatives as far as this budget is concerned," he said. By way of the Government's response to tackle the supply-side constraints in future, Dr. Singh said that a number of schemes such as the National Programme of Pulses, Ground Water Resources and the strengthening of the Rain-Fed Authority should provide a fresh momentum in this direction. On the hardships of the "aam aadmi", Dr. Singh argued that the expectation of the masses had been taken care of by way of the hike in the income tax exemption limit by Rs. 10,000 to Rs. 1.10 lakh. On developing infrastructure, he said the Government was considering a proposal to utilise a part of the country's foreign exchange reserves. The matter was under discussion with the Reserve Bank of India (RBI). "We are toying with the idea of utilising foreign exchange reserves for infrastructure development. Things are under discussion with the RBI in this regard... This will materialise in due course," he said.

5414. (1-3-2007) BANGALORE: Chief Minister H.D. Kumaraswamy and Deputy Chief Minister B.S. Yediyurappa have said that the Union Finance Minister P. Chidambaram should have followed the "Karnataka example" in extending support to the farm sector. They have both voiced their concern on the growing inflation and the lack of specific measures to check it in the Union Budget. Mr. Kumaraswamy said: "I am afraid the common man will be increasingly burdened by higher prices in the coming financial year."

5415. (1-3-2007) GULBARGA: The All-India Democratic Women Association (AIDWA) on Wednesday demanded that the Union Government extend the National Rural Employment Guarantee Scheme (NREGS) to all districts in the country to prevent the migration of agricultural labourers, particularly women, to urban pockets in search of employment. Addressing a press conference here, president of AIDWA and former MP Subashini Ali pointed out that 40 per cent of the women agricultural labourers in the rural areas migrated to urban areas every year due to the absence of employment opportunities in their villages. The Government could effectively curb the migration of rural workers to urban areas by ensuring at least 100 days employment during the lean period by covering the whole country under NREGS. Ms. Ali said the migration could not be effectively stopped mainly due to the ineffective implementation and failure of the officials in charge to provide a minimum 100 days work. She said Karnataka, which had a strong panchayati raj, system had a good opportunity to utilise the scheme by effectively curbing the migration. Andhra Pradesh had done extremely well in utilising the funds under NREGS. Ms. Ali praised the Bidar district administration for providing 80 per cent of employment to women under NREGS and this should be copied by others. The Union Government, which was harping on reforms in all sectors, should change the rigid rules in NREGS and direct the implementing agencies people seeking employment should be compulsorily provided 100 days of employment. Ms. Ali said the period between April and July was the lean season in rural areas when there is no agriculture work and officials should take up employment generating works in villages.

5416. (1-3-2007) NEW DELHI: The Union Budget has made a provision of Rs.150 crore for the Union Ministry of Youth Affairs and Sports and Rs.350 crore for the Delhi Government for creation of infrastructure and facilities for the Commonwealth Games-2010 to be held here in Delhi. As per the note on Demands for Grants 2007-08, the Commonwealth Games-2010 are scheduled to be held in Delhi from October

3 to 14, 2010. The Government of India has agreed to guarantee free entry fcr all accredited athletes and delegations of all participating countries as well as to underwrite any shortfall between revenue and expenditure of the Organising Committee. The Government has constituted a core Group of Ministers (GoM) for coordination of all the work related to the conduct of the Games. The GoM in turn has approved constitution of various other committees including the Organising Committee. According to the note, the GoM has re-confirmed the site of the Games Village and recommended the manner of funding and utilisation of the Games Village. The GoM has also approved disciplines and venues for various events for the Commonwealth Games-2010. The agencies concerned have been requested to take necessary action with regard to finalisation of their concept plan and design based on global tendering. The final documents would then be placed before the GoM for its consideration. During the Games, competitive events would be held in 19 disciplines namely athletics, archery, aquatics, badminton, billiards and snooker, boxing, cycling, gymnastics, hockey, lawn bowls, netball, rugby, shooting, squash, table tennis, tennis, weightlifting and wrestling.

5417. (1-3-2007) CHENNAI: Chief Minister M. Karunanidhi has urged Prime Minister Manmohan Singh to implement 27 per cent reservation for students from Other Backward Classes (OBCs) in the Central quota seats in State government-run medical institutions. These seats are filled up through all India entrance examinations (AIPMPD and AIPGMEE), he said on Wednesday. In a communication addressed to both the Prime Minister and Union Minister for Health and Family Welfare Anbumani Ramadoss Mr. Karunanidhi said, "Considering the fact that only these examinations account for the huge number Central quota seats in medical colleges and the large number of OBC students aspiring for professional education, it is imperative that the reservation for OBCs should logically be extended to these examinations also." Welcoming the move to provide reservation for SC/STs in seats filled by the All India Post Graduate Medical Entrance Examination introduced recently, he suggested that it be implemented in terms of individual courses offered through a roster system so that these students benefit. This pattern was successfully followed by Tamil Nadu and the All India Institute of Medical Sciences, he said.

5418. (2-3-2007) NEW DELHI: President A.P.J Abdul Kalam on Thursday called upon the Sangeet Natak Akademi to study how satellite communication could be effectively harnessed to use the expertise of established performers and teachers to train talented students in the remotest villages of the country. He asserted that the medium could also be used to spread the culture of villages to urban areas."In addition to the pure art topics, the Akademi also has to address the Intellectual Property rights and create avenues for sustained income for the artists. Development of 'rasikas' itself is an important aspect of encouragement for artists in this world of electronic media and its strong hold on the masses," Mr. Kalam said at the Sangeet Natak Akademi Awards function here.

5419. (2-3-2007) KOCHI: Spices export from the country has achieved the target for the financial year 2006-07, in terms of rupee and dollar values, by January.Spices Board sources has said that the cumulative export is estimated at 2,80,658 tonnes, valued at Rs. 2,675.25 crore ($ 588.85 million). It was 2,71,591 tonnes, put at Rs. 1,945.12 crore ($ 440 million), during the corresponding period of 2005-06. The increase in value in rupees is 38 per cent and dollars 34 per cent. The target was 3,06,000 tonnes, valued at Rs. 2,500 crore ($ 545 million), and the achievement is 92 per cent in quantity, 107 per cent in rupee terms and 108 per cent in dollars. During January, 23,390 tonnes of spices, valued at Rs. 249.77 crore ($ 56.35 million), were exported, as against 21,160 tonnes, valued at Rs. 163.31 crore ($ 36.79 million), in that month of 2006. Spice oils and oleoresins such as mint products contributed 46 per cent of the earnings. Chilli contributed 19 per cent, followed by pepper 9 per cent, cumin 7 per cent, and turmeric 5 per cent. Export of pepper, cardamom (large), chilli, turmeric, cumin, nutmeg and mace, vanilla, curry powder and paste, mint products, other seed spices, tamarind, asafoetida and so on are higher, in terms of quantity and value, than that during the corresponding period last year. In the case of coriander, fennel and fenugreek, the increase is in value only. Other major spices have shown a decline in quantity and value. A total of 22,270 tonnes of pepper, valued at Rs. 230.32 crore, was exported as against 13,513 tonnes, valued at Rs. 114.18 crore, last year. Chilli accounted for 98,000 tonnes, valued at Rs. 513.25 crore, as against 94,715 tonnes, valued at Rs. 330.53 crore, last year. For cumin, this was 23,500 tonnes, valued at Rs. 179.25 crore, as against 8,304 tonnes, valued at Rs. 63.74 crore, and vanilla, 98 tonnes, valued at Rs. 15.98 crore, as against 30 tonnes, valued at Rs. 6.38 crore. Exports of curry powder is estimated at 7,800 tonnes, valued at Rs. 70.58 crore, as against 7,200 tonnes, valued at Rs. 61.99 crore, last year. During the period, 12,500 tonnes of mint products, valued at Rs. 833.97 crore, was shipped as against 9,850 tonnes valued at Rs. 527.75 crore.

5420. (2-3-2007) NEW DELHI: The United Progressive Alliance (UPA) Government came in for criticism from the Opposition and the Left parties on Thursday for its failure to keep its word on the aam admi. The price rise, the agrarian crisis and the "deteriorating" internal security situation dominated the motion of thanks on the President's address.Leader of the Opposition L.K. Advani said the fact that the Government failed to fulfil its promises had been proved by the results of the Punjab and Uttarakhand elections, and earlier in Bihar and Kerala. "I may have a difference of opinion with a major UPA ally, but I agree with the party when it said the Government should learn lessons from the recent losses."Referring to the aam aadmi, Mr. Advani said it comprised the lower middle class or labourers in the urban areas and farmers in the rural set up, both of whom were affected by the price rise. The President's speech made no mention of the challenges rising from the agricultural crisis and rising inflation. As far as internal security was concerned, the speech made a fleeting reference to the United Liberation Front of Asom's activities, naxalism in Andhra Pradesh and terrorism in the Northeast.Similar sentiments were expressed by Communist Party of India (Marxist) leader Basudeb Acharia. He said it was paradoxical that even as the Government claimed that the economy was growing at 9.2 per cent, unemployment was also rising.Forward trading, introduced in 2003, had led to speculation in the agriculture market. He criticised Finance Minister P. Chidambaram for setting up a committee to look into the issue of forward trading instead of abolishing it completely. According to Mr. Acharia, incidents of communal riots had also not found a place in the President's address. The Muslims in Gujarat and the Christians in Madhya Pradesh and Chhattisgarh were living under a deep sense of insecurity.

5421. (2-3-2007) NEW DELHI: The impasse in Parliament over the Ottavio Quattrocchi issue ended on Thursday with Prime Minister Manmohan Singh asserting that the Government had done no wrong and allowed the Central Bureau of Investigation full freedom to do its job."We are not afraid. We have done no wrong and have nothing to hide," he said.Responding to Opposition concerns over the inappropriateness of the Prime Minister making a statement outside the House on the issue, Dr. Singh said he had responded to a question from the media and had made no statement.The Government never shied away from having any discussion. Minister for Personnel Suresh Pachauri, who sought to make a statement on the issue, was not permitted to do so and the Government had to table it.The Prime Minister's remarks, in both Houses, came after Rajya Sabha Chairman Bhairon Singh Shekhawat mediated to end the stalemate that saw disruptions of Parliament for the third day. Leader of the Opposition L.K. Advani explained the rationale behind the deadlock linked to the demand that the Prime Minister respond. Dr. Singh, he said, instead of making a statement in the House, chose to address the press outside Parliament, which was "not appropriate." In the Rajya Sabha, BJP leader Jaswant Singh quoted from various documents to underscore that Argentina was included in the list of countries with which India had a pre-independence extradition treaty that was still in place. He said he was "aggrieved" that the Prime Minister did not find it convenient to come to the House and share whatever he had to say about the "shabby" matter. "He is the Prime Minister because Parliament made him ... A day will come when Parliament too will not pay attention to him and that is not a happy situation." Earlier, during a meeting initiated by Mr. Shekhawat between the Government and the BJP, it was agreed that the Leader of the Opposition in both Houses would seek a response from the Government, to which the Prime Minister would reply. However, after Mr. Jaswant Singh made his remarks in the Rajya Sabha, Opposition parties, including the Samajwadi Party, the All-India Anna Dravida Munnetra Kazagham and the Telugu Desam Party, also sought to speak on the issue. The United Progressive Alliance's supporting ally, the Communist Party of India (Marxist), also wanted to speak.

5422. (2-3-2007) NEW DELHI: Finance Minister P. Chidambaram on Thursday asked India Inc. to hold the price line and help the Government rein in inflation, even as he defended the differential duty structure announced in the Union budget as a reward and punishment for cement companies.Mr. Chidambaram hailed the captains of industry for bringing about a structural shift in the economy that could sustain the momentum for the next 10 years.A day after presenting his budget, which evoked a mixed response from industries, the Minister commended the industry sector for playing catalyst in the higher economic growth. In his customary post-budget interaction with top industry representatives here, he said the structural shift came about mainly because of industry and services. "A structural shift which can be reinforced, a structural shift which can be made permanent, a structural shift which can give us this high growth for 10 years as the East Asian economies demonstrated in late 1980s and China continues to demonstrate for the last six-seven years. It happened mainly because of the ladies and gentlemen gathered here and in similar chambers all over India." Noting that the domestic industry had come of age and was scouting for acquisitions abroad, the Minister said: "I am quite happy to look at your top lines. Quarter after quarter, you are recording double-digit growth rate. There is huge demand in this country for product and services. People have money in their pockets, people are willing to spend." However, as he expected yet another year of high growth during 2007-08, he appealed to industry to contain prices and help in fighting inflation. Referring to the differential excise on cement, Mr. Chidambaram said the Government intended rewarding companies which held the price line while taxing those which sought to rake in huge profits in the wake of increasing demand. "I am happy that most industries have not pushed up prices. But in cement, prices have gone beyond all reasonable limits. Therefore, we say, we will try to reward those having an inclination to hold the price line, but we will tax anyone using that opportunity [of huge demand] for making huge profit." The Government received no cooperation from the cement sector although the companies, when cautioned, promised to cut prices. Although cement units were scattered all over India, competition in prices was non-existent in view of the transportation cost, which rendered cross-country sale uncompetitive. "I am sure [the] cement industry will hold a meeting with us, we will discuss with them and encourage them to hold the price line." Inflation, Mr Chidambaram said, could be tackled in three ways - through fiscal measures such as duty cuts, monetary steps undertaken by the Reserve Bank of India and improved supply-side management.

5423. (2-3-2007) NEW DELHI: Perhaps for the first time in independent India, an Army court has sentenced a jawan to death for killing an officer following an altercation.A General Court Martial (GCM) sentenced sepoy K.C. Behra to death for killing Lieutenant-Colonel Saket Saxena on the outskirts of Srinagar on October 31 last. The GCM was held near Srinagar and headed by a Colonel-rank officer from a regiment other than that of Lt. Col. Saxena, said reliable Army sources.Both the soldier and the officer were posted with the Rashtriya Rifles, the Army's specialised counter-insurgency force operating in Jammu and Kashmir. The sentence is subject to confirmation by the Chief of the Army Staff and can be challenged in the civil courts. "In my 32 years of service, I have not come across a case like this," said a former Army spokesperson. Claiming that the sentence was "harsh," serving officers said such a punishment was never meted out in previous cases of killing of officers by other ranks. They said it indicated a carrot and stick policy by the Army to curb distress deaths. Last year, deaths due to suicides and fratricide (killing of colleagues) in the armed forces touched a record high prompting Defence Minister A.K. Antony to set up a committee of experts from the Defence Institute of Psychological Research (DIPR) to examine the trend and submit a report "within two months." However, further action was stalled for some time as he sought a presentation from the DIPR team. Mr. Antony, in the meanwhile, persuaded the Army to take remedial measures, including a liberalised leave policy and training select junior commissioned officers (JCOs) in the northern and eastern command - two theatres of insurgency where the Army is involved - to detect early any indications of angst among jawans. The Minister has also written to Chief Ministers requesting them to pay special attention to the families of jawans posted far away from their homes in an era of splintering of the joint family system that earlier absorbed most of the stress. On Thursday, Mr. Antony said in the Rajya Sabha that 50 JCOs from the Army Medical Corps had been trained as counsellors in both the commands.

5424. (2-3-2007) MANGALORE: The Federation of Indian Export Organisation (FIEO) has welcomed the Union Budget proposals for 2007-08. Walter D'Souza, convener of the FIEO committee on agro exports, told The Hindu that the proposal to reduce the import duty from 7.5 per cent to 5 per cent on equipment and machinery meant for drip irrigation, sprinklers and food-processing machinery was a welcome step. He said that 100 per cent Central Excise exemption for the food-processing sector and generation of bio-diesel would also give impetus to growth in the agriculture sector. These would sharpen the competitive edge of Indian agro exports in the global markets. "We are of the opinion that Indian agro exports can generate higher return for the Indian agriculture produce provided the benefits proposed in the Budget are substantially raised to the desirable levels," Mr. D'Souza said. According to the Central Statistical Organisation, 65 per cent of the Indian population was engaged in agriculture and accounted for about 18.5 per cent of the GDP, Mr. D'Souza said. In such a situation it was desirable for the Finance Minister to have made result-oriented large-scale budgetary allocations for critical agricultural infrastructure developments exclusively to strengthen agro exports, he added. The employment generation for the foreign trade of $78 billion was estimated at 160 lakh during 2004-05. This was projected to be at 296 lakh in 2009-10 with the foreign trade rising to about $150 billion, he said. This would be possible only if the agricultural exports grow at an average of 20 per cent a year, as against the present 10 per cent. To achieve this, the Finance Ministry should makes supplementary allocation to bring the Indian agro exports industry on a par with global standards, Mr. D'Souza said.

5425. (2-3-2007) NEW DELHI: Noting that the agriculture sector had witnessed sharp ups and downs, Union Finance Minister P. Chidambaram in his budget proposals said that the average agriculture growth during the 10th Plan period was estimated at 2.3 per cent, which was below the desired level of 4 per cent a year.Announcing that the goal for doubling farm credit had been achieved before time, he set a target of achieving Rs 22,000 crore as farm credit in 2007-08 and for adding 50 lakh new farmers to the banking system. Until December 2006, 53.37 lakh new farmers were brought into institutional credit system. Concerned over the stagnation in the production and productivity of pulses, Mr. Chidambaram proposed the expansion of the Integrated Oilseeds, Oil Palm, Pulses and Maize Development programme with sharper focus on scaling up the production of certified seeds. The government will offer a capital grant or concessional financing to double the production of certified seeds within three years. Public as well as large private sector companies would be invited to submit plans to scale up production of seeds. Financial mechanisms would be put in place for coffee, rubber, spices, cashew and coconut on the lines of the Special Purpose Tea Fund for re-plantation and rejuvenation of tea. To augment irrigation potential and speed up completion of water projects, the Accelerated Irrigation Benefit Programme outlay of Rs 7,121 crore in 2006-07 has been increased to Rs 11,000 crore in 2007-08. Of this the grant component to the States would be Rs 3,580 crore, an increase from Rs 2,350 crore. He also proposed a scheme for ground water recharge by diverting rainwater into 'dug wells' with each structure costing Rs. 4,000. The requirement has been assessed for two million structures. The government will provide 100 per cent subsidy to small farmers and 60 per cent to other farmers. NABARD would hold Rs 1,800 crore in escrow for disbursement to beneficiaries under the Water Resources Ministry. He invited State Governments to come forward with proposals for repair, renovation and restoration of water bodies for management of water resources on the lines of the loan agreement signed by the World Bank with Tamil Nadu and proposed to be signed with Andhra Pradesh. Under the Rs 2,182 crore pact with Tamil Nadu, 5,763 water bodies having a command area of 400,000 hectares would be restored. The Andhra Pradesh agreement, to be concluded in March, would cover 3,000 water bodies with a command area of 250,000 hectares. Similar projects are being finalised with Karnataka, Orissa and West Bengal. In addition, the ICAR would set up teaching-cum-demonstration models of water harvesting in 32 selected State Agriculture Universities and ICAR institutions. To strengthen extension the Agriculture Ministry would work out a Training and Visit programme in 300 districts. The outlay for this has been raised from Rs. 50 crore to Rs. 230 crore. Mr Chidambaram has reduced the duty on drip and sprinkler irrigation and food processing machinery from 7.5 to 5 per cent. He maintained a "status quo" on crucial areas. For instance, he announced that the interest subvention scheme for short-term crop loan; the National Agricultural Insurance Scheme, the Rehabilitation Package for Farmers in 31 suicide districts would "continue."

5426. (2-3-2007) NEW DELHI : The Supreme Court on Thursday said its verdict in a case involving Railway Minister Lalu Prasad and his wife Rabri Devi could not be applied to the case of disproportionate assets against U.P. Chief Minister Mulayam Singh.Mr. Singh, citing a majority judgment in that case, said that public interest litigation petitions could not be filed to settle personal scores.The Bench maintained that "the said decision has no application to the facts of this case. The case against Mr. Lalu pertained to a pending criminal case and PIL is totally foreign to pending criminal proceedings. The case on hand does not relate to any pending criminal proceedings."The Bench said: "We are concerned in this case not with the merits of the allegations. An enquiry should not be shut out on the threshold because a political opponent of a person with political differences raises an allegation of commission of an offence."In this case, voluminous documents by way of sale deeds, income tax returns and assessment orders and photographs of the properties allegedly acquired by the accused had been filed. "In our opinion, the minuteness of the details furnished by all the parties has to be carefully looked into and analysed only by an independent agency with the assistance of a chartered accountant and other accredited engineers and valuers of property."On Mr. Singh's contention that the properties had been accounted for and the Income Tax department was looking into the matter, the Bench said: "The Income Tax department is concerned only with the source of income and whether tax was paid or not. Therefore, only an independent agency or the CBI could, on court direction, determine the question of disproportionate assets." The Bench directed the CBI ``to conduct a preliminary enquiry into the assets of Mr. Singh and all his family members (respondents) and if a case was made out then to take further action in the matter." The Bench asked the Registry to send, in a sealed cover, all the documents, sale deeds and statements filed by the parties to the CBI. On receipt of the report, the Government might take further steps, depending upon the outcome of the preliminary enquiry, the Bench said.

5427. (2-3-2007) MUMBAI: The Reserve Bank on Thursday said banks would continue to be exempted from maintaining the average cash reserve ratio (CRR) on liabilities of four categories - liabilities to the banking system in India, credit balances in ACU (USD) accounts, transactions in collateralised borrowing and lending obligation (CBLO) with Clearing Corporation of India (CCIL) and demand and time liabilities in respect of their offshore banking units.

5428. (2-3-2007) NEW DELHI: The Union Cabinet on Thursday cleared the merger of the state-owned carriers Air India and Indian, Information and Broadcasting Minister Priyaranjan Dasmunsi told reporters here. The Civil Aviation Ministry might be authorised to take all consequential and ancillary actions for a smooth and time-bound merger . The merger would enable the airlines to leverage their assets and capital better, and build a stronger and sustainable business. The combined airline would become the largest carrier in the country and would be comparable to other major airlines in Asia. It is expected that at the end of the third year of merger, the synergy benefits of approximately Rs. 820 crore a year would be available to the merged entity as against the estimated integration cost of Rs. 200 crore, some which would be a one-time cost. Therefore, the potential recurring synergies are expected to enhance profitability by over Rs. 600 crore, about four per cent of the current combined assets. The Ministry and the airlines are expected to complete the legal and procedural formalities in 16 weeks. After the legal merger, it would take 24 months for implementation, a Cabinet note said. The Cabinet nod came nine days after the proposal was cleared by a Group of Ministers, headed by External Affairs Minister Pranab Mukherjee.

5429. (2-3-2007) BUENOS AIRES: "We are carrying hundreds of documents and we have come fully prepared to convince all concerned - the judges, the government and the diplomats - that we have a watertight case," CBI Director of Prosecutions S.K. Sharma told The Hindu here on Thursday. These voluminous documents were presented to the Argentinean Foreign Office in a bid to obtain the extradition of Ottavio Quattrocchi, detained in this country on February 6 on the basis of an Interpol Red Corner alert.

5430. (2-3-2007) NEW DELHI: The Army has started implementing measures to curb incidents of distress deaths, which reached record levels last year, Defence Minister A. K. Antony said in the Rajya Sabha on Thursday. In order to detect signs of distress early among jawans, 50 junior commissioned officers from the Army Medical Corps have been trained as counsellors in Northern and Eastern Commands, the two theatres where troops are engaged in counter-insurgency operations.

5431. (2-3-2003) NEW DELHI: In a relief to those living in border areas, the Government on Thursday allowed mobile phone service providers to operate up to 500 metres of the country's international borders. Till now, the service was allowed only up to 10 km. "There shall be a 'no-service zone' of 500 metres width along the international border, where licensees are not permitted to provide wireless or mobile service. The licensee shall use requisite technology to ensure that the signals become unusable within 500 metres of international boundaries," the Department of Telecommunication said in a letter to all licensees (mobile operators). The telecom operators will also be required to create a 10-km 'buffer zone' along the Line of Control, the Line of Actual Control, Akhnoor and Pathankot areas in Jammu and Kashmir, where cell sites and radio transmitters cannot be deployed. "Periodic surprise checks may be carried out by the DoT or its authorised representatives, including security agencies, to ensure compliance with the conditions. In case any violation in respect of usable mobile signals in the 'no-service or buffer zone is detected, stern action will be taken according to the terms and conditions of the licence agreement, including imposition of financial penalty," the DoT said. In surprise checks conducted recently, the DoT's Vigilance Department found that most private cellular operators were violating the norm of restricting mobile signals within 10 km of the international border. But the operators said it was technically not feasible to restrict signals.

5432. (2-3-2007) NEW DELHI: The Lok Sabha on Thursday wished the Indian cricket team best wishes as it left the shores to take part in the World Cup Cricket competition in the West Indies. "The cricket team left for the West Indies and let us convey our best wishes," Speaker Somnath Chatterjee told the House amid thumping of the desks. And when Ramdas Athawale said "we want the cup," the Speaker remarked for that there has to be discipline and suggested "let the players not follow us." The remarks came after Mr. Chatterjee congratulated MP Navin Jindal for winning a gold medal in skeet shooting at the 5th Sardar Sajjan Singh Sethi memorial master competition at Jaipur recently. "I am sure the House would join me in congratulating Mr. Jindal on his commendable achievements," the Speaker said as the Congress MP stood up acknowledging greetings from fellow MPs.

5433. (2-3-2007) NEW DELHI: The Sports Broadcasting Signals (Mandatory Sharing with Prasar Bharati) Bill, 2007, providing for compulsory sharing of advertisement-free live sports broadcasting signals with all platforms of the public broadcaster on a revenue-sharing basis, was introduced in the Lok Sabha on Thursday. The Bill, introduced by Information and Broadcasting Minister Priyaranjan Dasmunsi, seeks to replace the Ordinance promulgated in early February to provide widest possible access to sporting events. Once the Bill enters the law books, sporting events of national importance can be accessed on All-India Radio and Doordarshan's national network. Besides DD1 and AIR's national hook-up, matches will also be available on Doordarshan's direct-to-home platform. The revenue-sharing format has also been incorporated in the Bill. In the case of television coverage, 75 per cent of the advertisement revenue earned will go to the rights holder and the remaining will be with the public broadcaster. For radio coverage, a 50:50 revenue-sharing model has been provided for. According to the Bill, the Centre can mandate that the Prasar Bharati will use a percentage of the revenue received for broadcasting other sporting events, which lament for sponsorships and space on television. Through the Bill, the Ministry proposes to provide legislative teeth to the downlinking and uplinking guidelines issued in late 2005 as some television channels challenged their legality in court. Penalties for violation include suspension or revocation of licence, permission or registration besides a fine not exceeding Rs. 1 crore. Once it becomes law, it will be effective with retrospective effect from November 11, 2005, when the guidelines were notified.

5434. (2-3-2007) BANGALORE: Key personnel from two global aircraft engine manufacturers who are competing to partner the Gas Turbine Research Establishment (GTRE) in the joint design and development of the Kaveri engine for the indigenously built Light Combat Aircraft are here to hold joint as well as independent meetings with officials from the GTRE. Snecma Moteurs of France and Russian combat aircraft design giant NPO-Saturn, both who are yet to reply to the GTRE's second (issued last December) request for proposal (RFP), are seeking to know the details and clarifications required. It is hoped that the meetings, meant to be debriefing sessions, would help resolve these issues. In 2005, the GTRE, a

Bangalore-based Ministry of Defence (MoD) research and development laboratory, realised that they could not independently develop a combat aircraft engine. They sent an RFP to three global engine manufacturers - Snecma Moteurs, NPO-Saturn and the U.S. Pratt and Whitney - looking to choose a partner who would join it in forming a 50:50 joint venture company (JVC) that would develop the Kaveri engine. Declaring a two-month deadline for replies to the RFP, a timeframe that ended in October 2005, the GTRE said they wanted the resultant JVC to get working by January 2006. But with the Hindustan Aeronautics Limited (which will produce the Kaveri engine once it is developed) raising issues over the methodology to be employed during the production stage of the engine, the GTRE was forced to issue a revised RFP last December, seeking more details. Both competitors (the second RFP was not sent to Pratt and Whitney) were unable to understand the clarifications sought by the GTRE in the revised RFP. Talking to The Hindu during a recent visit, Jean Paul Bechat, Chief Operating Officer of the Safran Group (of which Snecma is a subsidiary company), said: "We don't understand what GTRE wants. We gave a full proposal to their RFP. We answered what we were asked." Both Snecma and NPO-Saturn want the JVC to be involved in not just engine design but with production as well; for it is here that the real business lies. As per estimates, around 300 Kaveri engines could be sold. Mr. Bechat said: "We are interested in entering a full production programme. We have said that just designing an engine is not of interest to us. Just to undertake research on an engine, which we have anyway already done in the past, will be a waste. [The company] can't afford to spend money researching the same thing twice." According to Mr. Bechat, the full developmental cost of a fighter aircraft engine like the Kaveri would cost around Euro 1 billion and take four to five years to fructify. Currently, the Kaveri engine prototype K-9, a research and development effort undertaken by the GTRE, has been able to deliver 95 per cent of the desired thrust of 47 kilo Newton in stationary test bed conditions.

5435. (3-3-2007) CHENNAI: The All India Council for Technical Education is thinking in terms of letting engineering colleges in each region to form clusters. One of the colleges could then be designated as a nodal institution. The cluster colleges could invest money and send expert faculty to the nodal centre to train fresh teachers.Such an effort would address the problems of infrastructure and teacher shortage in engineering colleges, says AICTE Chairman Prof. Damodar Acharya. Explaining the AICTE's thinking, Prof. Acharya, told The Hindu here on Friday that the Council was aware of the situation where the number of colleges had grown and there was a faculty shortage. Even the available faculty was not adequately qualified - 50 per cent of them were mere B.E graduates. "Most of the colleges, rightly or wrongly, are in private hands. We cannot expect the private colleges to release their faculty over months or years to get additional qualifications... We will now ask 15 to 20 colleges in an area, say Coimbatore or Chennai, to form a cluster. One of the colleges could be a nodal centre, which can provide teacher training and upgradation," he said. "The nodal centre can do two types of training. One, train fresh teachers in lesson preparation, conduct of classes, classroom interaction, tests, etc. Secondly, we can take subject experts from different colleges, pool their expertise to improve teaching and thus raise education standards within the clusters," said Dr. Acharya, who was in Chennai to participate in an international conference on engineering education. The nodal centre could offer post-graduate education where teachers from the cluster can take the course work and go back to their own colleges for project work. By taking the experts in each cluster, "we can also create a national list of teachers or subject experts." Individual colleges could lend the services of teachers even for a week or so to train themselves in modules offered by the subject experts. This way, "we can cover the entire country without the teachers having to stay away for long from their colleges," he added. The AICTE Chairman said the colleges could invest a few lakhs of rupees each in the nodal centre to create centralised infrastructure and teacher training facilities. Dr. Acharya noted that corporate recruiters had not been visiting all the colleges within a given region. The proposed nodal centre could serve as a platform to offer a large number of students to such recruiters.

5436. (3-3-2003) NEW DELHI: A day after the Union Cabinet cleared the proposal for merging the two state-owned carriers, Air India and Indian Airlines Limited, Civil Aviation Minister Praful Patel on Friday said the technical and procedural formalities for the merger would begin immediately."One company with one name, one brand, one logo, one code and single financials is expected to be in place within the coming 16 weeks. This new airline, with about 112 aircraft with both international and domestic footprint, will set fresh benchmarks for efficiency and reliability, thus benefiting the civil aviation sector in the country, specially the travelling public," Mr. Patel told both Houses of Parliament. He said the Government was committed to ensuring that all legitimate employee interests, including their current compensation and status, were protected. "There will be no retrenchment and all employees will continue in the merged company. Besides, to keep the exercise as smooth as possible, the integration of manpower will be completed in a phased manner, on the basis of transparent and objective criteria. A well-defined grievance redress machinery will also be put in place." The new firm to be created by merging the two carriers will be registered under the Companies Act within the next fortnight, official sources said. As the first step, a new company will be incorporated under Sections 391-394 of the Companies Act of 1956. The Government proposes to register the new airline firm as a hundred per cent government-owned public company, keeping in mind the Cabinet decision to maintain the public sector character of the merged entity. However, the actual amalgamation and integration process will be carried out in phases over two years, especially to cater to the integration of the combined workforce of over 30,000. "It is estimated that this decision would result in the net benefit of Rs.600 crore at the end of third year of merger," Mr. Patel said. During the next week, the Minister is likely to hold talks with the managements of the two airlines and their employees' representatives in a bid to ensure a smooth and painless merger, sources said. The merged entity will be comparable with UAE carrier Emirates, which has a fleet of 93 aircraft, Singapore Airlines with 118 planes and Malaysia Airlines 110. The new company will work on a model, under which separate strategic business units will be created to look after different streams such as passenger airline, cargo, low-cost carrier, Maintenance-Repair-Overhaul, engineering and catering.

5437. (3-3-2007) NEW DELHI: The Centre on Friday announced a package for promotion of micro and small enterprises that called for a comprehensive study to assess the needs and scope of government intervention required for enhancing the competitiveness of micro and small enterprises in the service/business sector.Making a statement in the Rajya Sabha, Minister for Small Scale Industries and Agro and Rural Industries Mahavir Prasad said, the package fulfilled the requirement in the National Common Minimum Programme for promoting economic growth that was employment-oriented. The Government would soon enact a law on limited liability partnerships covering among others, micro, small and medium enterprises to facilitate infusion of equity and venture capital funding in these enterprises. A technological mission would be established to assist small and medium enterprises in technology development, energy conservation and pollution mitigation. Mr. Prasad said that 50,000 entrepreneurs would be trained in information technology, catering, agro and food processing, pharmaceuticals and biotechnology through specialised courses. A new scheme would be formulated to provide financial assistance to select management/business schools and technical institutes to conduct tailor-made courses. Five select universities/colleges would be financed to run 1,200 entrepreneurial clubs. Under the package, the existing guidelines of the Small Industries Cluster Development Programme—renamed Micro and Small Enterprises Cluster Development, would be reviewed to accelerate holistic development of clusters. The Small Industries Development Bank of India (SIDBI) would scale up and strengthen its credit operations for micro enterprises and cover 50 lakh additional beneficiaries over five years beginning 2006-07. The Government would provide grant to the SIDBI to enable it to create a Risk Capital Fund, as a pilot scheme, in 2006-07 to provide demand-based loans to micro enterprises. The SIDBI's direct lending operations would be expanded by increasing the number of branches from 56 to 100 in two years beginning 2006-07. The eligible loan limit under the Credit Guarantee Fund Scheme would be raised to Rs.50 lakh. The credit guarantee cover would be raised from 75 per cent to 80 per cent for micro enterprises for loans upto Rs.5 lakh. The Government would examine the feasibility of increasing the General Excise Exemption limit, he said. The Minister said that four training-cum-product development centres for agro and food processing industries would be set up at identified existing Small Industries Service Institutes. The Central Footwear Training Institute at Chennai and Agra would be further strengthened. Vertical Shaft Brick Kiln Technology would be promoted for adoption by small and micro enterprises engaged in manufacturing bricks to make them energy efficient and eco-friendly. For this one time capital subsidy, limited to 30 per cent of the cost or Rs 2 lakh, whichever is less would be provided. Under the Credit Guarantee Fund Scheme,

80 per cent guarantee cover would be provided to micro and small enterprises operated or owned by women.

5438. (3-3-2007) HYDERABAD: Director-General, Ordnance Services, Lieutenant General D. D. S. Sandhu on Thursday said focus would be laid on modernising weaponry as the Centre had hiked allocations to the Defence sector this year.The Central Government had allotted Rs. 96,000 crores in the budget that was presented on Wednesday. This was an increase of Rs.7, 000 crores when compared to last year. Interacting with media persons, Lt. Gen. Sandhu said that it was a good budget would be helpful for army, navy and air force to procure modern equipment. The capital expenditure of Rs.41, 922 crores in this year's budget would fund latest equipment in all the three wings. He came to the city to attend a two-day biennial conference of senior ordnance officers of Army Ordnance Corps (AOC). Forty-five officers would attend the conference to discuss various issues related to the management of ammunition, indigenisation and enhancement of material support to the army. The conference would also review achievements in sports, adventure and other regimental activities in AOC. Referring to a series of suicides reported in the army, he said necessary steps were being taken to prevent such incidents in the future. "We are utilising services of psychiatrists for giving treatment to soldiers," he said, and added that a foolproof mechanism was also adopted for recruiting soldiers. Lt. Gen. Sandhu, earlier, reviewed the parade presented by AOC contingent.

5439. (3-3-2007) NEW DELHI: Business in both Houses of Parliament was affected on Friday with the Samajwadi Party, along with the Telugu Desam Party, the Asom Gana Parishad and the All-India Anna Dravida Munnetra Kazhagam, staging a noisy protest. They were agitated over the ordering of a Central Bureau of Investigation probe into the assets of Uttar Pradesh Chief Minister Mulayam Singh. They alleged that the Congress was behind the "political conspiracy."The solidarity among the parties, demonstrated the other day outside Parliament over the anti-media order of Andhra Pradesh, was witnessed in the Lok Sabha. As SP members, led by Akhilesh Yadav, trooped into the well of the House, AGP and TDP members stood in the aisle or at their desk.Congress members from Uttar Pradesh, Rajesh Mishra, Surendra Goyal, Jitin Prasad and Bijender Singh, and Sarvey Satyanarayana from Andhra Pradesh countered the slogan-shouting by the SP members, even as Rahul Gandhi and Sonia Gandhi watched the happenings.Speaker Somnath Chatterjee adjourned the House twice during question hour and later adjourned it for the day, expressing anguish over the behaviour of some members. Appealing for cooperation, he said people were criticising MPs for the goings-on in the House.In the Rajya Sabha too, there was a furore over the CBI probe ordered by the Supreme Court, causing two adjournments.SP leader Amar Singh was seen displaying a compact disc, allegedly containing a conversation between a correspondent of a television channel and the person whose public interest litigation petition against Mr. Mulayam Singh in the apex court on disproportionate assets led to the CBI probe.

5440. (3-3-2007) NEW DELHI: The Centre has accorded clearances to three irrigation projects — Godavari Lift Irrigation Scheme, Guthpa and Alisagar— located in Telangana region and lift irrigation schemes.The projects were held up after the Central Water Commission held that they were not comparable to the gravity projects while the Chief Minister Y.S. Rajasekhara Reddy argued that these projects were in drought-prone districts and there was no alternate water source for providing irrigation to these areas. The move is bound to give a major fillip to 'Jalayagnam' programme. Four projects have been cleared by the Central Water Commission. The Technical Advisory Committee (TAC) of the Union Water Resources Ministry, which met here on Friday, considered these four projects, a release by the State Information said. It is understood that the TAC has recommended the clearance of Godavari Lift Irrigation Scheme (GLIS), Guthpa, Alisagar Lift Irrigation schemes and Musurumilli Reservoir Project. With this all the necessary clearances have been accorded to these four project, barring Planning Commission's investment clearance. Meanwhile, on the power front, the Centre has assured the State of additional help to tide over the crisis during summer. A delegation of MPs from Andhra Pradesh led by the Minister of Energy and Information Mohd. Shabbir Ali met Union Power Minister Sushil Kumar Shinde and apprised him of the looming power crisis in the State. The Union Minister said that he would review the situation and announce by next week what the Centre could do to ease the power situation in Andhra Pradesh. The delegation consisted of D. Vital Rao, Nizamuddin, A. Venkatarama Reddy, A. Saipratap, Y.S. Vivekananda Reddy, Rajamohana Reddy, Nandi Yellaiah, K.S. Rao, Madhu Yakshi, Girish Sanghi, Botcha Jhansi.

5441. (3-3-2007) NEW DELHI: Whenever a labour court or an industrial tribunal orders reinstatement of a workman, payment of back wages is neither automatic nor consequential, the Supreme Court has held."There is also a misconception that whenever reinstatement is directed, 'continuity of service' and 'consequential benefits' should follow as a matter of course. The disastrous effect of granting several promotions to a person who has not worked for 10 to 15 years and who does not have the benefit of necessary experience for discharging the higher duties and functions of promotional posts is seldom visualised while granting consequential benefits automatically," said a Bench consisting of Justices B.P. Singh and R.V. Raveendran. Writing the judgment, Mr. Justice Raveendran said: "Any income received by the employee during the relevant period on account of alternative employment or business is a factor to be taken note of while awarding back wages. Therefore, it is necessary for the employee to plead that he was not gainfully employed from the date of termination [of his service]" The Bench said: "When the punishment is reduced by a court as being excessive, there can be a direction either for reinstatement or for a nominal lump sum compensation. And if reinstatement is directed, it can be effective either prospectively from the date of such substitution of punishment [in which event, there is no continuity of service] or retrospectively, from the date on which termination [from service] was imposed." The Bench said,

"In cases where misconduct is held proved and reinstatement itself is a consequential benefit arising from imposition of a lesser punishment, award of back wages for the period the employee has not worked may amount to rewarding the delinquent employee and punishing the employer for taking action for misconduct. That should be avoided. In such cases, even where continuity of service is directed, it should be only for purposes of pensionary/retirement benefits, and not for increments, promotions, etc."

5442. (3-3-2007) NEW DELHI: Officers at the rank of Joint Secretary in the Centre can authorise orders for tapping of telephone "in unavoidable circumstances," according to the new telephone tapping guidelines that came into effect on Friday.According to the guidelines, only the Union Home Secretary at the Central level and Secretary, in charge of the Home Department at the State-level, can issue directions for interception of any message."In unavoidable circumstances, such order may be made by an officer, not below the rank of Joint Secretary at the Centre, who has been duly authorised by the Union Home Secretary or the State Home Secretary," the notification said. The direction for interception will remain in force, unless revoked earlier, for not more than 60 days from the date of issuing. These directions can be renewed, but cannot remain in force beyond a total period of 180 days. The guidelines require telecom operators to appoint two nodal officers for scrutiny of all the requests for interception from authorised security agencies. The Supreme Court, which is hearing the phone tapping controversy involving Samajwadi Party leader Amar Singh, on Friday granted one week to the Centre to place on record the fresh guidelines issued by the Department of Telecom. The Bench headed by Justice C.K. Thakker asked the Centre to furnish a copy of the guidelines to Mr. Amar Singh's counsel while adjourning the matter for two weeks.

5443. (3-3-2007) NEW DELHI: The Centre on Friday announced a package for promotion of micro and small enterprises that called for a comprehensive study to assess the needs and scope of government intervention required for enhancing the competitiveness of micro and small enterprises in the service/business sector.Making a statement in the Rajya Sabha, Minister for Small-Scale Industries and Agro and Rural Industries Mahavir Prasad said, the package fulfilled the requirement in the National Common Minimum Programme for promoting economic growth that was employment-oriented.The Government would soon enact a law on limited liability partnerships covering among others, micro, small and medium enterprises to facilitate infusion of equity and venture capital funding in these enterprises

5444. (3-3-2007) CHENNAI : The Telecom Regulatory Authority of India has released a consultation paper on issues relating to DTH (Direct-To-Home) services. Various regulatory issues arising out of the provision of the DTH television service have been discussed in the paper, says a release.

5445. (3-3-2007) NEW DELHI: Even as the rate of inflation eased marginally to 6.05 per cent during the week ended February 17, thanks mainly to the effect of cheaper transportation fuels and decline in prices of certain essential food articles and a few manufactured goods, a section of the core sector, such as cement and steel, appears to be headed for a confrontation with the Government. Having put in place a differential excise structure in the budget for 2007-08 as a sort of reward/punishment system for cement companies, Finance Minister P. Chidambaram, at his customary interaction the very next day, appealed to the captains of industry to hold the price line and help the Government in staving off inflation. However, instead of obliging the Minister, not only certain large cement companies but also a number of primary steel producers almost promptly responded by revising upwards the prices of their commodities in an act of apparent "defiance". What steps the Government takes to counter the challenge now remains to be seen. In the event, although the point-to-point inflation based on the wholesale prices index (WPI) had just about started its downward journey from the level of 6.63 per cent in the previous week but still far away from the Reserve Bank of India's "comfort zone" of 5-5.5 per cent for the current fiscal, the higher prices of the essential construction materials are likely to reverse the trend again. However, the fact remains that the measures announced in the budget to fight inflation would take some time to make an effective impact.

5446. (3-3-2007) NEW DELHI: Holding that prima facie there were irregularities in the appointment and promotions of 164 Assistant Professors of the All-India Institute of Medical Sciences (AIIMS), the Supreme Court on Friday directed the High Court to examine afresh a PIL challenging their legality. A Bench of Justices S.B. Sinha and Markandeya Katju felt that since the allegations were serious in nature the High Court ought not to have dismissed the PIL merely on the question of the locus standi of the petitioner. When Addtional Solicitor-General Vikas Singh, appearing for the Centre, tried to defend the appointments, the Bench remarked, "The AIIMS is ailing, it needs a cure," and accordingly directed that the High Court will examine the complaint on the merits of the case. The Bench passed the directions while disposing of an appeal filed by Dr. Sarman Singh an Additional Professor challenging the appointment of 164 Assistant Professors of whom 84 were subsequently promoted as Associate Professors. The said appointments were made between 1995 and 2000 and 84 of them were granted ad hoc promotions. Dr. Singh filed a PIL in the High Court challenging the appointments and promotions as illegal, but a Division Bench dismissed the same on the ground that the petitioner had no "locus standi."

5447. (3-3-2007) NEW DELHI: Sabyasachi Bhattacharya, former Vice-Chancellor of Visva-Bharati University (Santiniketan), has been appointed Chairman of the Indian Council of Historical Research (ICHR). He will hold the office for three years from the day he takes charge.

5448. (3-3-2007) NEW DELHI: Lt. Gen. Saibal Mukherjee took over as Director-General of the Army's Medical Services (DGMS) here on Friday.

5449. (3-3-2007) NEW DELHI: The Union Cabinet has approved the re-introduction of the bill for prevention and control of communal violence and for effective rehabilitation of victims of such incidents. "The Communal Violence (Prevention, Control and Rehabilitation of Victims) Bill" provides for speedy investigation, imposition of enhancement punishment for those involved in communal violence and provision of adequate rehabilitation and relief facilities for the victims. The Bill, among other things, provides for creating institutional arrangements to meet the objective and envisages the empowerment of Central and State authorities in discharging their duties effectively. Announcing the decision, Parliamentary Affairs Minister and Cabinet spokesperson Priyaranjan Dasmunsi said the legislation would be introduced in the Rajya Sabha and efforts would be taken to ensure that both Houses passed it in the current session.

5450. (3-3-2007) NEW DELHI: In another attempt to boost infrastructure, Rail Vikas Nigam Limited under the Union Ministry of Railways has formed a new special purpose vehicle (SPV) named Bharuch-Dahej Railway Company Limited (BDRCL) to implement the 62.36-km Bharuch-Samni-Dahej gauge conversion project in Gujarat. This is one of the port connectivity projects under the National Rail Vikas Yojna being implemented by RVNL. Western Railway had proposed to build a third line from Virar to Vadodara. The Bharuch-Samni narrow gauge line conversion has been proposed as part of this line. Conversion of the spur line to Dahej has been proposed to provide connectivity of Dahej port to the broad gauge network serving the hinterland.

5451. (3-3-2007) NEW DELHI: Haryana's annual Plan for 2007-08 was finalised at Rs.5,300 crore at a meeting here on Friday between Planning Commission Deputy Chairman Montek Singh Ahluwalia and Chief Minister Bhupinder Singh Hooda. The outlay includes a one-time additional Central assistance of Rs.80 crore for priority projects of the State. Initiating the discussion, Dr. Ahluwalia hailed the State Government for its fiscal performance, especially in terms of expenditure realisation and revenue growth. The State, he said, had set an example for others in development and private participation. In the last two years, while the Plan expenditure went up, the per capita income in the State also showed consistent improvement. Besides, initiatives taken by the State Government such as introduction of the VAT regime, he said, had also led to growth in revenue. The State, Dr. Ahluwalia added, should accord priority to further improvement of the rural and urban infrastructure so as to provide a strong base for development of productive sectors such as agriculture, horticulture, industry and tourism. Improvement in access to basic facilities would not only benefit the people below poverty line (BPL) but also act as catalyst for accelerating the growth process itself. The Commission members also drew attention to the growing demand for water and electricity in the National Capital Region (NCR) and said the issue was to be taken up with the concerned States: "Joint efforts should be made to meet the requirements for the region, with focused attention on accelerating development and improving the civic amenities in the State's Mewat district." Briefing the Commission, the Chief Minister said the development strategy was aimed at ensuring more inclusive growth and further improvement in the State's infrastructure so that the climate created for greater investment was further strengthened. He said a large number of projects were being taken up in public-private partnership mode. Rural infrastructure, he said, was being improved and a sum of Rs.350 crore would be spent next fiscal through the Marketing Board and Rural Development Fund. The power transmission system was also being developed at a cost of Rs.2,280 crore. For Mewat, a drinking water project was under implementation at a cost of Rs.425 crore. Mr. Hooda sought introduction of Metro rail in NCR towns such as Faridabad, Bahadurgarh, Sonipat and Kundli on the pattern of Phase-II of DMRC's project in Delhi. On agriculture, he said the State was pursuing crop diversification so compensation to farmers would be required. Among other new initiatives were the mega-petrochemical hub near Panipat and development of four new model industrial townships. On the strategy for the Eleventh Plan, the Chief Minister said top priority would be given to expansion and improvement of social services. Over 46 per cent of the Plan outlay would be earmarked for this sector.

5452. (4-3-2007) NEW DELHI: Demanding a high-level inquiry into the alleged burning and ransacking of Dalit houses by a group of Rajput men in Salwan village of Haryana a couple of days ago, social activists and political leaders charged here on Saturday that the attack was "planned."Accusing the police and administration of inaction and apathy towards Dalits, the fact-finding team of National Campaign on Dalit Human Rights (NCDHR), that visited the village on Friday, claimed that nearly 200 houses were destroyed in the arson and that the situation was still very "tense."

5453. (4-3-2007) NEW DELHI: Prime Minister Manmohan Singh has ruled out, for now, troops reduction in Jammu and Kashmir. He said such a step could be contemplated if terrorist activities ended in the troubled State.The Prime Minister rejected the contention that the Army was an "army of occupation." Troops were in the State to protect the citizens, their lives and liberties from those who believed in violence and terror.Dr. Singh's remarks on Saturday constitute a refutation of the statement made by All Parties Hurriyat Conference chief Mirwaiz Umar Farooq on Friday that India and Pakistan had agreed on troops reduction.The Prime Minister described his statement as "speculation." Apart from Pakistan and separatist voices, which have been demanding "demilitarisation," the People's Democratic Party, a partner in the ruling alliance with the Congress in the State, has raised the question of troops reduction. Dr. Singh's remarks, made on the sidelines of a book release function at his house here, assume significance because PDP leader Mehbooba Mufti met him two days ago. She met External Affairs Minister Pranab Mukherjee and Congress president Sonia Gandhi also. Ms. Mehbooba's argument is that since the Centre has been maintaining that militancy has come down, it is about time the Army made way for the local police. According to her, the Army, over the years, occupied orchards, school buildings, hospitals and private land for its use; the very presence of these pockets of security men constituted symbols of alienation. She told her interlocutors in New Delhi that should the Army vacate, say, from a village, there would be no reason for terrorists to target that village. On the contrary, the villagers would acquire a vested interest in making sure that militants did not come back to their area.

5454. (4-3-2007) NEW DELHI: Airing his disquiet over the disruption of Parliament since the commencement of the budget session, Prime Minister Manmohan Singh on Saturday said he was "relieved" that the impasse has ended."If Parliament does not function, it is not a source of rejoicing," Dr. Singh told reporters when asked about the deadlock in the Lok Sabha and the Rajya Sabha with the Opposition stalling proceedings over the issues of Ottavio Quattrocchi's detention in Argentina and the CBI probe against Uttar Pradesh Chief Minister Mulayam Singh. The BJP-led Oposition accused the government of initiating a "cover-up" by not acting swiftly to secure the extradition of the 69-year-old Quattrocchi. Calm was restored after Dr. Singh assured Parliament that he was ready for a discussion on the issue and that the CBI had full freedom to pursue the case. The Samajwadi Party, which withdrew support to the UPA at the Centre, also disrupted proceedings and accused the Congress of involvement in a "political conspiracy" behind the CBI inquiry to probe charges of disproportionate assets against Mr. Mulayam Singh. The Prime Minister was dismissive of the tirade launched by Samajwadi Party leader Amar Singh, saying "there is no basis in his allegation". Decrying the tendency to be suspicious of foreign influences, Dr. Singh asked people to take a more liberal view of the outside world while deriving confidence from the "greatness of our past". "Why should we be inward-looking and suspicious of foreign influences when we have so much to offer the world?" he wondered while releasing the book Cultural Heritage of India edited by art historian Kapila Vatsyayan. Emphasising the need to defeat forces that believed in an "exclusivist" culture, he asked "people to take a more liberal view of the outside world". Dr. Singh contested remarks in the media by some who thought that China was a closed society with an open mind and held the reverse true for India. "This should not be the case. We must derive confidence from the greatness of our past to be able to deal more confidently with the present and the challenges of the future," he said. Dr. Singh also spoke about the pluralistic values of Indian culture, which he said, proved resilient enough to withstand the test of time and impact of change.

5455. (4-3-2007) NEW DELHI: By-elections to the two Rajya Sabha seats from Punjab and Haryana that fell vacant following the death of sitting members, Sukhbuns Kaur Bhinder and Sumitra Mahajan, would be held on March 29, the Election Commission announced on Saturday. The election process will begin on March 12 with the notification, and nominations can be filed till March 19. The last date for withdrawal of candidature has been set for March 22. Polling will take place between 9 a.m. and 4 p.m. on March 29, and the results will be announced within an hour.

5456. (4-3-2007) NEW DELHI: There will be no retrenchment of employees due to the merger of the two state-owned carriers Indian and Air India, a top Civil Aviation Ministry official said on Saturday. "The Government has already made this clear to the employees' representatives and there is no change in the stance,' Civil Aviation Secretary Ashok Chawla said at a meeting of the Indian Association of Tour Operators (IATO) here. "In fact, it is going to be the other way round. There will be parity in pay scales and those getting lower pay scales may hope to look up," Mr. Chawla said. The pay scales and perks of Indian employees are generally lower than those in Air India. He said the merger would only lead to a win-win situation.

5457. (4-3-2007) NEW DELHI: The plea by various States against an increase in their share of funding for the Sarva Shiksha Abhiyan (SSA) from XI Plan has found support from the Parliamentary Standing Committee on Human Resource Development (HRD) at least in the case of the northeast. The committee - in its report on implementation of the SSA, the Mid-Day Meal Scheme and the Integrated Child Development Services Scheme in Jammu and Kashmir and the northeast - has favoured a further reduction in the State's share from the ratio of 75:25 to 90:10. Under the SSA, the Centre has been providing 75 per cent of the funds right through the 10th Plan period. As per the Memorandum of Understanding it entered with each State, this funding pattern is to change to 50:50. However, most States have expressed inability to pick up half the tab from the coming fiscal. In view of the small internal revenue base of the northeast and Jammu and Kashmir, the committee has said their plea for revising the funding pattern to 90:10 should be given serious consideration. It has also supported the demand by some northeastern States for making the SSA a 100 per cent centrally funded scheme. For, with the annual increase in the allocation for this programme, the States' share rises in direct proportion, causing an additional burden on their exchequer. Effectively, the funding for the seven sister States now is in the 90:10 ratio. While the allocation from the HRD Ministry stands at 75 per cent of the total cost, an additional 15 per cent goes to each of the seven States from the non-lapsable funds of the Union Ministry of Development of North-Eastern Region (DONER) as a special case. But the northeastern States are making out a case for the 90 per cent funding coming from the HRD itself. A similar 90:10 funding ratio has been suggested for the northeast by the committee for the ICDS Special Nutrition Programme also. At present, the Centre and States meet the cost equally.

5458. (4-3-2007) NEW DELHI: Finance Minister P. Chidambaram expects interest rates to moderate once the inflation rate declines. He made it clear on Saturday that the Government was ready to take further fiscal, monetary and supply-side steps to curb inflation. "Interest rate is a function of the monetary policy adopted by the

RBI. When there is tightening of the monetary policy, interest rates will also go up," he told PTI in an interview. In the last one year the Cash Reserve Ratio (CRR) and Repo rate had been revised four times in order to tighten the monetary policy, Mr. Chidambaram said. "Once inflation moderates and the RBI adopts a more accommodative policy, the interest rates will also decline. Interest rate is directly linked to inflation." Asked if inflation was a matter of concern, he said: "It is. If inflation is a matter of concern, high interest rates are also a matter of concern. If inflation moderates, high interest rates will also moderate." In the long-run, various measures undertaken for the agriculture sector would ensure higher production of wheat, rice and other cereals. That would lead to an improved price situation. The Fringe Benefit Tax (FBT) on Employee Stock Options (ESOPs) proposed in the budget was payable by the company and it would also apply to the ESOPs not cashed, Mr. Chidambaram said. "What has been stated is that ESOP is a fringe benefit and it will be taxed. The rules have not been worked out and the method of calculation has not been prescribed. It is only a policy announcement," the Minister said. Asked whether the company or the employee would be required to pay the FBT, he said, "it is a fringe benefit and obviously it will be on the company." Would it apply to ESOPs given before the budget and not encashed? "Of course, it will. The gain is taxed only when the ESOP is exercised. When the ESOP is not exercised, there is no gain at all." He shrugged off criticism, notably by the corporate sector, saying that it was on expected lines. "I don't think one should get too despondent about criticism or get too flattered by praise. One should take both in one's stride." Mr. Chidambaram said "the corporate sector gets an unduly large share of coverage in the visual media and the print media." The physically challenged who were promised a hundred thousand jobs did not get access to media, he said. When it was pointed out that corporate leaders who criticised the budget immediately after its presentation did a U-turn the next day during an interaction with him, Mr. Chidambaram remarked: "I didn't speak to them overnight." Nevertheless, he thought that the negative business and corporate reaction was expected because "everybody looks for what the budget gives him or her." He said reforms also meant changes in the agriculture sector, health and rural development and uplift of the Scheduled Castes and Scheduled Tribes, which is inclusive growth. He said the Petroleum Ministry's proposal for issuing smart cards for providing subsidised LPG and kerosene and improvement in delivery services for the farmers were a major reforms measure. "I believe we have not paid enough attention to the problems of HIV-AIDS, polio and problems like recharge of ground-water. I believe that we are opening the process for the neglected sections." Reforms meant providing funds for recharging 70 lakh water structures, their repair and restoration and massive programmes to improve production of seeds. "If all these are not reforms, then I don't know what are reforms," he said.

5459. (4-3-2007) LUCKNOW: To ensure smooth conduct of the upcoming elections in Uttar Pradesh, the Election Commission has directed that video films of the public meetings of all major leaders of the recognised political parties be prepared and screened. The District Magistrates have been directed to screen the videos and send their reports to the Commission, according to State election office sources here. Only officials on election duty would be permitted to enter the 100-metre radius area within the polling centres with gunners or shadows, they said.

5460. (4-3-2007) MAYILADUTHURAI: Conversion of the 122-km Villupuram-Mayiladuthurai section to broad gauge will be completed by December-end and train service will resume from January next, Minister of State for Railways R. Velu said here on Saturday. Sophisticated equipment worth Rs.16.50 crore had been purchased from Italy, Germany and Holland for laying the rail on bridges, including the one across the Coleroon. The section would have 15 crossing stations and five halt stations. Mr. Velu was speaking to reporters after inspecting development works being taken up at the Mayiladuthurai junction and between Mayiladuthurai and Kollidam. He said gauge conversion between Tiruvarur and Nagore would be completed by June. It was proposed to link Velankanni, Thirukkuvalai, Ettukudi and Tiruthuraipoondi. Railways planned to complete gauge conversion between Karaikudi and Manamadurai, Mayiladuthurai and Villupuram, Tirunelveli and Tiruchendur, Tiruvarur and Nagore, Vellore and Tiruvannamalai and Podanur and Coimbatore during 2007-08. early Rs. 1,076 crore had been allocated in the railway budget for various projects in Tamil Nadu. It was 60 per cent more than last year's allocation. Four new sections - Morapur-Dharmapuri, Madurai-Karaikudi (through Melur), Needamangalam- Pattukottai (through Mannargudi) and Dindigul-Kumuli (through Bodinaikanur) were being surveyed for laying rail lines. Mr. Velu said he would consider running an express shuttle service between Mayiladuthurai and Tiruchi, and the possibility of extending some trains. There was good scope for laying a broad gauge line between Nagore and Karaikal in the Union Territory of Puducherry. It would cost Rs.40 crore. If the Puducherry Government gave Rs.20 crore, the work could be started quickly, he said.

5461. (5-3-2007) THIRUVANANTHAPURAM: Union Minister for Overseas Indian Affairs Vayalar Ravi has said he is dissatisfied with the Union Budget as it has failed to make allocation for a Rs.100-crore corpus for establishing a welfare fund for overseas Indian workers. Replying to a question on what the Union Budget held for his Ministry, Mr. Ravi told The Hindu here on Sunday that he had sought a welfare fund for overseas Indian workers considering their contribution to the country's economy. He said the Government was offering many concessions, including tax concessions, to corporate houses and Special Economic Zones. While accepting the initiatives of the Union Cabinet, of which he was a part, to promote employment generation, investments and boosting exports, Mr. Ravi said overseas Indian workers, particularly those in the Gulf, were a community that was earning foreign exchange without expecting anything from the Government. He said the welfare fund would enable the Government to take up several programmes, including skill upgradation, resettlement of returnees, and steps for their welfare and protection in the destination countries during the Eleventh Plan. Remittances from abroad came to about 1.5 per cent of the GDP. The economic and social significance of this important segment could be judged by the spectacular growth in remittances from the Gulf. In 2005-06, India was the highest recipient of remittances from overseas Indians estimated at over $23 billion. About 45 per cent of these remittances, over $12 billion, were the contribution of unskilled and semi-skilled workers. There is an urgent need to undertake a slew of welfare measures for this segment, including returnees. The temporary migration of unskilled, semi-skilled and skilled workers, mostly to the Gulf, was unique in that the social cost of education or vocational training was modest while the economic and social benefits derived from remittances were significant. Mr. Ravi said there was evidence to suggest that remittances in the aggregate as well as per capita from the overseas Indian workers were significantly higher than remittances from others. Overseas Indian workers were at the lower end of the income scale; their remittances, however, not only support household consumption back home, but also provide resources for investments in the rural sector, particularly agriculture. Return migration could increase the incidence of unemployment by exerting pressure on the scarce job opportunities, he said.

5462. (5-3-2007). NEW DELHI: Child rights activists expressed unhappiness over the "inadequate" allocations for children's welfare in the Union Budget, particularly in the wake of the Nithari killings, an incident that focussed attention on the need to safeguard children's rights. f every Rs. 100 in the Union Budget, only Rs. 4.84 was set aside for children, according to HAQ: Centre for Child Rights. The Union Finance Minister reduced the allocation for children this year as against last year, when he had allocated Rs. 4.90. Despite claims to increase the social sector allocation, particularly for education and health, the child's share reduced by 1.23 per cent, the HAQ said. Education and child protection received better allocations in the budget compared to child health and child development. Out of the Rs. 32958.33 crore promised for children in the country, the share of development is 16.65 per cent, health 10.02 per cent, protection 0.92 per cent and education 72.4 per cent. With education receiving the maximum attention, the Government, once again, failed to focus on the child holistically, the HAQ claimed. With children being increasingly plagued by malnutrition, disease burden, the fall in allocation for health was a matter of concern. The allocation for child health fell from 0.55 per cent in 2006-07 to 0.48 percent this year. There was an increase of Rs. 673.46 crore in fund allocation for the Integrated Child Development Scheme (ICDS). However, this was inadequate to meet the Supreme Court's directive to universalise the ICDS in 17 lakh habitations. There was a shortfall of 8.2 lakh anganwadi centres in the beginning of 2007-08, with only 8.8 lakh anganwadi centres being operational. "In fact, the promised allocation of Rs. 4,761 crore is insufficient to meet the cost of the operational anganwadi centres. On a simple calculation, if we divide the increase of Rs. 673.46 crore in the ICDS allocation this year into the sanctioned number of 1,33,235 centres to be established, only about Rs. 51,000 seems to have been allocated per centre per year. Further, dividing the amount by 12 months, it comes to only Rs. 4,209 per centre per month," the HAQ said. The minimal increase of 0.01 per cent for child protection is largely due to the introduction of the Integrated Child Protection Scheme (ICPS) that was introduced in the current budget with an allocation of Rs. 85.5 crore. Child protection constituted a mere 0.04 per cent of the Union Budget. While the total allocation for education has increased by 34 per cent this year, the share of child education has gone up by only 21.34 per cent.

5463. (5-3-2007). NEW DELHI: The Centre has sought a report from the Jharkhand Government on the killing of JMM MP Sunil Kumar Mahato. The Union Home Ministry is understood to have asked the Chief Secretary and the Director-General of Police to submit a report by Monday. Home Minister Shivraj Patil condemned the killing of Mr. Mahato and described the incident as a cowardly act of naxalites. A Ministry of Home Affairs spokesman said that the security establishment would not be cowed down by such incidents. "The Government will continue to pursue its multi-pronged strategy to fight the naxals," he said. The Centre is in touch with the Jharkhand Government and has assured it all assistance to deal with the situation.

5464. (5-3-2007). KOCHI: Attempts to evolve a modern solid waste management system for Kochi received the much-needed impetus with the Jawaharlal Nehru National Urban Renewal Mission (JNNURM) clearing a city corporation proposal. The project appraisal committee of the Mission cleared a Rs.88-crore project for Kochi recently. The formal approval will be given on Monday.

5465. (5-3-2007). MUMBAI: Scientists and non-governmental organisations have demanded the scrapping of the Mashelkar Committee report, which has been criticised by the Left parties for alleged plagiarism. At a recent brainstorming session here, experts flayed the report on two counts - overlooking the amendments to the Patents Act and patentability of new chemical entities (NCEs). The desire of MPs, during a debate in April 2005 on the subject, should be respected and issues pertaining to the patentability of NCEs and micro organism should be addressed without bias for a cost-effective health care, they said. "This approach will also ensure an effective role of the domestic enterprises to promote access to medicine for all as recommended in the Doha Declaration on Trade Related Intellectual Property Rights (TRIPS) Agreement and Public Health." The scientists and members of NGOs included S.P. Shukla, Dinesh Abrol, Mira Shiva, Ashok Parthasarathi, B.K. Keayla, K.M. Gopakumar, Devendra Sharma, Amit Sen Gupta and Vandana Shiva. For the last two years, they said, the TRIPS amendment Section (3d) of 2005 had not been disputed by any member of the WTO and was a direct proof of the acceptance of the amendment made in Parliament. The technical committee, formed after the amendment, cannot deliberate on the amendment itself but had to decide whether any further improvement was necessary with respect to the scope of patentability of NCEs.

5466. (6-3-2007). MUMBAI: The Forward Markets Commission (FMC) on Monday said it would punish persons entering into real-time trading by opening terminals of foreign commodity exchanges in India, without prior approval of the government.

5467. (6-3-2007). MUMBAI: Indian stock markets closed deep in the red on Monday in line with other global markets and the benchmark Bombay Stock Exchange 30-share sensitive index (Sensex) lost 471.09 points on fears of recession in the world economy and sustained foreign institutional pullout. Among various sectors, automobile, capital goods, metal, pharmaceuticals and information technology are the major sector indices that ended negative. The Sensex dipped by 471.09 points or 3.66 per cent at 12415.04, and the Nifty lost 150.25 points or 4.03 per cent at 3576.5. Last week, some of the announcements in the Union Budget, especially the increase in the dividend distribution tax, hit the market sentiment negatively.

5468. (6-3-2007). NEW DELHI: The Centre has admitted in the Supreme Court that rules were "blatantly breached" by the All-India Institute of Medical Sciences (AIIMS) in the recruitment of 164 Assistant Professors in 2003.

5469. (6-3-2007). BALASORE: Pilotless target aircraft Lakshya was test flown from the Interim Test Range at Chandipur-on-Sea, about 15 km from here, on Monday.

5470. (6-3-2007). NEW DELHI: Faced with congestion in the airspace over Delhi, Mumbai and Bangalore, the Government is considering hiking the airport charges for airlines which operate flights during peak hours and slashing them by half during non-peak timings. The higher charges are likely to come into effect during the summer schedule, beginning March 25, Civil Aviation Secretary Ashok Chawla told reporters here on Monday. There was no move to increase the charges for the other airports. "We are trying to work out a system of incentives or disincentives for airlines operating services during peak hours [7 to 10 a.m. and 6 to 10 p.m.]. This will be a short-term measure," said Mr. Chawla, who took charge as Civil Aviation Secretary a month ago. He indicated that the airport charges, including landing and navigation charges, could even be doubled during peak hours and halved between midnight and 5 a.m. Preliminary discussions were held with the Director-General of Civil Aviation and the Airports Authority of India chief on decongesting the three airports. With the Delhi and Mumbai airports handling 30-35 landings every hour during peak time, on average an aircraft has to wait for 30-40 minutes before landing, burning fuel, let alone delays which have a cascading effect on subsequent flights. For a medium capacity Boeing 737 or Airbus A-320, the fuel cost is nearly Rs. 70,000 if it hovers at a height of not more than 10,000 feet for 30 minutes. Landing charges for this type of aircraft are between Rs. 12,000 and 14,000. Private airlines are already collecting Rs. 150 a ticket as congestion charge.

5471. (6-3-2007). NEW DELHI: A day after the killing of Sunil Kumar Mahato, Jharkhand Mukti Morcha MP, and three others in Jharkhand by naxalites, the Centre on Monday said the attack appeared to be a "retaliatory action" against the MP as he had been leading the anti-naxal campaign through a local citizens' body. Addressing a press conference at North Block here, Union Home Secretary V.K. Duggal said the Home Ministry had received a "first account" of the attack in a rather brief report sent by the Jharkhand Government. He said the JMM MP was also leading the Nagrik Suraksha Samiti (Citizens Security Council) and had been raising his voice against naxal cadres in the area. Replying to a question whether the Government would give security cover to all the MPs of naxal violence-affected States, Mr. Duggal said that a thorough review of all "sensitive and hyper-sensitive" areas in such States would be done. "Security is provided on the basis of threat perception and it is reviewed periodically. We will undertake the exercise in respect of MPs coming from sensitive constituencies." Mr. Duggal said the Ministry was in constant touch with the Jharkhand Chief Secretary and Director-General of Police and combing operations were already going on. " Neighbouring West Bengal has also been appraised of all developments and it is lending a helping hand to Jharkhand to catch the persons who were behind the attack," he said. "Joint action and joint task force which were launched in 2005 will continue on the basis of intelligence inputs. There is no need for a unified command on the lines of Jammu and Kashmir and Assam," he said. Admitting that the Centre had been "anticipating" such a daring attack on a high profile target by naxal cadres, he said the reason behind it was "marked improvement" on naxal front in Andhra Pradesh, Orissa, Bihar and Chhattisgarh where "good counter operations" had been launched by security personnel. To another question, Mr. Duggal said the Centre and the intelligence agencies were aware of the Ninth Congress of Maoists which was held recently somewhere in Jharkhand where naxalites had warned of launching mobile attacks. "This is an act of desperation by naxalites. The Government condemns it strongest possible terms. This incident will only strengthen our resolve to fight the menace of naxalism firmly on all fronts be it developmental, social and security."

5472. (6-3-2007). KOCHI: Chief Justice of India K. G. Balakrishnan on Monday urged the media to be a little more constructive while criticising judiciary. Speaking at the release of Neethi, a magazine on law, here, he said the judiciary was working under tremendous pressure. The infrastructure available to judiciary was not good. "There are a large number of pending cases. While criticising various judgments, the media may not be aware of the time taken for decision-making." The media should help in drawing the attention of policy makers for providing adequate infrastructure for judiciary. It should highlight the public impact of enactments made in Parliament. He pointed out that a recent enactment was passed in Parliament in five minutes. "People should get time to discuss such issues. Media should try to create awareness among the public on legal topics." He termed the increasing media coverage on judgments delivered by the Supreme Court and High Courts as a "good trend."

5473. (6-3-2007). JAMSHEDPUR: The Centre will consider in a day or two the Jharkhand Government's recommendation for a CBI probe into the killing of Jharkhand Mukti Morcha MP Sunil Kumar Mahato, Minister of State for Home Sriprakash Jaiswal said on Monday. There should be a thorough investigation into the circumstances leading to the killing on Sunday. "Whatever the State Government asks for will be considered." Its request for additional paramilitary forces would be looked into." The Minister dismissed allegations of misuse of Central funds provided for modernisation of the State police. He, however, cautioned that misuse, if found, would not be tolerated. Union Minister of State for Food Processing Subodh Kant Sahay, who accompanied Mr. Jaiswal, however, said funds meant for combating extremist activities and police modernisation were not properly utilised by the State Government. Praising Andhra Pradesh's efforts to control the naxalite menace through joint operations, Mr. Jaiswal suggested that Jharkhand follow a similar strategy. The Centre was prepared to provide all help to the State to ensure that such incidents did not take place at any cost, he said. Mr. Sahay said half-hearted measures to curb the naxal menace would not yield the desired results. The merciless killing of Mr. Mahato has sent out an important signal for officials and the State Government to put their act together and combat naxalism.

5474. (6-3-2007). NEW DELHI: Reiterating that the effective corporate tax rate in the country was already very low, Finance Minister P. Chidambaram on Monday ruled out any further cut until the tax exemptions were removed. In a post-budget interaction with members of the Federation of Indian Chambers of Commerce and Industry (FICCI) here, Mr. Chidambaram said: "[The] effective tax rate is not only moderate, but very moderate... the effective tax rate in India is 19.2 per cent. Show me one Asian country, one ASEAN country which has an effective tax rate of less than 19 per cent." It was not the scheduled rate but the effective tax rate that mattered, he said. Only when the effective corporate tax rate went up on removal of the existing tax exemptions, would there be scope for further moderation of the tax rates. On the issue of differential excise on cement as proposed in the budget, he said that the Government was not trying to resort to price control and invited industry players for talks. "We are not reinforcing price control... Government owes responsibility to the people of India to moderate prices where prices seem to have risen unreasonably. Whether they have risen unreasonably could be discussed. But if they have risen unreasonably, surely the Government has obligation to moderate prices." To a suggestion by a member that a committee should look into moderation of corporate tax rates, he said: "While I welcome your offer to join a committee to examine what the moderation would be, that committee should also examine how the effective tax rate can rise to ASEAN level." The withdrawal of the 10 per cent surcharge on corporate tax for small firms and companies was a clear indication that the Government wanted to moderate taxes.

5475. (6-3-2007). NEW DELHI: An influential section of the legal fraternity strongly favours association of an "outsider" with the proposed National Judicial

Council, a mechanism meant for dealing with errant judges. At a seminar last week, organised by the United Lawyers' Association, former judges and senior lawyers were nearly unanimous that the disciplinary mechanism proposed in the Judges (Inquiry) Bill, 2006 [Bill no. 97 of 2006] remained a closed shop and ought to be re-examined. The former Attorney-General of India, Soli Sorabjee presided. In his opening remarks, Mr. Sorabjee contexted the proposed measure in the larger felt need for transparency in all democratic institutions. He referred to considerable disquiet over the absolute powers the apex court had come to enjoy in the matter of appointments while the existing "disciplinary" provisions of the Constitution [article 124(4) and Article 218] had not proved very practical or effective. Mr. Sorabjee objected to the categorisation of "minor measure" as a form of penal action against an errant judge. He also pointed out the curious provision that a penalised judge "could prefer an appeal to the Supreme Court." Former Chief Justice of India J.S. Verma thought that exclusion of the Chief Justice of India from the jurisdiction of the Judicial Council was indefensible. He argued that the parallel between the Prime Minister (who remains excluded from the Lok Pal regime) and the Chief Justice was misplaced; according to him the Prime Minister had to be necessarily entrusted with enormous executive functions whereas the CJI was merely obliged to deal with judicial duties, and therefore, there was no reason why the CJI should be excluded from any disciplinary arrangement. Justice Verma argued that the Prime Minister or the Vice-President should be associated with the Judicial Council. Senior advocate K.K. Venugopal endorsed the idea of opening up the Judicial Council and suggested that the executive should not be excluded from any disciplinary regime. However, he thought that presence of the Vice President or the Prime Minister would bring in questions of protocol, and, therefore, his preference would be for the inclusion of the Law Minister in the Judicial Council. His concern was that the chief should preside over the deliberations. Justice Rajinder Sachar, former Chief Justice of the Delhi High Court, strongly advocated opening up of the appointment and disciplinary mechanisms. He noted that society had a stake in such functions and these could "not be the preserve of a small freemasonry of the judiciary." Harish Khare, Senior Associate Editor of The Hindu said the judiciary had disappointed civil society by the manner in which it had wielded so far its total and absolute control over its affairs. He said the proposed National Judicial Council would not go very far because it failed to address the source of the mischief: the collegium arrangement. There was general consensus against various provisions such as "misbehaviour" before the commencement of the proposed Act would be beyond the scope of the Judicial Council or the provision that "no such complaint shall be entertained and inquired into with respect to any act or conduct constituting misbehaviour which has taken place two years prior to the filing of complaint."

5476. (6-3-2007). NEW DELHI: The Punjab Government should await the Supreme Court order on sharing the Indus river water with neighbouring States before taking any decision on scrapping Section 5 of the Punjab Termination of Water Agreements Act, 2004, as declared by Chief Minister Parkash Singh Badal, Union

Minister for Water Resources Saifuddin Soz said here. "It is in the interest of Punjab that Mr. Badal resolves the issue through dialogue and discussion," Mr. Soz said speaking to journalists on his completion of one year in office. If the States concerned asked, the Centre would mediate. On Sunday, Mr Badal said his government would scrap the provision, which allows Haryana and Rajasthan to get water as per their share existing in 2004, when the Congress government passed the Act. At election meetings Mr. Badal promised the people that the Akalis would scrap the provision if elected to power. He said the State did not have surplus water to share with other States.The Congress Government enacted the Act, under which the State terminated all inter-State treaties/tribunal awards with neighbours, which was yet to be given effect to. Section 5, however, allowed sharing of water with Haryana, Rajasthan and Himachal Pradesh. The Punjab Government's move came a day before the Central Public Works Department was to undertake reconstruction of the Sutlej-Yamuna Link canal that carries water to Haryana. Mr Badal, who was then in opposition, supported the Amarinder Singh Government move. Through a Presidential order the Act was referred to the Supreme Court. The Government sought to know whether the Act discharged the State from enacting the water agreements on the Indus river. With this, the construction of the SYL was put off.

5477. (6-3-2007). CHANDIGARH: Haryana Irrigation Minister Ajay Singh Yadav on Monday described as unfortunate and unconstitutional the new Punjab Chief Minister Parkash Singh Badal's statement that appeared in the media recently about a proposed amendment to the Punjab Termination of Agreements Act, 2004, to delete its Section V. Talking to media persons here, Capt. Yadav said Punjab had taken plea of being a riparian State and Mr. Badal was reiterating that no other State, except Punjab, had the right over the waters flowing through its areas. He said the Punjab Termination of Agreements Act, 2004, enacted by Punjab was itself unconstitutional and an encroachment upon the judicial powers. It was enacted without any legislative competence, was inconsistent with the statutory order of March 24, 1976, the statutory agreements of December 31, 1981, and the provisions of Section 78 of the Punjab Reorganisation Act, 1966, and Section 14 of the Inter-State River Water Dispute Act, 1956, he said. Referring to Punjab's contention that Haryana and Rajasthan were not entitled to surplus Ravi-Beas waters because of being non-riparian states, he said that the doctrine of riparian rights had been discussed and rejected internationally while determining the rights of States in inter-State rivers. Several Tribunals appointed by the Government of India for resolving Inter- State River Water Disputes had also rejected the riparian principle of sharing water, he added. He reminded Mr. Badal that the surplus Ravi-Beas waters had been exchanged in lieu of Chenab and Jhelum waters with Pakistan by the Government of India by paying Rs. 110 crore under the Indus Water Treaty in 1960. Haryana, being a part of the then Punjab, had full right to Indus River waters on the basis of equity.

5478. (7-3-2007). CHENNAI: The Reserve Bank of India (RBI) on Tuesday announced regulations on inter-bank liability (IBL) to control "concentration risk" on the asset side and also systemic risks that might arise as a result of uncontrolled ABLs. In a circular to commercial banks, the RBI said the IBL of banks should not exceed 200 per cent of its net worth as of March 31 of the previous year. However, individual banks may, with the approval of their boards, might fix a lower limit, keeping in view their business model. The new measures will come into effect from April 1. The apex bank said that banks whose CRAR (capital-to-risk-weighted assets ratio) was at least 25 per cent more than the minimum CRAR of nine per cent, namely, 11.25 per cent, of the previous, year, would be allowed to have a higher limit of up to 300 per cent of the net worth for IBL. The limit prescribed will include only fund based IBL within India (including inter-bank liabilities in foreign currency to banks operating within the country). The limits will not include collateralised borrowings under the CBLO (collateralised borrowing and lending obligation) and refinance from National Bank for Agriculture and Rural Development (Nabard) and Small Industries Development Bank of India (SIDBI), it said. The existing limit on the call money borrowings will operate as a sub-limit within the abovementioned limits. Significantly, the RBI also cautioned that "banks having a high concentration of wholesale deposits should be aware of potential risk associated with such deposits" and advised them to frame suitable policies to contain the liquidity risk arising out of excessive dependence on such deposits. Banks which are not in a position to comply with these requirements from April 1 should furnish a plan for approval to the RBI indicating the date by which they would comply with them, the circular said. In a bid to check hidden costs and inject more transparency, the RBI made it mandatory for banks and financial institutions (FIs) to mention in its loan applications the fees, processing charges and other details. In a circular, the RBI also made it clear that if a loan or credit card application was rejected, banks and financial institutions should give in writing the reasons for it. It also wanted banks and FIs to work out a transparent policy in this regard with the approval of their boards.

5479. (7-3-2007). NEW DELHI: There was no agreement between MPs from Karnataka and Tamil Nadu, who met Lok Sabha Speaker Somnath Chatterjee here on Tuesday evening, on a discussion in Parliament on the final award of the Cauvery Water Disputes Tribunal on the sharing of the river water.

5480. (7-3-2007). NEW DELHI: Union Home Minister Shivraj Patil on Tuesday said the slain Jharkhand Mukti Morcha MP Sunil Mahato had not informed the police of his visit to a social function at Bakuria in East Singhbhum district, where he was shot dead on Sunday, allegedly by naxalites. Giving clarifications sought on his statement in the Rajya Sabha, marred by a BJP-led walkout, Mr. Patil said though Mr. Mahato was provided with Y category security in view of a threat to his life, "I can categorically say that no information [about his visit] was given to the district police." The MP was surrounded by alleged naxalites including women and shot dead along with two security personnel and a party worker. Acknowledging that inter-State police coordination would prevent naxalites from taking advantage of contiguous borders to escape after committing a crime in a State, he said the Centre had convened several meetings to deal with this problem. However, some States had reservations about a permanent coordination mechanism or listing certain offences as federal crimes, in solving which the Centre could take an active part. "That is why we have asked for an understanding among States on the movement of the police from one State to another [in pursuit of naxalites]." The Soli Sorabjee committee had been asked to give its views on this issue and the Centre was keen on cooperating with the States in tackling certain types of crimes. "But finally the States would have to cooperate. If they don't, it will be very difficult." Earlier, Mr. Patil said the Government condemned the killing of Mahato and the Home Ministry was keeping a "close watch" on the situation. He listed the steps taken to help the States counter naxalites. Seeking clarifications, a large number of members including the former Union Minister Yashwant Sinha, sought enhanced security for themselves. Among the exceptions were Brinda Karat (CPI-M), Ram Deo Bhandari (Rashtriya Janata Dal) and S. S. Ahluwalia (BJP) with the latter opposing the plea on the ground that a tighter security cordon would cut them off from the public. Ms. Karat referred to the problem of State boundaries and pointed out that naxalites from Jharkhand were targeting CPI (M) workers in neighbouring West Bengal for politically campaigning against them. Digvijay Singh (Janata Dal-United) wanted to know why Mr. Patil did not visit the site of killing of a sitting member. Mr. Sinha said that since Mr. Patil had acknowledged the success of the Andhra Pradesh police's anti-naxal squad `Greyhounds' it should be replicated in other States. Arun Shourie (BJP) said it took an incident like Mahato killing to "change the Government's tune on matters like this."

5481. (7-3-2007). NEW DELHI: United Progressive Alliance (UPA) chairperson Sonia Gandhi has stressed the need for focussing attention on gender issues, including female foeticide, illiteracy and discrimination, against women. "Women may have more opportunities now. But we still have a long way to go," she said after unfurling a multi-coloured flag to mark the International Women's Day celebrations titled `Ananya' (The Incomparable) here on Tuesday. She asserted that the Government was giving top priority to the welfare of women and children. Ms. Gandhi said the Constitution entitled women to equal opportunities and rights, but in some parts of the land the rate of female foeticide was high and the gender ratio terribly skewed. "Girls are not being sent to school in many places and women face prejudice and discrimination at the workplace," she said. These issues should get focus at the Women's Day celebrations, she said. According to Ms. Gandhi, the Panchayati Raj system had brought women to positions of responsibility. About 12 lakh women in panchayats had disproved the scepticism that they would just be proxies for men or mere rubber stamps. Earlier, Ms. Gandhi unfurled a theme flag on women's empowerment designed by Farook Ambalapurathe of the United Nations Population Fund. Minister of State for Women and Child Development Renuka Chowdhury and Panchayati Raj Minister Mani Shankar Aiyar were present at the function, which was attended by a large number of women panchayat leaders and rights activists. The flag, which depicts the colours of a muted rainbow under the national tricolour against a white background, will be hoisted all over the country on International Women's Day on March 8. The weeklong celebrations of the International Women's Day began on Monday with the inauguration of a film festival here that will showcase movies based on women-related themes.

5482. (7-3-2007). NEW DELHI: Claiming that there was always a time lag in dampening inflationary pressures, Union Finance Minister P. Chidambaram said he was confident of a moderating effect on price rise after the new crop came in and monetary and other policies, implemented by the Government took effect. Rejecting charges of a "disconnect" among the Union Ministries of Agriculture, Commerce and Finance in countering the price rise, Mr. Chidambaram said in the Rajya Sabha on Tuesday that in 2002-03 and 2005-06 too, inflation was brought down after a time lag of 12 to 18 months. He faced some trying moments during Question Hour especially after economist Arjun Sengupta (Independent) accused the Government of "gross mismanagement" of the economy. "The problem today is on the supply side. With $180 billion as foreign exchange reserves, as a short-term measure, no attempt was made to flood the market with imported commodities [that were contributing to the price rise]. These have to be imported at subsidised prices," added Dr. Sengupta. Mr. Chidambaram listed the commodities that were freely importable and said the Government had no hesitation in importing more but "some items are simply not available." Pulses, for instance are under the open general licence, "but where are the pulses? Myanmar, which partly meets India's needs, says it does not have enough exportable surplus. The answer to this for a country like India is to be self-sufficient [in food]." Pointing out that forward trading in wheat, rice, urad and toor had been restricted, he said the Government would take further action on the basis of a report to be submitted by the Abhijeet Sen committee within two months. Although the Parliamentary Standing Committee on Agriculture had suggested banning of forward trading in most commodities, the Government had decided to await the report, he said.

5483. (7-3-2007). NEW DELHI: Haryana Chief Minister Bhupinder Singh Hooda on Tuesday vowed that the State would give a "fitting response" to the intended move by Punjab to deny river water to Haryana. Mr. Hooda, who met Water Resources Minister Saifuddin Soz here, attributed "unconstitutional and questionable motives" to Chief Minister Parkash Singh Badal's move towards scrapping a section of the Punjab Termination Agreement's Act, 2004 which states that "all existing and actual utilisations through the existing systems shall remain protected and unaffected." Accusing the Punjab Chief Minster of indulging in cheap publicity, Mr. Hooda said the President had made a reference to the Supreme Court regarding the constitutional validity of the 2004 Act. "It is not understood how a piece of legislation, the constitutional validity of which is under the consideration of the Supreme Court, is sought to be amended," he said at a programme organised by the Press Club of India here. As a successor State, he said, Haryana was as much a riparian State as Punjab for the Ravi and the Beas. Haryana had inherent rights to the water of these rivers, he asserted and said the State would move the apex court for an early hearing on the matter. On whether he favoured nationalisation of rivers, he replied that as an MP he had said that every drop of water should be national property.

5484. (7-3-2007). NEW DELHI: The Lok Sabha adjourned for the day on Tuesday in memory of Jharkhand Mukti Morcha member Sunil Kumar Mahato. In his obituary reference, Speaker Somnath Chatterjee said: "A life of promise of a member of Parliament has been extinguished by senseless violence, seriously affecting the proper functioning of our democratic institutions and also creating insecurity and law and order problems." Informing the House about the details of Mr. Mahato's "tragic assassination," Mr. Chatterjee described him as a "dedicated social and active political worker" who worked tirelessly for the uplift of the tribals. "Through his interventions in the House, he vigorously championed the cause of the tribals and other deprived sections of society." Recalling Mr. Mahato's public life, the Speaker said he had actively campaigned for the creation of the State of Jharkhand. "He was associated with the social, cultural and religious activities of the people of the State and was a leading figure of JMM." After the obituary reference, the House observed silence for a while before adjourning for the day.

5485. (7-3-2007). HYDERABAD: The Nuclear Fuel Complex here, mainstay of supply for nuclear power reactors, has drawn up a Rs. 500-crore expansion plan to produce 1,350 tonnes by the end of the next Five-Year plan. Talking to The Hindu here on Monday, NFC chief executive R. N. Jayaraj said the plans included establishment of a new fabrication plant. It was not yet decided whether the plant should be located here or elsewhere. A committee would be constituted next month for recommending the site in about six months. The expansion was to help meet the target of generating 7,400 MWe by the end of the 11th Plan. The NFC had an installed capacity of 600 tonnes a year and was supplying 350-400 tonnes to 12 Pressurised Heavy Water Reactors (220 MWe each). It planned to augment production by 250 tonnes during 2008-09 to meet the requirement for another four plants. With the Nuclear Power Corporation of India proposing to establish four more PHWRs (of 700 MWe each) requiring 500 tonnes of fuel annually, the NFC's plans would come in handy. The NFC was also setting up a plant to fabricate andsupply core sub-assemblies for the Prototype Fast Breeder Test Reactor (PFBTR) coming up at Kalpakkam, near Chennai. "We have already standardised the fabrication technologies and got clearance for manufacturing," Mr. Jayaraj said. The required fuel and hexagonal tubes would be fabricated with hi-tech indigenous technology. These components were earlier imported. The NFC emerged as a potential global player, upgrading technologies for manufacturing critical components. Overseas enquiries were received for export of nuclear grade zircaloy and seamless calandria tubes for nuclear power plants. Asked about separation of civilian-military facilities when the India-U.S. agreement comes into force, Mr. Jayaraj said that only a single module of fuel fabrication dealing with imported natural uranium would fall under international safeguards. "The other modules for manufacturing natural uranium fuel will be under our control."

5486. (7-3-2007). NEW DELHI: Women's groups have asked the Centre to withhold the tabling of the Micro Finance Sector Development and Regulation Bill, 2007 (earlier known as NABARD Bill) slated to be tabled in the current session of Parliament. The bill needs to go through a process of re-drafting after thorough consultation with all organisations, groups, activists, academics and experts working in the field so that the full implication and impact of it can be assessed from the point of view of the people that it will affect, they said in a memorandum to the Union Finance Minister. The bill in its present form has certain fundamental flaws, which will put micro finance organisations (mostly comprising women's self-help groups) at the mercy of big corporate players in the sector. The exemption of micro financing institutions, non-banking financial organisations and non-profit Section 25 companies in the sector from the scope of regulation is unacceptable since the institutions are instrumental in channelling the savings of the poor into the hands of big players, the memorandum said. Further, the whole issue of high interest rates charged by the micro finance institutions has also been left unaddressed. At present, the bill states that the market should determine the rates of interest and that no ceiling has been placed on how much interest can be charged. This is extremely detrimental to the interests of women. Finally, the bill proposes NABARD rather than an independent body as the nodal authority without giving the federation of micro finance organisations any representation in the regulatory body. The signatories are: All-India Democratic Women's Association, All-India Women's Conference, All-India Federation of Anganwadi Workers and Helpers Association, Centre for Women's Development Studies, FORCES, Guild of Services, Joint Women's Programme, Muslim Women's Forum, National Federation of Indian Women, Nirantar, All-India Coordination Committee of Working Women and Young Women's Christian Association.

5487. (7-3-2007). NEW DELHI: The Union Tourism Ministry has prepared a Rs. 39.34-crore comprehensive project to improve the vicinity of the Taj Mahal. The Ministry has already sanctioned Rs. 7.67 crore for insfrastructure improvement from the East Gate and Rs. 7.58 crore from the West Gate as part of the "Agra revitalisation and visitor management for Taj Mahal" project, Tourism Minister Ambika Soni told the Rajya Sabha. The components will include covering of drains, development of a rose garden, upgrading roads, improvement of the Shah Jahan Park, an archaeological park and upgrading the green bus corridor to the monument.

5488. (7-3-2007). NEW DELHI: The Union Commerce Ministry is to bring together chiefs of various commodity boards and the North East Council in Guwahati this week. The meeting will be attended by Governors and Chief Ministers of the northeastern States and chaired by the Minister in charge of the Development of the North-Eastern Region (DONER), Mani Shankar Aiyar. This is an initiative of Union Minister of State for Commerce Jairam Ramesh. The delegation leaving for Guwahati comprises chiefs of the Tea Board, Spices Board, Rubber Board, Coffee Board and Agricultural and Processed Foods Export Development Authority. They will make presentations on the activities of their organisations in the region and get feedback from the Chief Ministers. Since he took over in February last year, Mr. Ramesh has been trying to revive the tea industry and expand spices, rubber, coffee and horticultural industries in the region. Accounting for over half of India's tea production and about eight per cent of natural rubber cultivation, the region can emerge as a major producing centre for organic spices such as turmeric, ginger, pepper and cardamom, organic coffee and organic fruits and vegetables. The Government has substantially liberalised freight subsidy for the movement of horticulture products from the northeast and is encouraging the setting up of cold-chain facilities at several airports in the region.

5489. (7-3-2007). NEW DELHI: The annual Plan for Sikkim for 2007-08 was pegged at Rs. 691.14 crore at a meeting here on Tuesday between Planning Commission Deputy Chairman Montek Singh Ahluwalia and State Chief Minister Pawan Chamling. The outlay, finalised on the basis of identifiable resources, includes a special Plan assistance and additional Central aid totalling Rs 65.72 crore for priority projects of the State. Initiating the discussion, Dr. Ahluwalia noted that Sikkim was doing well on all fronts and its socio-economic indicators were better than many other States. Hailing the State Government's performance in sectors such as health and education and the fact that panchayati raj institutions had been empowered, he said efforts should be made to further strengthen the small-scale industry and the production of seeds for which the weather conditions were suitable. For the Eleventh Plan period, Dr. Ahluwalia advised that efforts should be made to achieve self-reliance in food grain production. Besides, the public-private partnership (PPP) approach should be encouraged in all sectors, particularly in areas where the State has a natural potential. Eco-tourism, floriculture and traditional medicines should also be given priority, he said. The Commission's advice to the State Government was to concentrate on optimum use of Sikkim's abundant natural resources for sustainable economic development. Briefing the Commission about the State's priorities for the Eleventh Plan, the Chief Minister said tourism, horticulture, human resource development, hydel power generation and border trade-related infrastructure would be given focused attention. In the social sector, Mr. Chamling said emphasis would be laid on primary education and primary health care. On the financial side, consolidation of the devolution process along with downsizing of the Government would be the key to improving governance, he added. Education, Mr Chamling said, was also being given priority with an allocation of 18 per cent of the Plan outlay. Alongside, the construction of new school buildings to accommodate more children would also receive focused attention, he said. He also informed the Commission that private investments were coming into the State ever since the new industrial policy was implemented and a number of MoUs have already been signed.

5490. (7-3-2007). NEW DELHI: The National Mission for Manuscripts is caught in a turf war between the Union Culture Ministry and the Indira Gandhi National Centre for the Arts (IGNCA). Barely a month after the Mission celebrated its fourth birthday in grand style, the bank account it held with the IGNCA has been frozen. With over a crore of payments pending, employees of the Mission have gone without their salary for the month of February and all its projects have come to a grinding halt. This move is being viewed by observers here as IGNCA's attempt to get back at being reduced to a postal address for the Mission - it was to be the nodal agency when it was formed - but IGNCA maintains the shutting down of the account had nothing to do with the Mission. "The IGNCA has frozen its own account. It has nothing do to with the NMM. It was a bank account the IGNCA doesn't use. No institution that NMM has worked with has ever been paid through IGNCA. The NMM is an autonomous organisation and should have its own bank account. The Government has made it autonomous, it says so in all its publications. The IGNCA are not responsible for the financial problems that NMM may have," said an IGNCA staff member. While the IGNCA may take comfort in technicalities to prove its point, the current situation has become a crisis for an institution that has made a significant contribution to saving heritage that been ignored so far, point out experts. The freezing of the account at the end of a financial year is too much of a coincidence for the matter to be just a simple case of setting the record straight, say experts, especially as the IGNCA was strapped for funds and the Mission had been sanctioned large sums over the years. "It is petty politics. What else is it? The NMM has been too effective and that is the reason it is being targeted. The Mission was formed by the Government for a specific goal and has managed to do a lot. But it is now being penalised for being good at what it does. Why else would they suddenly shut down the account?" asked a conservationist who has worked with the Mission. The Ministry of Culture, which is at the centre of the controversy, admits that there was a problem and it is being handled. The director of the Mission, Sudha Gopalakrishnan, was unavailable for comment, but Neha Paliwal of the Mission said: "This is a matter between the Ministry of Culture and the IGNCA." The IGNCA may deny any "politics" behind the freezing of the account, but, it is pointed out, it sent a detailed note to the Ministry of Culture pointing out that the Mission had overstepped its original mandate and had disassociated itself from the IGNCA. In the note, the IGNCA is believed to have pointed out that the Mission had been using the IGNCA as a resource centre rather than the nodal authority. It has also frowned upon its "independence" as it has been shown as an independent autonomous organisation by the Central Department of Culture. However, IGNCA employees hint that there is more at stake in this issue. "This may seem like petty politics, but there is more to it than meets the eye. It is simply not a matter about an account. The truth will eventually come out," asserted an IGNCA staff member on Tuesday.

5491. (7-3-2007). NEW DELHI: Opposing the bail plea of former Union Minister and JMM leader Shibu Soren, sentenced by a trial court to life imprisonment for killing his private secretary Shashi Nath Jha, CBI today submitted in the Delhi High Court that there was enough evidence against him for having master-minded the murder. Appearing for CBI, Additional Solicitor General Amrender Sharan told the Bench of Justice Manmohan Sarin and Justice S L Bhayana that to establish the charge of kidnapping, the probe agency had evidence that Jha was pushed inside a white Ambassador car near Dhaula Kuan area in Delhi on May 22, 1994. The victim was also last seen in the company of Soren loyalists in a village near Ranchi next day, ASG argued. Claiming that the trial court had convicted Soren and five others on the basis of the evidence collected by CBI, he submitted that the past conduct of Soren had established criminal bent of mind as he had gone underground for few days soon after the news about Jha going missing spread. A Delhi trial court had on December 26, 2006, convicted Soren and four others for abduction and murder of Jha. According to the prosecution, Jha's body was exhumed from Piska village near Ranchi in 1998.

5492. (7-3-2007). TIRUCHI: Given their "unique and tough working conditions," the Government should treat railway employees as a special work force and pay them more, M. Raghavaiah, general secretary, National Federation of Indian Railwaymen, said on Tuesday. Addressing mediapersons here, he said the Railway Ministry should increase the productivity-linked bonus realistically. Employees worked round the clock, operating 15,000 trains a day that transport 1.5 crore passengers, helping the organisation earn profits and serve the public. Hence, all categories of the employees should be paid more. Mr. Raghavaiah, also chairman of the Joint Consultative Machinery, said the working conditions of the employees, especially those of technicians and Group D employees, had been conveyed to the Sixth Pay Commission. Over 5.5 lakh Group D employees worked for 10-14 hours a day, though their shift was only for eight hours. More than two lakh employees worked 12 hours a day, in miserable conditions, without any extra allowance. So, the federation appealed to the Ministry to appoint a high-powered committee to look into the working hours of employees, especially those in the operational and safety categories.

5493. (8-3-2007). NEW DELHI : Expressing resentment over alleged "inaction" and "indifferent" attitude of the Union Human Resource Development Ministry and the University Grants Commission towards its demands, the Federation of Central Universities Teachers' Associations (FEDCUTA) has pressed for resolving all the pending issues like raising of retirement age of teachers and implementation of career advancement scheme. At a recent meeting held at Jamia Hamdard University, the national executive of FEDCUTA reviewed the progress on its demands and discussed the various issues at hand. It has demanded that all pending issues like increasing of retirement age of teachers to 65 years, implementation of Career Advancement Scheme from January 1, 1996 and restoration of professorship in colleges be immediately resolved.

5494. (8-3-2007). HYDERABAD: Sam Pitroda, Chairman of National Knowledge Commission, has said reforms in Indian education is not the concern of India alone but a global issue since India's 500 million youth are going to be the world's workforce in the future. He called for a national-level discussion on the recommendations of the Knowledge Commission since only public pressure can compel the Government to bring in the necessary changes in the area of educational reforms. He expressed these views while addressing a gathering of educationists and policy makers through a videoconference from Chicago at the two-day seminar on 'Collaborative deliver of higher education programme in India: UK and India achieving best practice', being organised by UK India Education and Research Initiative (UKIERI), on Wednesday. Mr. Pitroda felt the education system must be restructured from the lowest level to the research level. He said improving teaching and faculty along with expansion of institutions was must as suggested in the Commission's recommendations. There was a need to debate these issues at all levels of power and also small towns. Mr. Pitroda expressed the view that it was time to examine the impact of reservations on society. Andhra Pradesh State Council of Higher Education (APSCHE) Chairman K.C. Reddy said private players' role was inevitable to improve quantum and quality. He, however, said there was need for strong regulatory mechanism that was not throat choking to ensure transparency in administration and fee and education that was relevant to society. Rod Pryde, Director, British Council, said UKIERI would promote India-British cooperation from school level to research level for mutual benefit. Seven projects that have been successful in their application would get funding from this year. A total of 40 projects were being planned in the next three years.

5495. (8-3-2007). HYDERABAD: The Council for Chartered Financial Analysts (CCFA) has urged the Centre to constitute a council for CFAs and consequently merge CCFA with it. The suggestion is contained in a draft bill prepared together with the Institute of Chartered Financial Analysts of India. The draft speaks of the imminent need for the CFA profession to be established on statutory lines to protect the interests of millions of investors participating directly or indirectly in the capital market. A press release asked CCFA members across the country to go through the draft bill prepared, together with the Institute of Chartered Financial Analysts of India (ICFAI) and invited suggestions, if any.

5496. (8-3-2007). NEW DELHI: The Union Finance Minister P. Chidambaram on Wednesday cautioned corporates that the government would examine all tax exemptions and withdraw most of them, if possible, to usher in an exemption-free tax regime in the coming years. Exceptions, however, would be made and the tax exemptions would be restricted to the most vulnerable sections of the society such as senior citizens, and for specific fields such as promotion of research and development (R&D) and frontier knowledge areas, he said. Announcing this at a post-Budget interaction with the Confederation of Indian Industry (CII) here, Mr. Chidambaram said: "Every exemption... as Prime Minister has said, will be examined. Every exemption that has to be removed will be removed." Deriding industry for seeking continued tax exemptions, he said: "Every exemption has a father, every exemption has a grandparent, parent or a foster parent," indicating thereby that while all its demands revolved around exemptions, some of them have to go. At the same time, Mr. Chidambaram gave an assurance that he was ready to consider the "grey areas", particularly those linked to the farm-related sectors, as agriculture was a priority focus area of the budget for the new fiscal. Declaring that he was not apologetic about the farm and rural focus in the budget, a point of criticism by certain sections of industry, he said: "As a Finance Minister of the coalition Government, I am obliged to implement the National Common Minimum Programme (NCMP)," which laid emphasis on rural India and agriculture. "While industry may desire that surcharge should be removed...in rural India, people have been waiting for roads for 5,000 years," he said. In this connection, he mentioned that the budget focus had been on credit, seeds, water, fertiliser and electricity for the farm sector to address the stagnating production of wheat, rice and pulses, in particular. Stating that the design of the budget was geared towards implementing NCMP promises, Mr. Chidambaram stressed that attention and money had been provided for a new thrust to the agriculture and social sectors. He emphasised that India's strong growth story would continue, based on robust growth of the global economy, high rates of investment and savings, the adaptability of the Indian corporate sector to new technology, and expanding external sector. The Dividend Distribution Tax, the Minimum Alternate Tax and venture capital pass-through for certain sectors, he said, came under the general category of exemptions, which were in the process of being reduced.

5497. (8-3-2007). NEW DELHI: Pointing out that there were intelligence inputs about terrorists planning to attack the Taj Mahal, CISF Director-General S.I.S. Ahmed on Wednesday said efforts were being made to provide unobtrusive security to the monument. Addressing a press conference here, he said the possibility of terrorists targeting the Taj Mahal was very high. However, as those managing its affairs and visitors were facing problems, the CISF now allowed mobile phones inside the monument.

5498. (8-3-2007). NEW DELHI: Over 11,000 Border Security Force men engaged in counter-terrorist operations will be pulled out of five of the worst violence-hit towns of Jammu and Kashmir next week. Though the withdrawal is part of a phased plan to remove the force from counter-terrorism duties, the details and timing of the withdrawal had been a closely held secret. Sources in the BSF told The Hindu that while eight battalions would move out of the Kashmir Valley - two each from Tral, Sopore, Pulwama and Chrar-e-Sharif, two would pull out of the mountain town of

Doda, northeast of Jammu. Officials said the pullout was expected to end by next weekend and these units would be relocated along the Line of Control after rest and retraining. Each battalion is being replaced with a newly raised Central Reserve Police Force formation. Each CRPF battalion has seven companies, compared to the BSF's six, and the additional manpower is made of those receiving on-the-job training. The withdrawal will, in practice, mean an increase in the number of personnel available to the Jammu and Kashmir Police for counter-terrorism operations. New Delhi's decision to go ahead with withdrawing the BSF comes days after Prime Minister Manmohan Singh rejected the People's Democratic Party (PDP) and the secessionist All Parties Hurriyat Conference demand to demilitarise the State. PDP leaders have threatened to withdraw from the State's coalition government unless the Army is pulled out of southern Kashmir. Officials in New Delhi contend that the continued presence of the Lashkar-e-Taiba and the Hizb ul-Mujahideen cadre means the demand is premature. Eleven battalions of the Rashtriya Rifles are now operating in southern Kashmir.

5499. (8-3-2007). NEW DELHI: The Government is considering changes in the Criminal Procedure Code to ensure that action is taken on first information reports filed in police stations. Law will also be changed to make the police act on reports of women/children missing, Home Minister Shivraj Patil said on Wednesday. He was replying, amid acrimonious scenes in the Rajya Sabha, to a question on the killings at Nithari in Noida, where hacked remains of children and women were found in a drain. The Minister said the Government was considering amending the Cr.PC because it was observed that the police did not take FIRs seriously. "We have decided that after an FIR is filed in the police station, a copy would be simultaneously sent to the judicial magistrate. This will ensure that even if the police do not register the FIR, action is taken." On a mechanism to trace missing children and women vigorously, Mr. Patil said the Union Ministry of Women and Child Welfare proposed making cases of persons missing a cognisable offence so that an FIR would be lodged and the matter taken more seriously. The Centre consulted States and asked them to give their views on a proposal it was drafting. The police have come under fire over the Nithari killings as they refused for a long time to register FIRs on missing children and women. It was later believed that the victims were sexually abused, their bodies dismembered and thrown in a sewer. Mr. Patil made his remarks amid commotion with Samajwadi Party members entering the well in protest against references to Uttar Pradesh Chief Minister Mulayam Singh. When a Congress member asked whether the Central Bureau of Investigation would seek a statement from Mr. Singh, the Minister said: "It is not our intention to direct any investigating agency to do or not do anything." But the question brought half-a-dozen protesting SP members into the well and they returned to their seats only after an assurance from Parliamentary Affairs Minister Priyaranjan Dasmunsi. Despite the interruptions and slogan shouting, Mr. Patil remained held his ground. "You apply your mind to my reply. Don't apply your mind to your question. Please sit down," he told a member who was interrupting him. "If your attempt is to create an impact, then I cannot do anything," Mr. Patil said on another occasion. Brinda Karat (CPI-M) and Supriya Sule (Nationalist Congress Party) did not want the issue restricted to Nithari and wanted members to rise above party divisions to discuss the "extremely alarming situation." Ms. Karat said that besides the disappearance of children all over the country, the condition of migrant families was worse. She called upon the Government to crack down on the mafias indulging in trafficking in children and instruct the police to pay special attention to large settlements of migrant workers.

5500. (8-3-2007). NEW DELHI: Distress deaths in the armed forces have continued into the New Year with 20 suicides being reported in the first two months, according to figures placed by the Defence Ministry in Parliament. While 15 Army personnel committed suicide till February 28, one naval and four Indian Air Force (IAF) personnel also killed themselves. Last year was particularly bad for the armed forces with a record 146 suicides. Of them, 120 were from the Army, two from the Navy and the Coast Guard and 24 from the IAF. The number of Army officers who have taken premature retirement is also on the rise but the number of IAF officers leaving the armed forces is on the decline. Last year, 811 Army officers wanted to quit the services but only 464 were permitted to do so. The figures for the previous two years were 365 and 290 respectively. In contrast, 244 officers took premature retirement in 2004 but the numbers fell to 175 in 2005 and 87 last year. The Government said the main reasons for seeking premature retirement were non-empanelment for promotion, being placed in a permanent low medical category and compassionate reasons - to look after ailing parents or children, resolve marital discord, attend to litigation and take care of ancestral property. The Ministry has decided against inducting women officers in all walks of Army life, including combat. A study on all aspects relating to women officers has among other recommendations suggested the exclusion of women officers for the present in close combat roles where "chances of physical contact with the enemy are high."

5501. (8-3-2007). NEW DELHI: The water wars of South India dominated proceedings in the Lok Sabha for over an hour on Wednesday as members turned the discussion on the Motion of Thanks on the President's Address into a forum for airing their differences on the vexed Cauvery water and Mullaperiyar dam issues. Differences between Kerala and Tamil Nadu over the creation of a separate Salem division by bifurcating the Palakkad Division of Southern Railways surfaced. Cutting across party lines, members identified themselves with their respective States so much that at one point Congress member Seeramesh Tejashwini crossed over to the Opposition side to picket the well along with Bharatiya Janata Party (BJP) members from Karnataka over the final award of the Cauvery Water Disputes Tribunal. As Karnataka members crossed words with their counterparts from Tamil Nadu across the Speaker's podium, Deputy Speaker Charanjit Singh Atwal adjourned the House for 25 minutes. The first salvo was fired by Ananth Kumar, BJP member from Karnataka, who said the President's Address made no mention of the water crisis facing the country. Bringing up the Cauvery issue, he urged the Government not to notify the final award and asked the Prime Minister to convene a meeting of the Chief Ministers of the affected States to arrive at a settlement. As Tamil Nadu members objected to him raising the Cauvery issue, Mr. Kumar wanted to know why they were shying from a structure discussion on the issue forcing the short adjournment. When the House met again, Parliamentary Affairs Minister Priyaranjan Dasmunsi's appeal to members to steer clear of the controversial issue - while Karnataka's request for discussion was under the Speaker's consideration - fell on deaf ears. Union Ministers Dayanidhi Maran and T. R. Baalu also joined the war of words with the latter maintaining that Karnataka had been opposed to the Cauvery Tribunal from the very beginning. With Tamil Nadu members, keeping up their chorus of protest to drown Mr. Kumar's voice, Kerala MPs joined their Karnataka counterparts in demanding a discussion. Though DMK member E. G. Sugavanam tried to cool matters by advocating reason in his intervention on the President's Address, tempers rose again when C. K. Chandrappan (Communist Party of India) brought up the Mullaperiyar issue. If the Mullaperiyar dam is not strengthened and repaired, and a new dam constructed, several districts of Kerala will be wiped out because of flash floods, he said. This again agitated the DMK, inviting a comment on their intolerance from Mr. Chandrappan. Dwelling on how Tamil Nadu and Kerala had gained from each other, the CPI member brought up the issue of creation of the Salem railway division much to the chagrin of Tamil Nadu members. Stating that there should be more tolerance for the other view, he asserted that issues such as Mullaperiyar and Cauvery could not be discussed in chambers and must be discussed in the House.

5502. (8-3-2007). CHANDIGARH: President Abdul Kalam on Wednesday unveiled his vision to make the Indian Air Force "a model for the rest of the world to emulate" by 2025. Speaking after the Presidential Fleet Review coinciding with the platinum jubilee of the IAF at the Air Force Station here, Mr. Kalam said that he visualized the IAF of 2025 to be based on India's scientific and technological competence in the development of communication satellites, high precision resource mapping satellites, missile systems, unmanned supersonic aerial vehicles and electronics and communication systems. He said this would enable it to succeed in the electronically controlled warfare in the midst of space, deep-sea and ballistic missile encounters. He said in future wars would be won by soldiers who could visualise the strength of the enemy using scientific capabilities, and develop suitable strategies. The nation was with the Air Force in its endeavour to "modernise and force multiply all your aerial platforms and ground support systems, so that you will excel in aerial warfare." Appreciating that the force had started acquiring unique capabilities by including several technologically advanced state-of-the-art platforms, sensors and weapon systems in addition to world class human capacity, he said it had the best of fighter aircraft in the world with multi-role capability, ability to carry unique payloads and the capacity to have long-range deep-penetration missions. It had also recognised the importance of the force multiplier in their flying machines with the addition of long-range air-borne radar capabilities, on board computers, MFD (Multi-function displays), various types of missile systems and electronic warfare systems. He turned nostalgic while recalling his experience of "flying" on a Sukhoi-30 MKI fighter plane on June 8 last. He hoped that the fighter, with modern weaponry and electronic warfare systems, would "very soon have the BrahMos missile integrated with it." An Akash-like system should be inducted for enhancing air defence capability, and an Airborne Warning and Control System would enhance surveillance capabilities manifold. An integrated imaging system, using multiple ground and satellite-based sensors, would be able to send battle-field scenarios to fighter squadrons in real time. "I visualise unmanned supersonic combat air vehicles, air-launched hypersonic cruise missiles, submarine-launched ballistic missiles, and anti-ballistic missiles integrated with long-range radars providing a high-technology combat scenario. High-power lasers and microwaves will dominate the war scenario." Mr. Kalam said the fourth fleet review was a remarkable event, with multiple squadrons participating and displaying the 41 standards and colours received by the force. The third Presidential Review of the Air Force was carried out in Chandigarh on January 19, 1976, by Fakhruddin Ali Ahmed. Air Force Marshal Arjan Singh, Punjab Governor S.F. Rodrigues, Haryana Governor A.R. Kidwai, Himachal Pradesh Governor V.S. Kokje, Haryana Chief Minister Bhupinder Singh Hooda, Chief of the Naval Staff Admiral Suresh Mehta and Air Force chief S.P. Tyagi attended the function. Earlier, Air Chief Marshal Tyagi made a unique entry, along with 74 others, by para-jumping from a helicopter. Another feature of the fly-past was the Jaguar formation of 17 aircraft, which made a figure of 75. The Sarang and Suryakiran aerobatic teams also gave a display of their prowess.

5503. (8-3-2007). BANGALORE: As another International Women's Day dawns, there is ample reason to celebrate the growing numbers of women who are joining the ranks of elected representatives in the three tiers of the panchayati raj. Of the 28 lakh elected representatives in India, 9.7 lakh are women. This is greater than the sum of elected women representatives all over the world, as T.R. Raghunandan, Secretary, Ministry of Panchayati Raj, put it. Karnataka has every reason to gloat too - with 43 per cent of its panchayat members being women. It is second only to Bihar, where women constitute 54 per cent of the total. Interestingly, 65 per cent of the seats reserved for Scheduled Tribes have been claimed by women, and 46 per cent of the Scheduled Castes category. The general category records a lower percentage of 37 per cent. "Poor women are increasing their presence in the panchayati raj, and over time, it is bound to change the way governance and administration is delivered in these institutions," Mr. Raghunandan told The Hindu. Closer home, Karnataka continues to be a trailblazer. More than 40,000 women of the 91,000 elected representatives are in the zilla, taluk and gram panchayats. There are 6,000 presidents and 6,000 vice-presidents in the panchayats. Karnataka was the first to launch a sisterhood of elected women representatives. The Karnataka Federation of Elected Women Representatives has emerged as a forum for the members to network, and find support to fight gender stereotyping, and bring about a women-sensitive aspect to governance at the lowest rung of political institutions.

5504. (8-3-2007). CHENNAI: Union Minister of Petroleum and Natural Gas Murli Deora urged Tamil Nadu Chief Minister M. Karunanidhi on Wednesday to allocate land for a 15 million tonne refinery proposed by Chennai Petroleum Corporation Limited (CPCL) at Ennore, about 30 km north of Chennai. The project would contribute to the industrial development of the State and generate a large number of employment opportunities. It would also be important from the perspective of earnings on export of petroleum products from the country, he told The Hindu in an interview here. Noting that around 20 million tonne petroleum products were being exported, the Union Minister pointed out that the export earnings were significant. (Sources in CPCL said a refinery-cum-petrochemical complex was planned. The land required for the project, including a naphtha cracker unit, downstream polymer units, and a paraxylene plant, was 3,000 acres. The project was estimated to cost Rs. 33,000 crore. The Indian Oil Corporation group company had initiated a preliminary feasibility study on the project.) Mr. Deora earlier visited the CPCL corporate office and reviewed the performance of the company that operates a refinery each in Manali, on the outskirts of Chennai, and at Panangudi near Nagapattinam. The selection of Ennore for the project was driven by the location of a port there. On the 2007-08 Budget allocations and proposals pertaining to his Ministry, the Union Minister said granting of infrastructure status for gas pipeline projects, which would provide 10-year income tax holiday, was welcome. It would contribute to expansion of the pipeline network in the country, and in particular assist in the promotion of the 'town gas supply' across the country. While hailing the Budget proposal reducing the ad valorem component of excise duty on petrol and diesel from 8 to 6 per cent, Mr. Deora said a further reduction to four per cent would have been ideal, at least on diesel. This became important in the context of the rising crude prices.

5505. (8-3-2007). NEW DELHI: The Rajya Sabha will discuss the recent incidents of discrimination by State Governments against two media houses - the Eenadu Group and North-East TV - according to a decision taken by the House's Business Advisory Committee. Raising the issue during Zero Hour, Ravula Chandra Sekhar Reddy (Telugu Desam Party) mentioned attempts by the Andhra Pradesh Government to "contain the media." Digvijay Singh (Janata Dal-United) alleged that the owner of NE TV, "a former Minister in the Prime Minister's office," is facing death threats from the United Liberation Front of Asom and denial of professional working space by the State Government. Union Home Minister Shivraj Patil said the Assam Government had been asked to provide adequate security to the NE TV owner. If that was not provided, "it will be asked why [this was not done]," the Minister added.

5506. (8-3-2007). NEW DELHI: Cutting across party lines, members of Parliament from Karnataka staged a dharna outside Parliament House building on Wednesday morning to protest against the final award of the Cauvery Water Disputes Tribunal. Among those who sat on dharna were former Prime Minister H. D. Deve Gowda and Bharatiya Janata Party leader Ananth Kumar. The dharna was staged a day after Lok Sabha Speaker Somnath Chatterjee convened a meeting of MPs from Karnataka and Tamil Nadu to decide on Karnataka's demand for a discussion on the award under Rule 193. With no consensus emerging, the matter is pending with the Speaker. Meanwhile, missing the Karnataka presence in the House, Mr. Chatterjee urged members from the State to attend proceedings. He also asked other members to make a similar appeal. However, it was soon pointed out that Mr. Gowda had come in for a while. And, a couple of backbencher members from Karnataka marked their presence by standing up.

5507. (8-3-2007). NEW DELHI: Indian women have outshone men in terms of employment growth rate with a 3.35 per cent rise in employment between 1998 and 2004 against a fall of about 8 per cent in case of males, according to the Assocham Eco Pulse Study on 'Women Employment Growth Rate and Gender Budgeting.' Keeping pace with the growth in GDP, the total number of women employed in the public and private sector has increased from 47.74 lakh in 1998 to 49.34 lakh in 2004, while the number of men employed has fallen from 233.92 lakh in 1998 to 215.09 lakh in 2004. "Growing employment opportunities for women mark a significant improvement in the social status and gender justice besides imparting economic power," said Chamber president Venugopal N. Dhoot. It said the public sector has been hiring women much more aggressively than the private sector. The number of women it employed has risen from 27.63 lakh in 1998 to 28.9 lakh in 2004, witnessing a growth of close to 4.6 per cent. The private sector added 0.33 lakh women staff with a growth of 1.64 per cent over 1998, taking the total number to 20.44 lakh.

5508. (8-3-2007). NEW DELHI: The presiding officers of both Houses of Parliament on Wednesday disallowed BJP and Trinamool Congress members to raise the issue of Congress MP M. K. Subba's nationality. A television news channel said Mr. Subba, representing Tezpur in Assam in the Lok Sabha, was of foreign origin. Raising the issue in the Lok Sabha, BJP deputy leader Vijay Kumar Malhotra wanted to know how a foreign national could be an MP. Speaker Somnath Chatterjee, however, said he had not given notice to raise the issue. In the Rajya Sabha, Dinesh Trivedi (Trinamool) said, "a fugitive is alleged to have become an MP. The House has the right to know." Deputy Chairman K. Rehman Khan pointed out that Mr. Subba was a member of the other House and so the issue could not be discussed in the Rajya Sabha.

5509. (8-3-2007). NEW DELHI: Naxal violence has declined by 6.15 per cent from 1,608 incidents in 2005 to 1,509 in 2006, Home Minister Shivraj Patil said in the Lok Sabha on Wednesday while making a suo moto statement on the killing of Jharkhand

Mukti Morcha member Sunil Kumar Mahato. After giving details about the attack on Mr. Mahato and his bodyguards, Mr. Patil said: "While the naxal problem is of serious nature, combined efforts of the State and Central Governments have shown some level of containment." In particular, Andhra Pradesh had achieved "noteworthy success" in controlling the problem. He said: "However, we need greater concerted and cooperative efforts between the States, as well as between the Centre and the States to achieve more acceptable results. "We expect that the motivation and dedication of the State police, coupled with financial, technical support that includes equipment and manpower support from the Government of India along with developmental programmes in the naxal affected areas will have a significant impact on this problem." The Minister said the attack on Mr. Mahato was a planned one. As for the assistance given to Jharkhand to tackle the naxal problem, Mr. Patil said under the Police Modernisation Scheme, Rs. 182.72 crore had been provided to the State over the last six years. In the current year, a special grant of Rs. 15 crore was being given to the State for purchase of telecommunication, weaponry and de-mining equipment. Besides, Jharkhand had been given Rs. 20.92 core under the Security Related Expenditure Scheme till date, he said.

5510. (8-3-2007). NEW DELHI: Union Minister for Rural Development Raghuvansh Prasad on Wednesday presented in the Lok Sabha a list of 130 new districts where the National Rural Employment Guarantee Act (NREGA) will be implemented from the next fiscal. The scheme is already operational in 200 districts. Mr. Prasad's presentation came a week after Union Finance Minister P. Chidambaram announced in his budget speech that it would be extended to the new districts in 2007-08. Making a suo motu statement, Mr. Prasad listed 113 districts, leaving out those located in Uttar Pradesh in view of the coming Assembly elections. He explained the criteria adopted while identifying the districts: 15 reported incidence of farmers' suicide; 34 were selected from the Planning Commission Ranking of Backwardness used for identifying the National Food for Work Programme districts; and 50 from among the Backward Regions Grant Fund districts. To ensure equitable distribution, at least two districts in addition were selected from each special category State as well as from States, whose minimum number was not covered by any of the other criteria. Through this route, 22 districts were selected. As the Minister sought to read out the list, Speaker Somnath Chatterjee suggested that it could be tabled. However, members insisted that it be read and the Minister went ahead saying he would take only a couple of minutes. Several members were unhappy over their districts being left out. Seeing their protest, the Speaker said: "This is why I did not want the list to be read out." The National Rural Employment Guarantee Act (Extension to Jammu and Kashmir) Bill 2007, providing for extension of the Act to the State, was introduced in the Lok Sabha on Wednesday. Mr. Prasad introduced the Bill. An employment guarantee scheme is already in operation in Poonch, Doda and Kupwara districts, on the lines of the NREGA, for which the Centre is providing funds.

5511 (8-3-2007). NEW DELHI: The Centre's decision to enforce 27 per cent reservation for Other Backward Classes in elite educational institutions from this year came in for scrutiny in the Supreme Court. "Without relevant determinable data how can we go ahead with the Act?" asked a Bench of Justices Arijit Pasayat and L.S. Panta on Wednesday. "Unless and until it is determined by the Centre who is socially and economically backward, this Act cannot really be given effect," it said as anti-quota petitioners opposed implementation of the law on the ground that a 75-year-old census could not be the basis for identifying OBCs.

5512. (9-3-2007). NEW DELHI: The Union Government on Thursday approved the guidelines on corporate governance for Central public sector enterprises, requiring all companies to have independent directors on their board. "The Union Cabinet approved the guidelines on corporate governance for public sector companies... The board of directors must have an optimum combination of executive and non-executive members," Information and Broadcasting Minister P R Dasmunsi told reporters. The board would have not less than 50 per cent of members as independent directors, he said after the Cabinet meeting chaired by Prime Minister Manmohan Singh. The exact number of independent directors on a company's board would depend on whether the chairman is executive or non-executive, he said.

5513. (9-3-2007). NEW DELHI: Observing that it is wrong to assume that entrepreneurship is confined to the private sector, Prime Minister Manmohan Singh on Thursday public sector enterprises (PSEs) to seize the opportunities for mergers, acquisitions, amalgamations and takeovers and creating new joint ventures. Inaugurating the conference of PSE chief executives here on Thursday, Dr. Singh assured them that revitalisation of the public sector was an integral part of the Government's strategy to promote inclusive growth. Expressing happiness over the fall in the number of loss making PSEs from 79 to 58, he asked the Board for Reconstruction of PSEs to come forward with time-bound programmes for the revival of sick PSEs. "It must help the Government take an early decision on all pending proposals," he observed. He underlined the need to improve corporate governance in PSEs and adhere to the code of corporate ethics and conduct. Referring to state level PSEs, which also required change and adapt, he emphasised the need to find viable means to revive and sustain such enterprises and ensure that the interests of workers and employees are not hurt owing to political interference and bad management. Pointing out that the PSEs today share business space with Indian firms and global multinationals, Dr. Singh complimented the PSEs for standing their ground against fierce competition. "This is a tribute to your managerial competence, to the dedication of your workers and employees and management to our joint national commitment to the revitalisation of public enterprises as a major engine of India's economic growth. I am happy to say that in these past two years you have done a creditable job in turning around many of our public enterprises. There has been an improvement in their financial and physical performance. I compliment you all for this solid achievement." The Prime Minister suggested that more PSEs should be listed on the stock exchange to enhance professionalisation of the board of directors and empower independent directors. PSEs should also grant adequate freedom to the chief executive and his senior management to take quick and difficult decisions. Excessive regulation restricted entrepreneurial drive and made management risk averse. "That is not the way to go forward in the fast changing world full of uncertainty - the overall environment in which our enterprises operate," he said. PSEs should also evolve their own code of corporate ethics and conduct and ensure adherence to such codes. The Government was working towards limiting the administrative ministries' role in their day-to-day management. "I hope the steps we intend to take will help our public enterprises to become more globally competitive," the Prime Minister observed.

5514. (9 -3-2007). NEW DELHI: Sharing MPs' concern over price rise, Prime Minister Manmohan Singh on Thursday appeared confident that the measures taken by the Government would moderate inflationary pressures over the next few months. "There are indications that the rate of inflation has declined by nearly one percentage point in the last two weeks," he told Parliament. Replying to the debate on the motion of thanks to the President's address, Dr. Singh said the Government was trying to "curb inflationary pressures." While supply-side shortages could be eased through imports, the Government's effort had been to bring in those imports without affecting the profitability of domestic agriculture. In almost similar replies in the two Houses before the motion of thanks was adopted, Dr. Singh dwelt on the need to revitalise the agricultural economy, the controversy surrounding the Special Economic Zones (SEZs), internal security and foreign policy. He said the monetary measures taken by the Reserve Bank to moderate the growth of money supply, and steps by the Finance Minister to reduce customs duty on essential commodities and arrangements to augment domestic supplies through imports would have the desired effect. Calling for a more effective strategy to increase production of foodgrains, vegetable oils and pulses, Dr. Singh said it would be a priority concern of his Government during the 11th Five-Year Plan. Region-wise plans would be prepared by the Agriculture Ministry and the Planning Commission to revitalise the agricultural economy and these would be discussed at a National Development Council meeting. In an obvious reference to the Cauvery dispute, the Prime Minister called upon all the political parties to treat water as a national resource and not as an issue that should divide the people. "The management of our water resources and putting in place viable and effective arrangements for the resolution of inter-State disputes are critical for sustained development in the years to come."

5515. (9-3-2007). NEW DELHI: The Lok Sabha on Thursday unanimously passed the Sports Broadcasting Signals Bill, 2007, which makes it mandatory for private broadcasters to share live feed of national events with Doordarshan and All India Radio on a free-to-air basis. The Bill will go to the Rajya Sabha on Friday. There was no alternative to bringing in the ordinance and now the Bill to replace it, for enabling cricket lovers to watch the World Cup starting on March 11, Information and Broadcasting Minister Priyaranjan Dasmunsi said. The Sports Broadcasting Signals (mandatory sharing with Prasar Bharati) Ordinance, 2007 was promulgated last month after Nimbus Communications, which holds telecast rights for all international cricket matches being played in India till 2010, refused to share signals with Prasar Bharati. Wishing the Indian cricket team success in the World Cup events, Mr. Dasmunsi clarified that the Bill was intended not for a particular game but to promote all sports, though the entire debate seemed to revolve round cricket. Though India generated 70 per cent of the advertising revenue from international cricket, Indians could not even watch matches involving their national team. Australia and the United Kingdom, which contribute only 5-10 per cent of the total advertising revenue from international cricket, had much more stringent laws on telecast of matches, he said.

5516. (9-3-2007). NEW DELHI: The National Council of Educational Research and Training (NCERT) will soon set up a Rural Education Cell to figure out the problems that plague rural schools and to strengthen their overall performance. The Council has also decided to create a new Reading Cell - to be funded by Sarva Shiksha Abhiyaan - that will focus attention on the reading skills and capabilities of students of Classes I and II. The Executive Committee chaired by Union Human Resource Development Minister Arjun Singh that met on Thursday approved of these two plans, NCERT Director Krishna Kumar said on Thursday. The Rural Education Cell that will be housed on the NCERT campus will make a deep analysis of the all-India education survey data to assess the condition of rural schools. "We will segregate the rural data gender wise and age wise to look deeply at patterns that emerge. We will try to get to the heart of the problem of rural education in terms of working conditions, infrastructure, teachers, poor performance and high drop-out rate of students," Prof. Kumar said. The cell will also conduct case studies in different States and organise conferences for rural teachers to help evolve a policy for rural schools. "Personally, I am happy that we will be doing something especially for rural schools. The rural-urban divide in the field of education in our country is something which we would very much like to study and bridge," he added. As part of the Reading Cell, NCERT would bring out graded self-reading series of "tiny books" for little children that will help to sustain their interest in what they read. These books comprising pictures along with text will be graded according to the level of vocabulary and difficulty for children. Regarding the second initiative, Mr. Kumar stated, "From our many surveys we have found out that the reading skills of students do not get fully consolidated in Classes I and II. The children can read mechanically but can't necessarily draw the meaning of the text. Reading is the basis of all understanding. If the child does not understand what he reads in Class I, then the path becomes tougher and tougher for him in future classes." Initially NCERT will zero in on one district that has a poor reading record for its intensive work. Following the go-ahead by the Executive Committee, the Council will now make its proposals to the HRD Ministry for implementation of the projects.

5517. (9-3-2007). NEW DELHI: Finance Minister P. Chidambaram on Thursday chided captains of industry for doing precious little by way of social responsibility while seeking relief and tax concessions for themselves. Putting the ball in the court of India Inc. during his post-budget interaction with members of the Associated Chambers of Commerce and Industry of India here, he said: "When we are promising 1,00,000 jobs to the physically challenged... it's a challenge not only for the Government but also for you. I did not hear any one of you speak about how you will provide jobs to physically challenged persons." While presenting the budget, Mr Chidambaram promised corporates that the Government would reimburse the employers' contribution to the EPF (Employees Provident Fund) and the ESI (Employees State Insurance) for the first three years if they provided jobs to the physically handicapped. The Minister rapped the corporate honchos for not coming forward to upgrade industrial training institutes (ITIs) despite the budgetary promise of interest-free loans for their modernisation. "When I offer 1,396 ITIs [for upgrading] and I promised Rs 2.50 crore [as interest-free loan] per ITI, I did not hear any one of you say this is [a] challenge for industry and we will come forward and take over it." Mr. Chidambaram asked the corporate sector to appoint CEOs and CFOs to take better care of its social responsibility to the vulnerable sections, and to avoid seeking fiscal concessions to help achieve inclusive growth. India Inc. needed to take care of that half of India which had no access to water, community toilets, sanitation, electricity, education and health, instead of insisting on repeated tax concessions. On inflation, he said it was a larger social issue and price rise would be moderated in the long run through increased supply of farm goods. "While fiscal steps will have some immediate impact, monetary side will take some time to transmit into the system. Supply-side is indeed a durable answer to inflation. More wheat, more rice, more sugar, more pulses, more oilseeds is [the] durable side." Just as increased supply of inputs was the durable answer to the growth of industry, higher supplies of these were the durable answer to agriculture. Explaining the rationale behind the shift in the budget focus to the farm sector during 2007-08, he said that just as in his "dream" budget of 1997-98 it was necessary to pull India Inc. out of its cocoon, now the stress on the rural sector was essential for "inclusive" growth. Issues such as fringe benefit tax, service tax, double taxation on cement and dividend distribution tax could be addressed through a composite dialogue between his Ministry officials and industry representatives. But the challenge before the Government and the corporates was to make rural India share the gains of current growth, which for the next couple of years would be nine per cent or more.

5518. (9-3-2007). MUMBAI: The Reserve Bank of India will shortly issue bank notes of Rs. 20 denomination with inset letter "R" in both the numbering panels in the Mahatma Gandhi series. It will also have additional new security features bearing the signature of RBI Governor Y.V. Reddy, the RBI said in a release. Except for the change in the inset letter, the design of these notes is similar in all respects to those issued earlier with additional security features on August 17, 2006. All Rs. 20 notes issued earlier will continue to be legal tender, it said.

5519. (9-3-2007). NEW DELHI: Prime Minister Manmohan Singh on Thursday said the Special Economic Zone (SEZ) policy was being reviewed to find out whether there was any pitfall in the existing framework. Recognising the need for a more humane approach, he assured Parliament that the Government would come up with an improved rehabilitation and resettlement policy. He was replying to the debate on the motion of thanks to the President's address. On the Sachar report, Dr. Singh said it brought out the stark reality of the condition of Muslims. The new 15-point programme was focussed on ensuring equitable sharing of the benefits of crucial development programmes, particularly in health and education. The Government was also formulating targeted programmes for districts where the minorities were concentrated. "In the long-run, as all communities catch up on their social indicators, there would be no need for such programmes but given the current disparities it is imperative that we carry all sections along." Dwelling on internal security, Dr. Singh asserted that his Government had an enviable track record, better than that of the previous regime, be it in the northeast, Jammu and Kashmir or naxal-affected districts. Even when there were terrorist incidents, the country never saw a breakdown of law and order and an upsurge of communal violence of the type that rocked Gujarat. "Compare the violence after the Godhra incident in Gujarat to the situation in Maharashtra after last year's Mumbai blasts." Describing naxalism as the "most widespread internal security threat" as seen in the recent killing of Sunil Mahato, a sitting Lok Sabha member from Jharkhand, Dr. Singh said the Government was following a two-pronged approach - supporting States in improving the performance of the security and police forces and going into the deep-rooted causes that gave rise to disaffection among tribals and other sections. In a clear message to terrorist groups, he said the Government could negotiate only with those who wanted peace, not with those who killed innocent people. "We will never hesitate to sit down and talk to a fellow Indian - howsoever misguided - if such conversations can bring peace to our people. But we will never compromise the unity and integrity of our country or allow those who kill innocent people to go unpunished." Dr. Singh was referring to recent talks with the United Liberation Front of Asom, which failed to make headway. On the foreign policy, he said India's relations with Russia, the U.S., the European Union, China, Japan and the ASEAN nations had grown and expanded to cover many new areas. As for Pakistan, he was confident that all outstanding issues would be resolved through dialogue.

5520. (9-3-2007). NEW DELHI: Women parliamentarians had their say in both Houses of Parliament on the occasion of International Women's Day on Thursday but were unable to secure a concrete assurance from the Government on the introduction of the Women's Reservation Bill. All they got was a reiteration of the Government's commitment to bring the Bill to Parliament before its term ended. In the Rajya Sabha, Prime Minister Manmohan Singh said: "Our Government remains committed to work towards broad based consensus on the Bill." Some months back the initiative "nearly succeeded but some problems arose and we could not bring it in the last session of Parliament." Responding to the demand for a commitment on the introduction of the Bill in the Lok Sabha, Union Parliamentary Affairs Minister Priyaranjan Dasmunsi said a consensus-building exercise was on since it was a Constitutional Amendment requiring two-thirds majority for passage. "We will introduce it before our term is over." Earlier, Lok Sabha Speaker Somnath Chatterjee made a reference to International Women's Day before setting aside time from Question Hour to allow women members to air their views. However, as the women MPs refused to confine themselves to a minute each and nearly half of Question Hour was taken up, the Speaker quipped: "I made a mistake, I find." Cutting across party lines, the refrain of women MPs was that every year platitudes are offered to women's empowerment - both inside and outside Parliament - but the Bill remained an elusive goal. First off the block was Sumitra Mahajan (Bharatiya Janata Party). Krishna Tirath (Congress) asked members to raise their hands if they supported the introduction of the Bill. Some members obliged; giving enough reason to other women MPs to continue taking digs at parliamentarians for paying lip service to women's empowerment. While P. Satheedevi and C.S. Sujatha (Communist Party of India-Marxist), Bhavani Rajenthiran (Dravida Munnetra Kazhagam), Sushila Kerketta (Congress), and Archana Nayak (Biju Janata Dal) raised the same issue, Ranjeet Ranjan (Lok Janshakti Party) also referred to the many unsung women who wage daily battles of existence all over the country. Of the view that the Women's Reservation Bill would never see the light of day, Maneka Gandhi (BJP) said that instead parties should give one-third tickets to women. And, a beginning should be made with the upcoming Assembly elections, she suggested.

5521. (9-3-2007). PANAJI : Goa Rajya Sabha MP Shantaram Naik on Wednesday met Union Finance Minister P. Chidambaram in New Delhi and submitted to him a memorandum demanding rollback of export duty of Rs. 300 a tonne on iron ore. Mr. Naik told The Hindu that the Minister had promised to take an appropriate view on the issue after a debate on the budget in Parliament. Mr. Naik said in the memorandum that ore from Goa was in the form of fines (80 per cent) and lumps (20 per cent) and was of low grade with Fe below 62 per cent. There was no market for such ore domestically and only recently with demand from China, this ore, which would have otherwise been discarded, had found a market and was earning substantial foreign exchange, the memorandum added. Mr. Naik said Goa's economy depended on ore exports and had been exporting medium-grade iron ore to long-term buyers in Japan, South Korea and Europe . "This nascent industry will be destroyed with the imposition of the export duty," Mr. Naik felt.

5522. (9-3-2007). NEW DELHI: For the second day on Thursday, the Bharatiya Janata Party raked up in the Lok Sabha the issue of the nationality of Congress member M. K. Subba and invited upon itself a reprimand from Speaker Somnath

Chatterjee for pressuring him on the matter. BJP deputy leader Vijay Kumar Malhotra raised the issue soon after question hour. He pointed out that on an earlier occasion - the cash-for-query scam - members were asked to stay away from proceedings pending a decision. Drawing the Speaker's attention to the presence of Mr. Subba in the House, he said the same practice should be followed in this case also. As Ananth Kumar (BJP) pressed with the demand that Mr. Subba be asked to leave the House, the Speaker said the Opposition should give him more time to take a decision. Also, he was agitated over the manner in which the BJP was trying to impute motives. With the BJP keeping up pressure, Parliamentary Affairs Minister Priyaranjan Dasmunsi intervened on Mr. Subba's behalf; asking "why should he not attend the House."

5523. (9-3-2007). NEW DELHI: Despite the stiff resistance put up by Tamil Nadu members against a discussion in the Lok Sabha on the final award of the Cauvery Water Disputes Tribunal, Speaker Somnath Chatterjee decided to allow the vexed issue to be discussed in the House. Disclosing this in the House on Thursday, he said, however, priority would be given to financial business. Mr. Chatterjee ended the suspense on the matter during a last-minute intervention by the former Prime Minister, H.D. Deve Gowda, on the Motion of Thanks to the President's address. Since a meeting convened by the Speaker on Tuesday to arrive at a consensus on allowing a discussion on Cauvery remained inconclusive, Karnataka members were particularly agitated over the issue. Though the discussion on the Motion of Thanks was wrapped up on Wednesday evening, the Speaker conceded a request by Mr. Gowda for time to make an intervention on the condition that he would not bring up the Cauvery issue, which forced a brief adjournment of the proceedings on Thursday. Stating that he would keep his promise of not raising the Cauvery issue, the former Prime Minister, however, wondered whether "the compulsions of coalition politics and exigencies of power play" could be allowed to gag the voices of five-and-a-half crore citizens who wanted to find expression through their elected representatives in Parliament. "Are these signs of a mature and vibrant democracy that we take pride in," Mr. Gowda asked, adding that it was important to send out the message that Parliament thinks, behaved and acted as one nation and not as "divided principalities of British India." Having said this, he articulated the request of Karnataka MPs for a discussion on Cauvery under Rule 193; bringing Tamil Nadu MPs on their feet.

5524. (9-3-2007). NEW DELHI : President A.P.J. Abdul Kalam has asked the National Commission for Women (NCW) to act as the nodal agency for creating rehabilitation centres for mentally ill and homeless women. He asked the Commission to take up the task of making the country free from uncared mentally ill women within the next five years by creating at least 300 compassionate organisations, which can take up the cause. Inaugurating a seminar on "Mentally ill women - Is destitution the only answer?" to mark International Women's Day, Mr. Kalam said the NCW, along with various Government Departments and State Women Commissions, could work to create a hundred rehabilitation centres and 1,000 after-care-homes in the country. The corporate sector and societal transformers, with the help of trained people, could also work for this cause. The programme should include welfare of the children of the affected persons and counselling for the family with the Ministries of Social Justice and Women and Child Development providing necessary funds and infrastructural support. He said the NCW could create a web site where societal members could report about the destitute they came across daily. This would enable treatment and rehabilitation centres to approach the destitute and persuade them to undergo treatment. The Commission could also seek the assistance of police, scouts and guides and volunteers for collecting and registering of data about the destitute on the web site. The police could be sensitised during the training process to take pro-active action to report the existence of persons with mental illness who are found in their jurisdiction to the nearest rehabilitation centre, besides advising the relatives of the affected persons to take the individual for treatment. "The developed status of society is indicated by the respect society gives to its womanhood," he said. There are about 2,500 mentally ill abandoned women in the capital. Of the total number of mentally ill people, nine lakh are women.

5525. (9-3-2007). NEW DELHI: There will soon be hope for unprotected monuments dotting the countryside that were earlier not on any list. With the promised National Mission for Antiquities and Monuments finally being launched on April 19, after being entangled in red tape for four long years, more ancient buildings will find space on the heritage map. The Mission for Intangible Heritage, however, also announced by former Prime Minister Atal Bihari Vajpayee four years ago, is yet to take off. The Mission for Antiquities and Monuments will operate under the Archaeological Survey of India (ASI) and will bank heavily on networking with State Governments, non-government organisations and even universities. "The Secretary Culture will be the chairperson while superintending archaeologist of the circles will be members. The ASI will train people. The Mission will be a little like the National Mission for Manuscripts (NMM) that has State level committees. They will then do the fieldwork. But ASI will release budgets," said ASI Director-General C. Babu Rajeev. However, learning from the NMM experience that has run into trouble with its nodal agency — the Indira Gandhi National Centre for the Arts (IGNCA) — and with the situation turning ugly, the ASI is planning to have its role clearly defined so as to leave no loopholes. While originally there were to be two separate Missions — one for Monuments and the other for Antiquities — they have now been clubbed into one. Looking at two diverse areas, experts point out that blending them into one may be diluting the mandate. However, the Mission has at least taken a purposeful step in the direction, while ASI has so far been unable to make any headway, point out observers. With over 3,000-odd monuments under its wing and limited manpower and resources being major restrictive factors, the ASI has its hands full. As such many significant buildings not on the list had been left to fend for themselves. But now this Mission is hoping to be able to then find ways to rescue such monuments. "The Mission will evolve along the way," said an official in the Department of Culture.

5526. (9-3-2007). LUCKNOW: With orders to carry out intensive checking on the borders of eight States neighbouring Uttar Pradesh to prevent inflow of illegal arms and explosives, the Election Commission has sought details from the State Government about the people given security cover, including elected representatives. The details will include those who have been provided with gunners after the announcement of the Assembly election schedule on February 21, their crime record, if any, and the nature of threat perception. The Commission has also sought districtwise break-up figures for criminal cases against persons with criminal antecedents, including elected representatives and candidates. These details have to be furnished before March 13, when nominations open for the first phase of the seven-phase polls. The Commission's move is seen as the first step towards keeping a tight leash on criminal elements from subverting the election process and weeding out those with criminal antecedents. Opposition parties have complained that several ruling party functionaries and leaders with alleged criminal records were given security cover. On Thursday, Chief Electoral Officer Anuj Kumar Bishnoi held a meeting with the Home Secretaries and Directors-General of Police of Bihar, Jharkhand, Chhattisgarh, Madhya Pradesh, Rajasthan, Haryana, Himachal Pradesh and Uttarakhand. The CEO told reporters that inter-State border checking had begun and the borders with the eight States would be sealed before the elections. The police in the border districts would remain in touch with their counterparts in Uttar Pradesh and exchange vital information and intelligence inputs. Officials of these States were asked to conduct raids on illegal arms units and illicit liquor distillation units, besides preparing a dossier on anti-social elements, criminals and gangsters. Plans were afoot to post police units as well as deploy foot patrol along the borders, Mr. Bishnoi said.

5527. (10-3-2007). NEW DELHI: The Union Government on Friday introduced a Bill in the Lok Sabha to provide greater operational flexibility to RBI in conducting monetary policy. The Banking Regulation (Amendment) Bill proposes to replace an Ordinance that was promulgated on January 23.

5528. (10-3-2007). MUMBAI: The Securities and Exchange Board of India (SEBI) on Friday proposed that nominee directors would not be considered as independent directors as part of Clause 49 of the listing agreement. "Consequently, the provision which allows nominee directors appointed by institutions to be considered as independent directors may be deleted," SEBI suggested. It is proposed that a provision be added stating that if the non-executive Chairman is a promoter or is related to promoters or persons occupying management positions at the Board level or at one level below the Board, he would not be treated as independent director and the company, in such a case, would be equired to have 50 per cent independent directors on the Board. It is also proposed to stipulate that an independent director who resigns or is removed from the Board shall be replaced by a new independent director within a time-gap of not more than 90 days from such resignation or removal. "Without any time limit, a company may continue to remain non-compliant and may take a plea that it has not been able to find an independent director," SEBI stated. Further SEBI suggested that companies shall disclose the relation between independent directors inter-se as well as other directors of the company not holding a management position, in all documents where the details of the Board of directors are incorporated or given for information of the public or shareholders. It is proposed that the minimum age of an independent director shall be 21 years. SEBI also stated "it may not be possible to stipulate that experience, maximum age or qualification for an independent director since it would differ from company to company based on the line of activities it is engaged in." SEBI has sought responses to the suggestions on or before April 2.

5529. (10-3-2007). CHENNAI: The Finance Bill 2007 has for the first time brought the Indian law fully in tune with India's obligations under the World Trade Organisation regime in the matter of transaction value of goods. The amendment to Sec. 14 of the Customs Act will help businesses, which have often been facing arbitrary action by Customs officials, according to Lakshmi Kumaran, advocate and consultant. Addressing a seminar organised by the Institute of Business Laws here on Monday, Mr. Lakshmi Kumaran pointed out that even in cases where there was an arm's length relationship between the buyer and the seller and there was no other payment involved, Customs officials tended to refuse to accept the declared value of the goods in view of the fact that the Revenue Department had only sought to give effect to the international norm, agreed to by India in 1998, through executive instruction, without amending the statute. Mr. Lakshmi Kumaran said a negative development was that the scope for intervention by the Settlement Commission (SC) (for indirect taxes) had been curtailed, and powers to grant immunity from prosecution under other laws, including the Indian Penal Code, had been removed as also the power to grant immunity from payment of interest. Submissions made to the commission could be used as evidence in law courts had also been withdrawn. These changes would lead to harassment for those who had committed genuine errors in filing returns and would discourage assessees from resorting to the services of the commission, Mr. Lakshmi Kumaran said.

5530. (10-3-2007). NEW DELHI: Asserting that all efforts would be directed towards making the Indian Railways a world class network, Railway Minister Lalu Prasad on Friday announced that special facilities would be provided for pregnant women and their kin while travelling in trains. Mr. Prasad also announced that the Railways planned to overhaul the food provided to passengers on all major trains and indicated that the menu could undergo a change for the better with an eye on providing healthy and nutritious diet to the travelling public. "Pregnant women travelling by trains can look forward to assistance from the Railway staff. Special package keeping this aspect in mind would be announced very soon. The deployed staff would be given instructions and training to put on alert railway stations in case of any urgent medical emergency for such passengers. Special coupe would be allotted to such couples or individuals during the journey on the train," Mr. Prasad said, while rounding up the debate on the Railway Budget 2007-08 in the Lok Sabha. The House approved vote on account for meeting expenses of the Railways for three months from April. Supplementary demands for grants of Rs. 7,579 crore and relevant Appropriation Bills also got the nod of the House through a voice vote. Charging the previous NDA Government with charting out a path to privatise the Railways, Mr. Prasad said: "There is no question of going in for blanket privatisation. All efforts would be directed towards making the Indian Railways a world-class network." This would address the concerns raised by the Left party members over the plans to privatise various operations. Seeking to brush aside the questions being raised about Bihar getting Rs. 1,199 crore allocation in the budget, Mr. Prasad said his home State had been discriminated against for long but now that wrong had been rectified. Terming as "irresponsible" the recent reported remarks by Shiv Sena chief Bal Thackrey that Biharis living in Mumbai would have to maintain a low profile, Mr. Prasad said people from Bihar have not learnt to live in fear. The Minister also denied that Railways planned to indirectly charge additional fare for women and senior citizens for providing them lower berths in trains, a scheme announced by Mr. Prasad in his budget. Mr. Prasad also spoke about the plans being drawn up to change the food menu in trains, suggesting items like salad should be dropped because they could be a source of infection. "We could limit the menu to pulses, rice, vegetables and some spicy meat," he said. Besides the eight pairs of trains proposed to be introduced this year, more would be added particularly to meet needs of the poor. As part of the strategy to beef up security in trains and stations, vacant posts in the Railway Protection Force would be filled shortly, he said. A dedicated freight corridor would be established for faster movement of goods and moves were already under way to build new-design coaches made up of aluminium.

5531. (10-3-2007). NEW DELHI: The Central Bureau of Investigation (CBI) told the Supreme Court on Thursday that it had requested the General Secretariat Interpol on March 3 last to continue the red corner notice pending against Italian businessman and Bofors case accused Ottavio Quattrocchi. Countering the allegations that the notice was no longer valid, the CBI informed the apex court that the Interpol Secretariat General confirmed on September 14 last that the red corner notice would be maintained. The relevant information would remain registered and accessible to all Interpol members, and the caveat "subject to legal review" would be removed, the Secretariat General said.

5532. (10-3-2007). HYDERABAD: Chairman of the Delimitation Commission Kuldeep Singh, has indicated that some of the Lok Sabha seats reserved for the Scheduled Castes in the State, which fall into clusters or contiguous belts, would be redistributed. After conclusion of a public hearing on the Commission's proposals for Adilabad, Karimnagar and Nizamabad districts here on Friday, Justice Kuldeep Singh told reporters that the Commission would consider constituencies with the next highest percentage of SC population to replace the ones mooted in the draft proposals. Karimnagar, Warangal and Ramagundem had been proposed as the Lok Sabha segments reserved for SCs, but the Commission could now reserve Chevella in Ranga Reddy district and, in addition, retain Nagarkurnool in Mahabubagar district. Similarly, Gudur could now become the new Lok Sabha seat reserved for SCs instead of Tirupati. A similar problem has arisen in Assembly constituencies in three coastal Andhra districts. Tiruvur, Nandigama and Nuzvid in Krishna district, Santanuthalapadu, Addanki and Kondapi in Prakasam district and Amalapuram, Razole and Allavaram in East Godavari districts are the contiguous segments. The Commission is likely to take a re-look at these constituencies too. Earlier, the Commission's proceedings were marred by slogan-shouting youth demanding creation of Korutla Assembly segment in Karimnagar district in place of the proposed Dharmapuri constituency.

5533. (10-3-2007). NEW DELHI: Last month's arrest in Argentina of Italian businessman Ottavio Quattrocchi, a key accused in the Bofors payoffs case, has generated much controversy over his extradition to India. He has since been freed on bail. Even as a two-member team of the Central Bureau of Investigation (CBI) team is camping in Buenos Aires to complete formalities for the lengthy judicial process, the agency is awaiting the extradition of 40 other fugitives from various other countries. Of the 40 criminals and economic offenders, 17 are wanted by the CBI and the others by the police in Gujarat, Punjab, Delhi, Bangalore and Chennai. In almost all cases, the extradition requests have been pending for the past three years or so. As many as 15 requests are pending with the United States, four with the United Kingdom, six with Canada and the others with New Zealand, Australia, Germany, Singapore, Sri Lanka, Italy, the United Arab Emirates and Kuwait. CBI sources pointed to the curious case of Amarendra Nath Ghosh, wanted by the agency's Kolkata branch in a bank fraud and cheating case, who swallowed a knife to escape extradition from Germany. He has remained admitted to hospital for the past few years, refusing surgery to remove the knife. The request for his extradition has been pending since January 31, 2003. The CBI was, however, successful in securing the extradition of 21 other fugitives in the past 11 years. They include underworld don Abu Salem, a key accused in the March 1993 Mumbai serial blasts case, and his companion Monica Bedi, who were extradited from Lisbon, Portugal, in November 2005; and Babloo Srivastav, wanted in several cases of organised crime, who was handed over from Singapore in 1995. Seven fugitives, against whom red corner notices had been pending, were deported over the past three years from Hong Kong, Canada, the U.S. and the UAE. The sources and former officials of the CBI said most of those extradited or deported were Indian nationals. Particularly distressing is the decade-old case of Turkish nationals Cihan Karanci and Tunkay Alankus, extradited in 1997 from Switzerland, and Brazilian Agnaldo Pinto, extradited from the U.K. in 1999. All three are accused in the Rs. 133-crore urea scam, which surfaced in 1995 during the Narasimha Rao regime. They are lodged in the Tihar jail here and the trial is yet to be concluded, a fact that only diminishes the image of India's criminal justice delivery system.

5534. (10-3-2007). NEW DELHI: After having demanded a meeting on the issue of nationality of Congress MP M.K. Subba, the Bharatiya Janata Party on Friday is believed to have said it was not prepared to discuss the matter with the Speaker. It would write to him in detail later. The Subba affair has resulted in an exchange of some unpleasant words over the last two days in the Lok Sabha between BJP MPs Jual Oram and V.K. Malhotra and Speaker Somnath Chatterjee, who had expunged alleged derogatory remarks made against the Chair. However, it is believed that Congress MP Devendra Prasad Yadav has given a privilege notice against Mr. Oram for allegedly denigrating the Chair. He is reported to have pleaded that although what they had said was expunged, the "offensive" remarks attributing motives to the Chair had been telecast live and heard throughout the country. It is learnt that the Speaker is yet to take a decision on the notice. On the request of the BJP that the Subba matter be discussed, the issue was raised at a meeting called by the Speaker on Friday morning. BJP's deputy leader V.K. Malhotra is reported to have said that he would write to the Speaker in detail, while Parliamentary Affairs Minister Priyaranjan Dasmunsi took the plea that it was for the Chair to decide whether the matter should be discussed in the House or not. However, the Government's view was that the subject was before the Supreme Court and it was there that the nationality issue should be decided before Parliament takes it up. The BJP's grouse is that while Parliament was quick to set up a committee to examine the "cash-for-questions" scandal following a sting operation - and later the MPs were disqualified - the Congress had been slow to react to the Subba affair. To that extent the BJP has charged the Congress with playing partisan politics. On the other hand, the ruling party has argued that the "cash-for-questions" scandal had shown some MPs to be corrupt and urgent action was needed to save the dignity of Parliament.

5535. (10-3-2007). CHENNAI: A group of activists has written to Prime Minister Manmohan Singh expressing deep concern about the neglect of children under six in the Union Budget 2007-08, terming it a "staggering and unacceptable imbalance in Budget priorities." The communiqu,, signed among others by economist Jean Dreze, Aruna Roy of the National Campaign for People's Right to Information and N.C. Saxena, former Member, Planning Commission, said it was shocking that the Government of India would be spending less than Rs. 5,000 crore this year on children under six, representing more than 15 per cent of India's population compared to Rs. 96,000 crore to be spent on defence. The allocation for ICDS (Rs. 4,761 crore) has barely increased in real terms, and was virtually unchanged as a proportion of GDP. The message to the Prime Minister has also been copied to UPA chairperson Sonia Gandhi, Union Finance Minister P. Chidambaram and Planning Commission Deputy Chairperson Montek Singh Alhuwalia. It recalls the Prime Minister's assurance to some of the signatories after the Bal Adhikar Samvad that the UPA Government was committed to the universalisation of ICDS and to fulfilling the Supreme Court ruling on ICDS. "We are, therefore, startled and dismayed that this commitment is not reflected at all in the Union Budget 2007-08." Shantha Sinha of the M.V. Foundation, Kavita Srivastava of People's Union for Civil Liberties, Harsh Mander of the Centre for Eqity Studies, Sudha Sundararaman of the All-India Democratic Women's Association, Vandana Prasad of Jan Swasthya Abhiyan, Annie Raja of the National Federation for Indian Women, Arun Gupta of Breastfeeding Promotion Network of India, Veena Shatrugna of the National Institute of Nutrition, and Mridula Bajaj of Mobile Creches also signed the letter. "It is a mystery to us how the CMP commitment and Supreme Court judgment can possibly be implemented within such meagre budget allocations," they wrote. The Supreme Court judgment requires an increase in the number of anganwadis from the present 9.4 lakh to at least 14 lakhs by December 2008. Higher allocations are also required to enhance the quality of ICDS services. Based on fairly conservative calculations of the requirements of "universalization with quality," the National Advisory Council recommended (in November 2004) an allocation of at least Rs. 9,600 crore for ICDS in 2007-08. "This figure needs upward revision in the light of the Supreme Court judgment, yet the actual provision in the Union Budget 2007-8 is not even half of this conservative estimate," they said. The contrast was shocking especially at a time of growing evidence (particularly from the National Family Health Survey) that there has been no substantial improvement in infant and young child nutrition, including optimal breastfeeding practices, during the last eight years. The signatories urged the Prime Minister to intervene and ensure a fairer deal for children in the Union Budget and in the 11th Plan. "We also take this opportunity to reiterate our appeal for more active political leadership on children's issues, including the universalisation of ICDS." **5536. (10-3-2007). NEW DELHI:** Social worker J.K. Mittal has been appointed Chairperson of the Central Adoption Resource Agency (CARA), an autonomous body under the Ministry of Women and Child Development. CARA functions as the central authority on the inter-country adoption of children. Immediately after taking over charge, Mr. Mittal reviewed the emerging issues on the protection and welfare of children with regard to adoption. In view of some unfortunate incidents in the recent past, he said the protection and welfare of children had become important. Mr. Mittal asked the officials to prepare a database of abandoned or relinquished children, who could be put up for adoption in the country or abroad. He also asked them to review the guidelines for inter-country adoption to ensure all safety measures and well being of children. The officials were directed to draw up training programmes for sensitising non-governmental organisations, officials, medical professionals and the judiciary on adoption.

5537. (10-3-2007). NEW DELHI: The one lakh jobs for the disabled people announced by the Centre in the Union budget will benefit the mentally challenged also, Union Social Justice and Empowerment Minister Meira Kumar has said. The private sector would also be given incentives for employing people with disabilities as announced by the Union Finance Minister in his budget speech. Speaking at the conclusion of the two-day seminar on "Mentally ill women: is destitution the only answer" organised by the National Commission for Women, Institute of Human Behaviour and Allied Sciences and Ashray Adhikar Abhiyan, here on Friday, Ms. Kumar said mentally ill people were entitled to all basic rights, including the right to live with dignity, treatment, physical protection, property and gainful employment. "However, while the problem of mental illness is far more complicated than physical illness, women also need more protection and destitution cannot be an answer in a civilised society," the Minister said. She called upon non-governmental organisations (NGOs) to set up rehabilitation and shelter homes for the mentally ill and abandoned women. Her Ministry supported 10 Halfway Homes for such people and "we want the NGOs to come forward to setting up and running similar homes, for which the Centre will provide financial assistance." Earlier, NCW chairperson Girija Vyas said the Mental Health Act, 1987 and the guidelines issued in 1982 must be reviewed to provide for rehabilitation after treatment of the mentally ill. Besides stringent legislative measures, sensitisation of the official mechanism and creating awareness among the people were equally important to overcome this huge problem which affected nationally 11 lakh people, of whom 3.5 lakh are women.

5538. (10-3-2007). NEW DELHI: All TV viewers and radio listeners will be able to follow the cricket World Cup live after Parliament approved a Bill making it compulsory for all private broadcasters to share their feed of major sports events with Doordarshan and All India Radio on free to air basis. The Rajya Sabha approved the Sports Broadcasting Signals (Mandatory Sharing with Prasar Bharti) Bill 2007 by voice vote on Friday. The Lok Sabha passed the Bill on Thursday. The Bill will replace the ordinance issued in February after Nimbus Communications, which holds rights of telecasting all international cricket matches in India till 2010, refused to share telecast signals with Prasar Bharati. The legislation seeks to ensure that access to sporting events is given to a large number of viewers and listeners, especially those who do not have access top satellite or cable television. Most of this section is in rural India and regularly denied access to sports events because a few dominant exclusive rights owners refuse to share the feed with Prasar Bharati, which is the exclusive owner of terrestrial platform. Winding up the brief discussion, Minister for Information and Broadcasting Priyaranjan Dasmunshi said the Government's downlinking and uplinking guidelines provided for mandatory sharing of sports signals. The Government was forced to take the ordinance route because the executive guidelines were challenged in the courts. In fact, during the recent West Indies-India one-day series, a large number of people were unable to watch the first match because the rights holders refused to provide live feed to Doordarshan. For these reasons, it became necessary to first promulgate ordinance and then formulate a law to give "immediate effect" to the Government's intentions.

5539. (10-3-2007). NEW DELHI: Lok Sabha Speaker Somnath Chatterjee has expressed the hope that the Women's Reservation Bill would be passed during his tenure. Speaking at a function organised here to felicitate women achievers, he said women contributed a lot to society and efforts should be made to encourage their participation in the political structure and public life. He, however, expressed unhappiness over the media coverage of the passionate speeches made by women MPs in both Houses on the occasion of International Women's Day on Thursday. Mr. Chatterjee said that most of the newspapers and television channels ignored the issue. Minister of State for Women and Child Development Renuka Chawdhary said that the Government had taken up women's development as a priority area and was working on various programmes to encourage women in every sphere of life. The women felicitated were: Anjali Gopalan, founder of Naz Foundation (India Trust); Archana Gupta, housewife working for self-help groups; Aruna Mishra, woman boxer; Indira Jaising, lawyer; Lalita Devi, a teacher working for Dalit girls' education in Gaya (Bihar); Monisha Behl, women's rights activist from northeast; Squadron Leader Namrita Chandi; Sabera Khoja, community radio broadcaster from Kutch; Vandana Vaibhav Gandhi, gynaecologist; and Veena Devi, woman sarpanch from Navada in Bihar.

5540. (10-3-2007). NEW DELHI: Raids by Income Tax and Enforcement Directorate officials on a Pune stud farm owner upset business schedule of the Lok Sabha on Friday, with the Opposition demanding a statement from Finance Minister P. Chidambaram. The Minister, however, did not oblige. Though all parties had agreed to dispense with the zero hour to allow time for discussion on the Railway budget, Bharatiya Janata Party (BJP) deputy leader Vijay Kumar Malhotra insisted on raising the issue after question hour. Since Mr. Malhotra insisted on bringing up the matter, the Speaker allowed other members, who had given notice for zero hour, to put up their issues. This led tofurther uproar as Congress member Madhusudhan Mistry drew attention of the House to police lathicharge on a Dalit rally in Gandhinagar. When BJP protested, Mr. Chatterjee said, "You did not stick to the decision to take up Railway budget after question hour. Now that I have let you raise an issue, others too will have to be allowed."

5541. (10-3-2007). NEW DELHI: The opposition Bharatiya Janata Party and the Communist Party of India (Marxist), on Thursday sought to know from the Government as to how the Indian Railways earned a whopping profit of Rs. 20,000 crore despite fall in passenger traffic by nearly seven per cent.

5542. (10- 3-2007) NEW DELHI: Prime Minister Manmohan Singh on Thursday said the Special Economic Zone (SEZ) policy was being reviewed to find out whether there was any pitfall in the existing framework. Recognising the need for a more humane approach, he assured Parliament that the Government would come up with an improved rehabilitation and resettlement policy. He was replying to the debate on the motion of thanks to the President's address. On the Sachar report, Dr. Singh said it brought out the stark reality of the condition of Muslims. The new 15-point programme was focussed on ensuring equitable sharing of the benefits of crucial development programmes, particularly in health and education. The Government was also formulating targeted programmes for districts where the minorities were concentrated. "In the long-run, as all communities catch up on their social indicators, there would be no need for such programmes but given the current disparities it is imperative that we carry all sections along." Dwelling on internal security, Dr. Singh asserted that his Government had an enviable track record, better than that of the previous regime, be it in the northeast, Jammu and Kashmir or naxal-affected districts. Even when there were terrorist incidents, the country never saw a breakdown of law and order and an upsurge of communal violence of the type that rocked Gujarat. "Compare the violence after the Godhra incident in Gujarat to the situation in Maharashtra after last year's Mumbai blasts." Describing naxalism as the "most widespread internal security threat" as seen in the recent killing of Sunil Mahato, a sitting Lok Sabha member from Jharkhand, Dr. Singh said the Government was following a two-pronged approach - supporting States in improving the performance of the security and police forces and going into the deep-rooted causes that gave rise to disaffection. In a clear message to terrorist groups, he said the Government could negotiate only with those who wanted peace, not with those who killed innocent people. "We will never hesitate to sit down and talk to a fellow Indian - howsoever misguided - if such conversations can bring peace to our people. But we will never compromise the unity and integrity of our country or allow those who kill innocent people to go unpunished."

5543. (10-3-2007). PUDUCHERRY: The Coast Guard (CG) has suggested the territorial administration to issue photo identity cards to fishermen and make registration of their boats compulsory. The issue was taken up by the maritime agency at the first district coastal security meeting, held under the chairmanship of District Collector G. Theva Neethi Dhas on Friday, which was initiated by the CG Station here. "We have requested the district administration to expedite the issuing of photo identity cards and registration of boats. The two things are necessary to thwart any infiltration attempt of the Liberation Tigers of Tamil Elam (LTTE) in the guise of fishermen," N. Somasundaram, Commandant CG Station, told The Hindu . The coastal security off Nagapattinam had been tightened and the LTTE may look for other places as landing sites, he pointed out. The tasks of issuing the photo identity cards and registration of fishing boats were given to the Fisheries Department. "We have asked the administration to closely monitor and regulate the supply of civil supply items such as rice and kerosene," he said. The Coast Guard wanted to speed up the dredging work at the Pondicherry Port to allow its vessels to anchor and implement International Ship and Port Facility Security Code (ISPS). The code provides for a framework for cooperation between vessels and port facilities in terms of maritime security. It was decided to have coastal security meeting every month. Another meeting would be held very soon in Karaikal, he informed.

5544. (10-3-2007). CHENNAI: Cinematographer-turned-director Velu Prabhakaran is not apologetic about his film 'Kadhal Arangam' having run into problems with the Censor Board. Rejecting criticism of "too much of exposure by the heroine", Shirly Das, Mr. Prabhakaran says the story itself is about how society views a woman's body. "I have approached the Central Board of Film Certification, which has refused a certificate for the film. Both the examining and the revising committee were apparently not able to see the true message of my film. I do not know why... " he says. "People today are openly talking about the spread of AIDS ... A few years ago no one would have talked about condom use to prevent AIDS, that too among students. My film is about the problem of sexual abuse... Why then is the Censor Board now allowing the movie?" he questions. The message of the film is to spread sex education. "My film conveys this in a unique manner." He says his conviction was strengthened by a recent survey that showed that a majority of crimes were sexually motivated. "In other countries, people do not gape at a bikini-clad woman in a swimming pool. Even here the Censor Board allows nudity in foreign movies or vulgar dialogues in recent movies. "But when I make a movie with a message, it is cut ruthlessly. We need a change in attitude ... " Mr. Prabhakaran says.

5545. (11-3-2007). NEW DELHI: The Central Board of Trustees of the Employees Provident Fund (EPF) Organisation on Saturday once again postponed a decision on fixing interest rates for its four crore subscribers. This was done to facilitate more consultations between the Labour and Finance Ministries, Minister of State for Labour and Employment Oscar Fernandes told journalists after the meeting here. Mr. Fernandes, as Chairperson of the Board of Trustees, told the meetingthat some more time was needed to fix the rate. The interest rates for 2006-07 and 2007-08 would possibly be announced at the next meeting. Members of the board belonging to trade unions rejected outright a suggestion for fixing the rate at eight per cent for 2006-07 and at 8.25 per cent for 2007-08. The rate for 2005-06 was fixed at 8.5 per cent. At the present rate of 8.5 per cent, the EPFO will have a Rs. 450-crore deficit and a reduction of half a per cent will leave it with a marginal surplus of Rs. 10.25 crore. Representatives of the Left-backed unions said the overall interest rates in the economy had gone up; some banks were paying 9.5 per cent on fixed deposits. Hence, the board should announce a higher rate for the subscribers, possibly over nine per cent. At its last meeting, the board rejected the Finance Ministry's proposal to invest five per cent of the EPF money in the equity market to increase its internal resources.

5546. (11-3-2007). BANGALORE: With the entry of China in the international sugar market in a big way coupled with stiff competition from Brazil and other countries, sugarcane growers and the sugar industry in the country will have a bleak future unless long and short term measures are taken, Union Minister for Agriculture, Public Distribution and Consumer Affairs Sharad Pawar said here on Saturday. Inaugurating a two-day national seminar on mechanised cultivation of sugarcane and safety-quality management in the sugar industry, Mr. Pawar said the situation called for a multi-pronged approach to face the challenge. The meet was organised by the Institution of Engineers (India), the Commissioner for Cane Development and Director of Sugar, the Indian Council for Agricultural Research and others. Mr. Pawar said the Union Government should bear the storing and stacking charges and both the Centre and the States should relax their taxes on sugar for the survival of the cane growers and the industry. With the sugar production around 240 lakh tonnes this year and a buffer of 40 lakh tonnes, the country will have 90 lakh tonnes of surplus after meeting the domestic consumption triggering a fall in the price. China, he said, was is commissioning 37 new plants with crushing capacity of 35,000 tonnes each and it will flood the market with sugar. Mr. Pawar said that the fall in the price would be a perennial problem for the farmers and the industry and all the stakeholders including the governments at the Centre and the States, should collectively take a decision to solve it. It is time for starting composite industry with cogeneration of power, ethanol, sugar and other industry related activities. The Union Minister leader called for reducing the pressure on land by weaning away rural people from agriculture, who accounted for 62 per cent, to industries and the service sector. There was an urgent need to go in for mechanisation as the cost of labour was increasing and was not available.

5547. (11-3-2007). BIDAR: The National Rural Employment Guarantee Assurance Scheme will be implemented in six more districts in the State from now on. The Centre has added Bellary, Hassan, Belgaum, Shimoga, Kodagu and Chikmagalur to the list of districts where the scheme is being implemented. Only Bidar, Gulbarga, Raichur, Chitradurga and Davangere districts were covered under the scheme so far. The scheme had been extended to six districts in Andhra Pradesh, five in Orissa, four in Tamil Nadu and two in Kerala. "These States had requested the Centre to extend the scheme to those districts. The Centre said that it considered issues like backwardness and prevalence of farmers' suicides," the Government sources said. Finance Minister P. Chidambaram said the Centre planned to extend the scheme to 130 districts this financial year. He had set aside Rs. 12,000 crore for the purpose. At the national level in 2006-07, the scheme had generated 65.35 crore mandays providing employment to 1.67 crore families spending Rs. 6,016 crore. In Karnataka, 4.78 lakh families had benefited by the scheme. The Government had spent Rs. 183 crore for this purpose.

5548. (11-3-2007). NEW DELHI: The Parliamentary Public Accounts Committee (PAC) has expressed concern at the technologies developed by the Indian Council of Agriculture Research (ICAR) not reaching farmers. In its 40th report on "Management of projects relating to utilisation and conservation of soil and water undertaken by the institutes of the ICAR," tabled in the Lok Sabha on Friday, the PAC noted that 16 technologies at a cost of Rs. 2.44 crore developed by four institutes of the ICAR had not been transferred to the end-users, farmers. It has recommended that the Department of Agriculture and Extension study the feasibility of setting up State-level Agricultural Research Extension Committees comprising representatives of the Ministry of Agriculture, ICAR, State Governments, farmers' organisations and NGOs to oversee effective coordination and supervision of activities relating to transfer of technologies. The panel, chaired by V.K. Malhotra, was unhappy that no records were maintained for 10 completed projects and 16 other projects affecting proper monitoring. While observing that projects were not completed within the stipulated time, the Committee suggested that the ICAR streamline its monitoring mechanism. The report is based on the audit review of the management of the in-house projects, sponsored projects and externally-aided projects undertaken by five ICAR institutes including the National Bureau of Soil Survey and Land Use Planning, Nagpur, the Indian Institute of Soil Science, Bhopal, the Central Soil Salinity Research Institute, Karnal, the Water Technology Centre for Eastern Region, Bhubaneswar, and the Central Soil and Water Conservation Research and Training Institute, Dehra Dun.

5549. (11-3-2007). NEW DELHI: The actions of the judiciary came under the scanner on Saturday at a people's convention organised by the Campaign for Judicial Accountability and Judicial Reforms. The two-day convention was addressed, among others, by the former Supreme Court judge, Justice P.B. Sawant, the former Law Minister, Shanti Bhushan, writer Arundhati Roy, the civil liberties lawyer, Prashant Bhushan, Dr. Bhaskar Rao of the Centre for Media Studies and Professor B.B. Pandey, former Dean of the Law Faculty, Delhi University. Criticising The Judges (Inquiry) Bill, 2006 intended to make the process of investigating complaints against Supreme Court and High Court judges more transparent, Mr. Justice Sawant held the amendments contemplated to be worse than the original provisions contained in the Judges (Inquiry) Act of 1968. He pointed out that under the existing Act, the enquiry committee to investigate judges consisted of a sitting judge of the Supreme Court, a Chief Justice of the High Court and one other independent jurist, all to be selected by the Speaker of the Lok Sabha. As against this, the proposed Bill provided for a National Judicial Council consisting of the Chief Justice of India, two senior-most judges of the Supreme Court and two Chief Justices of the High Court. This would make the judicial council an in-house council of sitting judges. Mr. Justice Sawant said credibility demanded that not all members of the enquiry committee were sitting judges. Mr. Justice Sawant also described as shocking the judiciary's attempts to place itself outside the purview of the Right to Information Act. He observed that the judiciary was perceived to be elitist because society, at large, was controlled by people who were anti-poor. He recommended the appointment of an independent judicial commission, similar to the senate judicial committee in the United States, where all relevant aspects of a proposed appointee's record and personality could be openly discussed. Mr. Justice Sawant also made a critical reference to a reported statement of the Chief Justice of India, K.G. Balakrishnan, that no self-respecting judge would be willing to discuss his assets. The former Press Council Chairman wondered whether it was the Chief Justice's case that all bureaucrats, ministers and electoral candidates, who were required to declare their assets, had no self-respect. Ms. Roy said the judiciary was perceived to be dysfunctional. In truth, it was dysfunctional only when it came to the poor. The Supreme Court's observations in several recent cases, including the case of the Narmada oustees, proved this amply.

5550. (11-3-2007). BANGALORE: Union Agriculture Minister Sharad Pawar on Saturday said the Centre was serious about implementing the recommendations of the National Commission on Agriculture headed by M.S. Swaminathan. He told The Hindu here that the voluminous report had been sent to the Ministries concerned, asking them to give their feedback in quick time. "Thereafter, I will place the report, with the views of the various Ministries, before the Cabinet for approval. I am confident that this exercise will be completed in about three months. We are privileged that an international agriculture scientist of repute headed the commission and the recommendations are highly valuable". Mr. Pawar, who is on a two-day trip to Bangalore, said the five-volume report had been sent to the Ministries of Rural Development, Water Resources, Forests, Rural Electrification, Finance, Planning and Women and Child Welfare. Appreciative of the commission's findings, he said all importance would be given to the recommendations. His Ministry was now laying stress on increasing the area under irrigation, providing quality seeds to farmers, ensuring availability of agricultural credit at reasonable rates of interest, enhancing post-harvest facilities including agro-processing, development of cold storages and remunerative prices for all produce. On sugar production in the current year, Mr. Pawar said he would draw the Cabinet's attention to surplus availability of about 90 lakh tonnes and the need to open up exports. The production this year was expected to be about 240 lakh tonnes and with last year's buffer of 40-lakh tonnes, the total availability would be around 280 lakh tonnes compared to the country's requirement of 180-190 lakh tonnes. "We have no choice but to export around 90 lakh tonnes." The major sugar-producing States were Uttar Pradesh (90 lakh tonnes), Maharashtra (75 lakh tonnes) and Karnataka (25 lakh tonnes). The others were Tamil Nadu, Andhra Pradesh and Gujarat. On the incidence of suicide by farmers, Mr. Pawar said that according to the latest reports from the vulnerable States of Andhra Pradesh, Maharashtra, Karnataka and Kerala, there was a drop in the number of suicides following the implementation of schemes for the benefit of farmers. The Union Government was closely monitoring the situation. The first part of the financial package granted to 32 districts in the four States related to waiver of interest on all farm loans and was totally implemented. Further, the loans taken by farmers from private financiers were transferred to commercial banks. Of the total of about 1.20 lakh suicides reported in the country every year, around 16,000 cases involved farmers (around 11 per cent). The suicides were not merely a fallout of crop failure. There were also those who had obtained loans for other reasons and committed suicide unable to repay. The second part of the package, relating to stepping up irrigation facilities in the 32 districts, would be implemented shortly.

5551. (11-3-2007). NEW DELHI: Taking time off political activities, parliamentarians participated in a sports meet organised by the Ministry of Parliamentary Affairs on Saturday. Jyotirmoyee Sikdar, Communist Party of India (Marxist) MP from West Bengal and former international athlete, held centre stage, capturing the first position in all races for women - 50 m, 75 m, and 100 m. While Ranjeet Ranjan of the Lok Jan Shakti Party was the runner-up, Anusuya Uikay of the Bharatiya Janata Party came third in all the races. In the men's 50 m race, Sandeep Dikshit of the Congress won the first position, followed by party colleague M.M. Pallam Raju and BJP member Ram Swaroop Koli. In the 75 m and 100 m race, Mr. Raju came first followed by Mr. Dikshit and Mr. Kohli. The results were mixed in the other contests also. The three-legged race was won by Ms. Sikdar and Ms. Ranjan, followed by Mr. Koli and G. Nizamudin of the Congress. In the musical chairs contest, Mr Nizamudin came first, and was followed by Ms. Uikay and Ms. Sikdar. The event also featured a kabbadi match and a tug-of-war contest. The parliamentarians won hands down against a team of journalists in both. Minister of State for Parliamentary Affairs and Chemicals and Fertilizers B.K. Handique gave away the trophies to the winners.

5552. (11-3-2007). BANGALORE: The Agriculture Ministry's focus is on impressing on farmers the need to look at allied activities if not other avocations. In other words, the effort is to wean people away from agriculture and thus prevent fragmentation of farmland. Union Agriculture Minister Sharad Pawar told The Hindu here on Saturday that the bane of Indian farming was that a large population was dependent on agriculture. With the size of each family increasing, more people were dependent on the same piece of land. Fragmentation added to the problem. While 56 per cent of the population was dependent on agriculture in India, in most of the developed countries it was only around five per cent. Thus, the per capita income of the farming community in such countries was much higher. "We have to spread this word and motivate our farm families to look at other occupations as well. This will help in increasing farm holdings and along with it will come mechanised cultivation."

5553. (11-3-2007). . SRINAGAR: The announcement that Kashmiri poet Rehman Rahi has been chosen for the Jnanpith Award for 2004 has sent a wave of jubilation among the people of the State. Since Friday, the poet himself has been flooded with congratulatory messages, and his home has been witnessing a never-ending queue of visitors. Talking to The Hindu , Prof. Rahi said: "I was happy to hear about the award but actually it is for the Kashmiri language." In his message, Union Water Resources Minister Saifuddin Soz described Prof. Rahi "as the embodiment of all that is best in the multi-hued and composite culture of Kashmir." Mr. Soz said: "By achieving this distinction, Prof. Rahi has brought dignity and honour not only to himself and his State but also to the lovers of art and literature all over. The fact that Prof. Rahi happens to be the first poet-writer of Kashmir to achieve this distinction is a matter of great honour and pride to the people of the State." Prof. Rahi, a recipient of the Padma Shree and the Sahitya Akademi fellowship, is considered a living legend in the State. Born in Srinagar in 1925, he was brought up by his uncle after being orphaned at an early age.

5554. (11-3-2007). GHAZIABAD: President A.P.J. Abdul Kalam on Saturday emphasised the need to analyse the frequency and the type of crime occurring in different establishments serviced by the Central Industrial Security Force and called for conducting a security seminar once every two years to review its performance. Making two suggestions to enable the force to constantly improve, Mr. Kalam said: "An analysis may be conducted about the frequency and the type of crime occurring in different establishments serviced by the CISF. Also, there is a need to network all the CISF units in the country and create a CISF e-governance grid so that rapid mobilisation of additional resources can be done in difficult areas at short notice." Secondly, the President stressed the need to conduct a security seminar once in two years, wherein all chief executives of establishments serviced by the CISF can participate and present their views based on the overall performance and utilise the feedback for making policy changes. Addressing the officers and men on the occasion of the 38th Raising Day of the CISF at its campus here in Indirapuram, Mr. Kalam said the force should aim at becoming an "invisible lean and thin smart security system" in the establishments under their cover, causing minimum disturbance to functionaries of the establishments and the clients. Monthly review meetings should be held to bring out incidents successfully handled and those where difficulties were faced. He also administered oath to the CISF personnel to lead an honest life and become a role model for others through their conduct, discipline and service with a smile.

5555. (11-3-2007). NEW DELHI: Asserting that a solution would be found in the next few days on the proposal to increase peak-time operation charges for airlines at key airports to reduce congestion, Union Civil Aviation Secretary Ashok Chawla said on Friday that ways and means to decongest airports at peak time had to be found. Speaking at India Aviation Forum 2007, organised by the Confederation of Indian Industry and KPMG, Mr. Chawla said the Airport Economic Regulatory Authority Bill to deal with airport tariffs and other disputes would be introduced in the ongoing Budget Session of Parliament. Bringing together key people in the aviation sector, the Forum aimed to highlight the problems that this growing sector was facing. A joint paper released by the KPMG and CII on the aviation industry pointed out the need to develop non-metro locations to support the domestic network. The paper recommended that brown field projects be given the same tax incentives as green-field projects owing to the fact that substantial investments are being made towards upgrading airport facilities, which result in creation of new assets.

5556. (11-3-2007). CHENNAI: The University Grants Commission is committed to an inclusive agenda for the disadvantaged sections in higher education as a means of equitable development, UGC Chairman Sukhadeo K. Thorat said on Saturday. The Commission was addressing multiple exclusions that denied the disadvantaged education rights and would follow an inclusive, holistic policy, he said at the inauguration of a national conference on 'Higher Education and Inclusive Development,' organised by the University of Madras' Department of Econometrics. From this year on, 13 universities would offer courses in inclusiveness. The commission would support educational institutions in backward regions. Inclusive education was the major focus of the Eleventh Plan. Exclusion in higher education fell into two categories: entire groups and individuals. Certain sections such as Scheduled Castes, religious minorities and women were at a disadvantage. While the national gross enrolment stood at 10 per cent in 2005, it was only 4.5 per cent for tribals, seven for Scheduled Castes and nine for Other Backward Classes. Among the other castes, it touched 90 per cent. The percentage of women in the gross enrolment was a mere seven per cent, while it was eleven per cent for men. The percentage of rural poor was less than two and seven among urban poor. As such, Indian society faced complex problems of exclusion, which had to be studied while designing higher education programmes, Mr. Thorat said. The recent budget was an "economic elaboration of the principles of social inclusion," since, for the first time, the allocation for education, health and agriculture had been increased by 34.2 per cent, 21.9 per cent and 53.7 per cent respectively, said M. Anandakrishnan, Chairman, Madras Institute of Development Studies. Education had been made the core of the development process in the last three years, and inclusion of the disadvantaged would have to be done at both the social and spatial levels. The feudal mindset that the higher education was the preserve of the elite had to change, he said. Deeper deliberations were needed to influence agencies such as the UGC to formulate higher education policies, Xavier Alphonse, member, UGC. Access, equity, affordability and opportunity should combine in the pursuit of excellence in education.

5557. (11-3-2007). COIMBATORE: Funds will not be a constraint for the Irugur railway line doubling and it will be completed by December 2007, Union Minister of State for Railways R. Velu said on Saturday. The Ondipudur and Ukkadam rail overbridges would be thrown open by April 14 and July respectively. Mr. Velu was here to inaugurate 'Swapnam', a multi-cuisine food plaza, at the Coimbatore Junction under the aegis of the Indian Railway Catering and Tourism Corporation. Asked about the inadequate allocation and inordinate delay in completion of the Irugur line doubling work, Mr. Velu said budgetary allocation or funds would never be a constraint in easing the single line bottleneck and said "Railways could cut corners in other schemes and ensure completion of this project". On the long-pending rail overbridges on Tiruchi Road at Ondipudur and at Ukkadam on the Sungam bypass road, Mr.Velu said the Ondipudur rail overbridge would be thrown open for traffic by April 14. The railway portion of the work at Ukkadam would be completed by May while the highways department would complete its remaining portion of the work by June. Denying reports of the Coimbatore region being neglected in the railway infrastructure, Mr. Velu said Rs. 8.40 crore was spent for various passenger amenities and work for basic infrastructure worth Rs. 58.78 lakh had been completed and works worth Rs. 187.19 lakh were in progress. Besides, projects worth Rs. 594.25 lakh had been accorded sanction. The major works included construction of a second sub-way besides waiting halls in the western entrance of the Coimbatore Junction. On a query for operating shuttle electric train services to Pollachi and Mettupalayam and increasing the frequency of services to Tirupur and Erode to ease the pressure on road traffic, the Minister said every train and track required periodical maintenance in a block of four hours or in two blocks of two-and-a-half hours each. Running trains beyond capacity would be at the cost of safety, he said. On the plea for a convenient train connectivity to Tirupur and Erode, the Minister said the passenger train timings would be revised. For the convenience of rail users and to decongest the Coimbatore Junction, the Intercity Express and the West Coast Express would be given a stoppage at North Coimbatore Junction. On the allocation of Rs. 30 crore for the gauge conversion work between Coimbatore and Dindigul via Pollachi, which would cost Rs. 330 crore, the Minister said for preliminary works this allocation would be enough. The demand for overnight train services from Coimbatore to Bangalore and Tiruvananthapuram would be considered, he said.

5558. (11-3-2007). COIMBATORE: Formation of the Salem Railway division would not affect the revenue or growth of the Palakkad division, Minister of State for Railways R. Velu said here on Saturday. On the delay in formation and functioning of the Salem Division, Mr. Velu said Rs. 3 crore had already been allotted for preliminary works and the division had started functioning. Employees transferred from the Palakkad Division had been relieved as per the headquarter orders, the Divisional Railway Manager, Palakkad, A.K. Harit, pointed out. To put in place complete logistics it would take some more time and the new division and its jurisdictions remained the same, Mr. Velu said. On food plazas, Mr. Velu said it was proposed to open 50 food plazas in major railway stations. Already 38 such plazas had been opened. Similar plazas would also be opened at Tambaram, Katpadi, Tirunelveli, Salem and Erode.

5559. (12-3-2007). BHOPAL: The ruling Bharatiya Janata Party has won the Gwalior parliamentary and the Udaipur Assembly seats, while the Congress won the Sidhi Lok Sabha seat in Madhya Pradesh. The byelection results were announced on Sunday. Madhya Pradesh Minister for Tourism, Sports and Youth Welfare Yashodhara Raje Scindia won the Gwalior seat by defeating Ashok Singh of the Congress by a margin of 35,602 votes. Ms. Scindia polled 2,10,465 votes, while Mr. Singh 1,74,863. The seat was represented by Congress MP Ram Sevak, who resigned in the wake of the cash-for-question scam. However, the Congress has managed to stage a comeback by wresting the Sidhi parliamentary seat from the BJP. Its candidate Manik Singh defeated Kunwar Singh of the BJP by a slender margin of 1,576 votes. Mr. Manik Singh polled 2,12, 998 votes, while the BJP candidate 2,11,412. The Udaipura Assembly seat was won by Shashi Prabha Ram Pal Singh of the BJP. She polled 52,544 votes against the Congress party's Sahib Singh Patel, who got 33,465 votes.

5560. (12-3-2007). NEW DELHI: The Central Bureau of Investigation will take the services of a "neutral team" of chartered accountants to scrutinise the material for a preliminary enquiry against Uttar Pradesh Chief Minister Mulayam Singh for allegedly amassing assets disproportionate to his known sources of income. After registering a Preliminary Enquiry (PE) on March 5 on the Supreme Court's direction, the CBI recorded the statement of petitioner Vishwanath Chaturvedi, an advocate who also claimed to be a Congress activist. His statements, very general in nature, were on sworn affidavits, CBI sources said. "We are proceeding with extreme caution and care. The preliminary enquiry will be conducted to ascertain if a case is made out or not. To ensure transparency, quick, fair and balanced probe, we will call for a panel of neutral chartered accountants either from their own institute or the Comptroller and Auditor-General or the Central Vigilance Commission," privileged sources told The Hindu. The sources said the CBI was also likely to seek a "correction" of the Supreme Court order, which said the agency should submit its report, after concluding the PE, to the Central Government. "We are also examining this aspect and may seek the view of the court to ascertain if it was legally tenable as it does not seem to be in line with the existing provisions in the law." The CBI was proceeding in "strict compliance" of the order in a "responsible manner" as per the law. In the initial phase, the agency would scrutinise the documents such as sale deeds and other statements filed by the parties along with the public interest litigation petition. It was on Mr. Chaturvedi's petition that the Supreme Court ordered on March 1 a preliminary enquiry by the CBI into allegations that Mr. Singh and his family had acquired assets disproportionate to known sources of income. Vehemently opposing a CBI probe, Mr. Mulayam Singh has alleged that the agency was neither "impartial nor unbiased."

5561. (12-3-2007). THIRUVANANTHAPURAM: The Indian Coast Guard will acquire three new specialised vessels this year to tackle oil spill disasters, A. Rajasekhar, Inspector General and Commander, Coast Guard Region (West), told The Hindu on Sunday. A massive oil spill disaster control exercise would be held off the coast of Gujarat in April, he said. It would also help the Coast Guard assess the in-house marine pollution fighting capabilities of private and public sector oil refining companies having facilities along the west coast. The western seaboard of the country has become highly vulnerable to marine pollution because of increased oil tanker and container ship traffic. Such shipments are at risk from terrorists and, more commonly, rough weather. Inclement weather caused at least six large cargo ships to run aground in 2006, raising the spectre of oil pollution. Three oil spill incidents were reported in Indian waters last year. In September last, the Coast Guard helped Sri Lankan authorities fight an oil slick caused by a sunken merchant ship off Galle harbour. The Coast Guard is set to acquire 15 new vessels and 23 aircrafts in the next five years. Seventy per cent of the new acquisitions will be deployed in the western region. Two new Coast Guard stations are coming up in Maharashtra. At Vizhinjam, the Coast Guard has asked for a separate docking facility when the proposed port materialises. Another priority of the force is to prevent terrorists and smugglers from using the 500-odd uninhabited islands dotting the Western seaboard as staging points for their operations. Recently, the State police had found that there were 74 hot spots along Kerala's 570-km coastline that could be exploited for such activities. The Coast Guard has launched a community interaction programme to win the "hearts and minds" of the coastal community. In return, the Coast Guard gets better intelligence on illegal activities. Such initiatives resulted in the seizure of contraband, including narcotic drugs, valued at Rs.238 crore last year. The unit conducted 237 search and rescue missions, including sorties, last year. As many as 48 poachers were arrested from Indian waters.

5562. (11-3-2007). CHENNAI: With the Centre turning down the State's proposal to introduce Tamil in the Madras High Court, Chief Minister M. Karunanidhi on Sunday wrote to the Prime Minister and the Union Ministers of Home and Law urging them to expeditiously obtain Presidential consent for use of Tamil in the High Court. In identical letters, a copy of which was released to the press, Mr. Karunanidhi said: "All concerned are surprised and shocked over the contents of this letter [disagreeing with the State's proposal], when the relevant provisions of the Constitution and the Law made by Parliament remain unchanged." High Courts in Bihar, Uttar Pradesh, Madhya Pradesh and Rajasthan had been authorised to conduct all proceedings in Hindi. "Therefore, in the case of Tamil Nadu a different stand cannot be taken," he said. The letter from the Centre said the matter was examined in consultation with the Supreme Court and the Chief Justice of India opined that for the present "it is not proper to introduce regional language in the orders, decrees and other proceedings of the High Court." According to the Chief Minister, the use of Tamil as High Court language was not exclusive but only in addition to English language. "Therefore, any judge who wants to have the proceedings or pass an order in English is not prohibited from using English. Also any order passed in Tamil shall always be accompanied by an official English translation. No judge who is not well versed in Tamil would face any difficulty either in hearing the argument or passing the orders." Pointing to the reference made to certain resolutions passed in 1966 on the issue of use of languages other than English (linguistic medium) in High Courts, he said: "The entire scenario in the country has undergone transformation since then. Regional aspirations have gained momentum ... in a multi-lingual country like India, there cannot be a permanent formula for the use of a single language." He said, "The rejection of request made by West Bengal Government for introduction of Bengali as the official language in Calcutta High Court may not be a valid reason to reject the request of Tamil Nadu. As already stated, the four states have been permitted ... and that the same cannot be denied to Tamil Nadu."

5563. (12-3-2007). THIRUVANANTHAPURAM: The City Corporation has been directed to revise three major project reports that were submitted to the Central Government for financial assistance under the Jawaharlal Nehru National Urban Renewal Mission (JNNURM). The Ministry of Urban Development has denied approval for the water supply, sewerage and solid waste management components of the City Development Plan. The project reports have been returned with recommendations for revision of the parameters. Mayor C. Jayan Babu who returned from New Delhi after signing the tripartite agreement involving the Central and State governments and the City Corporation for implementation of the JNNURM, said here on Sunday that the water supply and sewerage projects would have to be revised in accordance with national standards. Of the total estimate of Rs.842.34 crore that was submitted by the City Corporation, only the report on the improvement of basic services for the urban poor costing Rs.5.66 crore was approved.

5564. (12-3-2007). FEROKE: Historian and former chairman of the Indian Council for Historical Research (ICHR) M.G.S. Narayanan has contested Chief Minister V.S. Achuthanandan's comments that the ICHR had been instrumental in propagating communal interpretation of history. Professor Narayanan, who chaired the ICHR between August 2001 and December 2003, said that neither he nor the historical body had anything to do with communalising history textbooks. Mr. Achuthanandan, while inaugurating the 67th edition of the Indian History Congress at Farook College here on Saturday, alleged that attempts were made to rewrite textbooks on communal lines and to use institutions like the ICHR for propagating communal interpretation. Professor Narayanan told The Hindu that he, as chairman of the ICHR, had openly criticised the Bharatiya Janata Party Government, which was then in power at the Centre, for re-writing history books. He said it was the National Council for Educational Research and Training (NCERT) which tried to implement the RSS agenda through history books. "As a sister organisation we were never consulted by the NCERT," said Prof. Narayanan.

5565. (12-3-2007). NEW DELHI: The shortfall in the availability of wheat in the domestic market last year that pushed prices up, is expected to be made up this year with the expectations of a "good crop" this rabi. Although officials are still reluctant to make early predictions, it is estimated that wheat production will touch 74 million tonnes this season, as against 69.4 million tonnes produced last year. The target for wheat procurement for the Public Distribution System is set at 130 lakh tonnes as against the 92.5 lakh tonnes procured last year. With a ban on wheat exports and futures trading in wheat, it is expected that the mandi arrivals would be procured by the Food Corporation of India and government agencies. Sources said the farming community is hopeful of the government giving a bonus of Rs. 50 a quintal in addition to the minimum support price of Rs. 750 a quintal for wheat this season. Procurement commences in Punjab and Haryana from April 1. It will be earlier in Madhya Pradesh. So far most of the 55 lakh tonnes of imported wheat has arrived. The buffer stock of wheat on April 1 would be 45 lakh tonnes. With a procurement target of 130 lakh tonnes, the wheat availability would improve during the year which would help contain the price of wheat, atta, bread and various wheat products. Agriculture Minister Sharad Pawar too has expressed optimism on wheat output in view of the favourable weather so far. The recent rains and reports from farm commissioners from wheat producing States indicate that wheat production would cross the earlier estimates of 72.5 million tonnes, he told journalists on the sidelines of an India-Africa Agrifood Summit here. However, at a workshop on Wheat Management-Rabi, 2007 Food Secretary T. Nanda Kumar said the Centre would soon convene a meeting with State Governments to impress upon them the need to rationalise mandi taxes and levies that also contribute to the higher price of wheat. The Food Secretary said the government would not hesitate to import further quantities of wheat and to procure more wheat this season to maintain the Public Distribution System and welfare schemes. He countered the rumour that a ban on futures trading of wheat and rice was imposed to allow the Food Corporation of India to procure more. The Parliamentary Standing Committee on Food recommended the ban, he clarified. On his part, FCI Chairman Alok Sinha advised roller flour millers to collectively think how best to bring down prices of atta and wheat products. Despite the government releasing wheat in the open market the price of the commodity had not come down in the retail market, he pointed out. As yet another measure to prevent hoarding for speculation, the Central Government has extended its notification on empowering State Governments to impose stock limits on wheat and pulses to prevent speculation.

5566. (12-3-2007). COIMBATORE: The Union Finance Minister, P. Chidambaram, expressed confidence that public sector banks will be able to bring down the net Non-Performing Assets (NPA) to below 0.5 per cent in the next few years. Speaking at the opening of the Vadavalli branch of Indian Overseas Bank (IOB) here on Sunday, he said the net NPA level now was 1.3 per cent. Efforts were on to bring it to one per cent in one year and reduce it further in the coming years. With the banks and the borrowers cooperating by repaying the loans, the NPA level could be brought down. For three consecutive years, the country's average Gross Domestic Product (GDP) growth was 8.6 per cent. The Finance Minister was confident that the GDP would grow at 9 per cent this fiscal and next year too. The banks had disbursed Rs. 1.76 lakh crore of agricultural loans in two years (though the Government's target was to achieve it in three years). Hence, the target for next year was Rs. 2.25 lakh crore. He said that banks had given loans to 26 lakh self-help groups at the national level. Every year, five lakh to six lakh new groups got loans. Their repayment was 98 per cent. The groups should strive to achieve 100 per cent repayment, he said.

5567. (13-3-2007). NEW DELHI: Pleading the case of freedom-fighters from Telengana who have yet to get the status, a delegation of MPs from Andhra Pradesh met Prime Minister Manmohan Singh, urging his intervention and early resolution on the issue. "It is a matter of shame that 60 years after Independence, the status of the 13,500 members identified by a committee it has not been resolved. In the last 10 years, many have died. The question is not of pension or free railway tickets, but at least, that they be recognised," CPI(M) MP Sitaram Yechury said. The delegation included CPI leader S. Sudhakar Reddy, Telugu Desam Party's K. Yerrannaidu, C. Ramchandraiah and others. Mr. Yechury said nearly 500 representatives staged a protest sit-in at Jantar Mantar to highlight their problem. Mr. Yechury said that in 1996, a committee appointed by then Home Minister Indrajit Gupta identified 13,500 people as having taken part in the movement against the Nizam Government in Hyderabad region. He said these people fought for the integrity of the country at a time when there was a "conspiracy" to have the region go to Pakistan. He said this was the second time the Andhra Pradesh delegation had met Dr. Singh on the issue of freedom-fighters of the region and the Government for the third time, having petitioned the Home Minister earlier.

5568. (13-3-2007). NEW DELHI: Buoyed by a robust performance by the manufacturing sector, growth in industrial production in January this year was higher at 10.9 per cent as compared to 8.5 per cent in the same month a year ago. According to quick estimates of the Index of Industrial Production (IIP) released by the Central Statistical Organisation (CSO) here, industrial growth during the first ten months of 2006-07 was 11 per cent on the back of an eight per cent growth clocked during the same period in the previous fiscal.

5569. (13-3-2007). NEW DELHI: The Union Human Resource Development (HRD) Ministry has ruled out the possibility of accepting the National Knowledge Commission (NKC) recommendation for increasing fees in universities to meet at least 20 per cent of their total expenditure from this source. The Ministry indicated this in its reply in the Rajya Sabha to a question on "scaling up of higher education fees." According to the Ministry, it has already accepted the recommendation of the 2005 report of the Central Advisory Board of Education (CABE) Committee on "Financing of Higher and Technical Education" that "revenue generation through student fees beyond 20 per cent may seriously affect access to higher education." The NKC - in its note on higher education finalised earlier this year - recommended a more rational fee structure for resource generation. "As a norm, fees should meet at least 20 per cent of the total expenditure in universities. This should be subject to two conditions: needy students should be provided with a fee waiver plus scholarships to meet their costs and universities should not be penalised by the University Grants Commission for the resources raised from higher fees through matching deductions from their grants-in-aid." While the NKC said universities should generate at least 20 per cent of their expenditure from fees, the CABE Committee set 20 per cent as the outer limit. The CABE Committee report said: "Earlier committees have recommended raising of resources through fees and other sources to the extent of about 20 per cent of the recurring requirements of the universities. This may be considered an upper level.

5570. (13-3-2007) NEW DELHI: Yogi Adityanath, the Bharatiya Janata Party Member of Parliament from Gorakhpur, broke down in the Lok Sabha on Monday alleging a "political conspiracy" against him by the Uttar Pradesh Government. The

MP, who attended the House after spending 11 days in the Gorakhpur jail, wept while narrating his experience at the hands of the State Government, alleging that it was out to "malign and torment me". A third-term member from Gorakhpur, he broke into sobs after Speaker Somnath Chatterjee allowed him to raise the issue during zero hour and promised to look into the matter "Will we get protection or will our condition be the same as that of Sunil Mahato?" he asked the Speaker. Mahato, a Jharkhand Mukti Morcha member from Jharkhand, was assassinated near Jamshedpur last week. Yogi Adityanath alleged that he was being "framed". The cases in which he had been cleared by the CB-CID years back were being reopened as he was raising public issues and speaking out against corruption and the growing activities of the ISI along the Indo-Nepal border, he charged. Amid chants of "shame, shame" from BJP members, Yogi Adityanath claimed that 14 of his supporters had been booked under the National Security Act and he himself was not provided any reason for his arrest for seven days. The Speaker told the House that he had sought a report from the Union Home Ministry on the incident and would personally look into the matter. "We will do whatever is within our jurisdiction but we have to follow a procedure. There is a certain inadequacy of powers," Mr. Chatterjee said. The MP said if he failed to get protection from the House, "I have no intention of continuing as a member even for a minute." Several members including Gurudas Das Gupta (CPI), Prabhu Nath Singh (JD-U) and BJP deputy leader V.K. Malhotra came out in support of Yogi Adityanath.

5571. (13-3-2007). KOCHI: The Central Bureau of Investigation (CBI) on Monday submitted before a Division Bench that it could not take over the investigation into the Marad violence, as trial in the case was already on. The submission was made before a Bench comprising Acting Chief Justice K.S. Radhakrishnan and Justice M.N. Krishnan when writ petitions seeking a CBI probe into the case came up before it. The CBI further submitted that if an investigation was conducted into the aspects such as source of fund or suspected involvement of a foreign hand, it would be a partial investigation.

5572. (13-3-2007). THIRUVANANTHAPURAM : Indian Air Force (IAF) would receive the first batch of the British-made Advanced Jet Trainers, Hawks, by the middle of the year, Chief of the Air Staff S. P. Tyagi said on Monday. At a press conference here, Air Chief Marshall Tyagi said the IAF had ordered 66 Hawks, out of which 24 would be directly supplied by the British company. The rest would be assembled at the Hindustan Aeronautics Limited (HAL) facility in Bangalore. "The IAF is about to sign a contract for forty more Russian-made Sukhoi-30 MKI fighter aircraft," he said. It would soon have 80 new Russian-made MI-17 helicopters. The IAF would acquire three Advanced Warning and Air Control System (AWACS) aircrafts by December. The planes were made in Uzbekhistan, modified in Russia and were now being fitted with superior avionics in Israel. The IAF needed 126 more fighter planes but had not yet decided what types of aircraft to buy. Air Chief Marshall Tyagi said peninsular India was gaining strategic importance and more "combat assets" of the IAF "will be moving South." Two new airfields would be built at the IAF's Suloor airbase in Coimbatore. The base could become home to the Light Combat Aircraft (LCA), likely to be inducted in 2010. The IAF was also developing Tanjore as another strategically important base. The IAF has approached the Civil Aviation authorities in Thiruvananthapuram for the shared use of the Thiruvananthapuram International Airport. The Central Government was aware of the need to improve the pay of fighter pilots. The Air Chief is due for retirement soon. It was his farewell visit to the SAC. A veteran combat aviator, he has served in the IAF for over 43 years. "I have spent a life time with the IAF. If there is a rebirth, I would like to be back in the force as a fighter pilot," he said.

5573. (13-3-2007). NEW DELHI: The multicrore money laundering case unearthed in Pune figured in the Lok Sabha on Monday, when the Bharatiya Janata Party charged the United Progressive Alliance Government with orchestrating a "cover-up" operation. Participating in a discussion on the Union budget, BJP deputy leader V.K. Malhotra asked the Government to reveal the names of politicians and bureaucrats who were alleged to be having links with the Pune stud-farm owner Hasan Ali. According to the ongoing police investigations, Mr. Ali is said to have stashed away over Rs. 35,000 crore in Swiss bank accounts. "Who are the politicians? Who are the bureaucrats, said to be known to Hasan Ali, being questioned by police in Pune? Why are names of all these persons not being made public," Mr. Malhotra asked while noting that, according to reports, some terrorists were also known to Mr. Ali. Before turning to the budget proposals, Mr. Malhotra took a dig at Congress president Sonia Gandhi saying she could not "escape her responsibility" by merely "expressing concern" over issues such as rising prices and distance herself from the UPA Government's "failures." For, neither the Prime Minister nor the Finance Minister could take any decision without her consent. Noting that "this is not a budget for aam aadmi," Mr. Malhotra asked the Government to explain the reasons for the spiralling prices of vegetables, pulses and various other commodities. It was because of the Government's "wrong policies" and flawed procurement process that hoarders were making profits at the expense of the common man. The promises made by the ruling coalition in its Common Minimum Programme (CMP) were not being honoured and the salaried class was feeling "betrayed." "There is no mention of the 26-crore below poverty line people in the budget which is anti-poor and anti-common man." The budget would be more remembered for making cat and dog food cheaper, Mr. Malhotra said.

5574. (13-3-2007) FEROKE (KOZHIKODE): The curtain came down on the three-day, 67th session of the Indian History Congress with a call to the Centre to free the Archaeological Survey of India (ASI) and the National Archives of India (NAI) from bureaucratic control. A resolution adopted at the closing plenary here on Monday regretted the continuing tendency to place the administration of such organisations in the hands of government officials and keep professionals out of their helm. Despite strong protests from the Indian History Congress, the ASI has had no professional archaeologist as its Director-General for over a decade now. The NAI has similarly been placed in the hands of a government official with no professional credentials. The resolution, moved by historian Irfan Habib, pointed out that for a long time the Jawaharlal Nehru Memorial Museum and Library too was deprived of an academic director on mere technicalities and maintained as a bureaucratic fief. A similar situation often occurred in the autonomous institutions. The Indian Council for Historical Research (ICHR), which should have an 'eminent historian' as its chairman, had during long periods of interregnum been saddled with Human Resource Development Ministry officials assigned to it as chairmen. This congress was happy that a recent interregnum was brought to an end with the appointment of eminent historian Sabyasachi Bhattacharya as ICHR chairman. The resolution came out strongly against the "attempts" being made by various Ministries to wrest control of autonomous institutions by taking over the entire process of selection and appointment of their 'chief executives.' Thus the Department of Personnel identified the member-secretary and not the chairman as the 'chief executive' of the ICHR, and the HRD Ministry, therefore, put forward the claim that it had the sole powers to control the selection and appointment of the member-secretary, contrary to the process prescribed in the ICHR charter. Such measures made a mockery of the autonomy of academic institutions and ought to be immediately be rescinded. The History Congress hoped that Parliament and the Ministers concerned would give serious attention to the issue, that professional control of the ASI and the NAI would be restored and the attempt "to ride roughshod" over the prescribed process of selection of officers of autonomous organisations would be abandoned. A second resolution welcomed the passage and enforcement of the Right to Information Act and called upon the Government to make the principles underlying the Act applicable to the NAI and the State Archives so as to grant scholars larger and freer access to all records. The ASI too should provide easy access to its physical finds, field notes and unpublished reports, the resolution said.It expressed happiness over the American Historical Association's efforts to end all restrictive measures to control the flow of information taken in the U.S. in the wake of the aggression in Iraq and the so-called 'war on terror'. The right of the people to know was of worldwide application and Indian historians expressed full solidarity with their U.S. colleagues. Through a third resolution, the History Congress appreciated the Union Government's decision to earmark Rs. 3.20 crore for the upkeep and preservation of invaluable manuscripts in the Bhandarkar Oriental Research Institute, Pune.

5575. (13-3-2007) FEROKE (KOZHIKODE): Historian Irfan Habib has disputed former Indian Council for Historical Research (ICHR) chairman M.G.S. Narayanan's statement that the ICHR had played no part in attempts at communal interpretation of history during the Bharatiya Janata Party-led National Democratic Alliance regime. Prof. Habib said the ICHR did play a part in the decision not to publish the volumes of the 'Towards Freedom' project that contained chapters on the Hindu Mahasabha's support for Britain's War effort because such contents were not to the liking of the Rashtriya Swayamsevak Sangh and the Sangh Parivar. It is equally noteworthy that no such evidence could be found against the Communist Party, he said. Responding to the allegation that the Indian History Congress (IHC) is interpreting history with a narrow political perspective, Prof. Habib said no organisation could function outside politics. As for the charge that the History Congress is a camp follower of the Left, he said membership of the IHC is open to persons subscribing to all shades of political opinion. He pointed out that at the session of the IHC where a resolution against the demolition of the Babri Masjid was adopted, only two persons had opposed it, despite 67 of the delegates having earlier voted against those who subscribed to a Leftist perspective. Asked why the IHC had failed to recognise the importance of 'Contemporary History' and allot a special section for it in its session, the eminent historian said this is mainly because there has been a strong argument that 'Contemporary History' is too contemporary for rigorous evaluation. However, it has been decided to include it as a separate session of the IHC annual conference. This has been done basically because several papers concerning contemporary history were coming in and being included in the 'Modern India' section, 'which is bursting in its seams,' he said.

5576. (13-3-2007). NEW DELHI: The Government was put in the dock in the Rajya Sabha on the high rate of dropout of girl students. It was said to be as high as 64.92 per cent before the tenth standard. Several Opposition members expressed dissatisfaction at the Government's reply on the steps being taken to ensure that girl students stayed back or returned to school. Minister of State for Human Resource Development D. Purandeswari said lack of access to school, lack of transportation facilities and teacher absenteeism were some of the reasons for this state of affairs. She said the Government was seized of the matter and had initiated "bridge-schools" such as Innovative Education and Education Guarantee Schemes to bring girls back to school.

5577. (13-3-2007) NEW DELHI: The Bharatiya Janata Party has written to Speaker Somnath Chatterjee demanding an investigation into allegations against Congress MP Mani Kumar Subba by a Lok Sabha committee and expulsion of the member. BJP deputy leader V.K. Malhotra pointed out one of the basic qualifications for contesting the Lok Sabha polls was that the candidate must be an Indian citizen. Now there were serious doubts about Mr. Subba's nationality. Also there was a precedent of disqualification of MPs on the recommendation of a House committee as in the case of those involved in the cash-for-questions scandal. Along with the two-page letter dated March 12 - the BJP released copies to the press - Mr. Malhotra sent to the Speaker the full transcript of a recent investigative story telecast by CNN IBN. Parliamentary Affairs Minister Priyaranjan Dasmunsi said it was for the Speaker to take a decision (on setting up a committee). Congress sources maintained that the cash-for-questions issue was one of corruption and ethical standards. Mr. Malhotra said that while Mr. Subba's birthplace and date of birth as mentioned in the records of the 12th Lok Sabha were Tejpur in Assam and March

16, 1951, the current Lok Sabha records mentioned Debgram in Darjeeling and March 16, 1958.

5578. (13-3-2007). CHENNAI: Union Law Minister H.R. Bhardwaj has asked his department to "process the matter [on the introduction of Tamil as the official language in the Madras High Court] afresh, keeping in view the points raised" by Chief Minister M. Karunanidhi. He conveyed this in a letter to Mr. Karunanidhi on Monday. He has also asked his department to follow up the processing of the matter with obtaining the "consent of the President... as expeditiously as possible." After the Law Ministry disagreed with the proposals sent earlier, the Chief Minister had written to the Union Law Minister expressing shock over the rejection of the proposal and had also pointed out that there were four States where proceedings were also available in their official language. Introduction of Tamil was also in line with Article 348 (2), Mr. Karunanidhi had pointed out. The State had completed the other requirements such as taking the Governor's consent and passing a resolution in the Assembly.

5579. (13-3-2007). NEW DELHI: A delegation of Members of Parliament belonging to the ruling DMK and allies in Tamil Nadu and Puducherry met Prime Minister Manmohan Singh here on Monday and requested him to expedite the Presidential assent to the resolution passed by the Tamil Nadu Assembly authorising the use of Tamil as court language in the Madras High Court. Led by Union Transport Minister T.R. Baalu, the delegation presented a memorandum to the Prime Minister stressing the need for making Tamil as the court language in the High Court.

(1)

A DRAFT OF THE PROPOSED BROADCASTING SERVICES REGULATION BILL, 2007

Whereas airwaves are public property and it is felt necessary to regulate the use of such airwaves in national and public interest, particularly with a view to ensuring proper dissemination of content and in the widest possible manner;

Whereas the Broadcast media is a powerful purveyor of ideas and values andplays a pivotal role in not only providing entertainment but also disseminatinginformation, nurturing and cultivating diverse opinions, educating and empoweringthe people of India to be informed citizens so as to effectively participate in thedemocratic process; preserving, promoting and projecting the diversity of Indianculture and talent;

Whereas Government has issued guidelines from time to time for regulating the Broadcasting Services and it is felt necessary to give a statutory effect to these guidelines and provide for a comprehensive legislation;

Therefore this is a Bill To promote facilitate and develop in an orderly manner the carriage and content of Broadcasting,

To provide for regulation of broadcasting services in India for offering a wide variety of entertainment, news, views and information in a fair, objective and competitive manner and to provide for regulation of content for public viewing and matters connected therewith or incidental thereto.

To provide for the establishment of an independent authority to be known as the Broadcast Regulatory Authority of India for the purpose of regulating and facilitating development of broadcasting services in India.

To encourage Broadcasting services to be responsive to the educational, developmental, social, cultural and other needs and aspirations of people and include in their programming public service messaging and content BE it enacted by Parliament in the Fifty –Eighth Year of the Republic of India as follows: -

CHAPTER 1

PRELIMINARY

1. Short title, extent and commencement: (1) This Act may be called the Broadcasting Services Regulation Act, 2007.

(2) It extends to the whole of India.

(3) It shall come into force with immediate effect.

2. Definitions: In this Act, unless the context otherwise requires: -

(a) "Authority" means the Broadcasting Regulatory Authority of India established under section 14;

(b) "Authorized Officer" with respect to a Broadcasting Service means

i) an officer of the Central Government or the Authority or the State Government for such limits of jurisdiction as may be notified by the Central Government

ii) on being empowered by the Central Government to notify , an officer of the Authority or State Government for such limits of jurisdiction as may be notified by the Authority or the State Government

(c) "Broadcaster" means any person who provides a content broadcasting service and includes a broadcasting network service provider when he manages and operates his own television or radio channel service.

(d) "Broadcasting" means assembling and programming any form of communication content like signs, signals, writing, pictures, images and sounds, and either placing it in electronic form on electro-magnetic waves on specified frequencies and transmitting it through space or cables to make it continuously available on the carrier waves so as to be accessible to single or multiple users through receiving devices either directly or indirectly; and all its grammatical variations and cognate expressions;

(e) "Broadcasting Service" means assembling, programming and placing communication content in electronic form on the electro-magnetic waves on specified frequencies and transmitting it continuously through broadcasting network or networks so as to enable all or any of the multiple users to access it by connecting their receiver devices to their respective broadcasting networks, and includes all the content broadcasting services and the broadcasting network services;

(f) "Broadcasting Network Service" means a service, which provides a network of infrastructure of cables or transmitting devices for carrying broadcasting content in electronic form on specified frequencies by means of guided or unguided electro-magnetic waves to multiple users, and includes the management and operation of any of the following:

i. Teleport / Hub / Earth Station

ii. Direct-to-Home (DTH) Broadcasting Network

iii. Multi-System Cable Television Network.

iv. Local Cable Television Network

v. Satellite Radio Broadcasting Network

vi. Such other Network Service as may be prescribed by the Central Government

(g) "Cable Operator" means any person who manages and operates, or is otherwise responsible for, a multi-system or a local cable television network

(h) "Cable television channel service" means the assembly, programming and transmission by cables of any broadcast television content on a given set of frequencies to multiple subscribers.

(i) "Cable Television Network" means any system consisting of closed transmission paths and associated signal generation, control and distribution equipment, designed to receive and re-transmit television channels or programs for reception by multiple subscribers;

(j) "Carrier" means the electro-magnetic waves that can travel on air or cable and are capable of carrying communication content in electronic form on specified frequencies

(k) "Chairperson' means the Chairperson of the Authority appointed under section 15;

(l) "Channel" means a set of frequencies used for transmission of a programme;

(m) "Competent Authority" means the Authority designated by the Government for the purpose of this Act;

(n) "Community radio service" means terrestrial radio broadcasting intended and restricted only to a specific group & within specified territory;

(o) "Content" means any sound, text, data, picture (still or moving), other audiovisual representation, signal or intelligence of any nature or any combination thereof which is capable of being created, processed, stored, retrieved or communicated electronically;

(p)"Content Broadcasting service" means the assembling, programming and placing content in electronic form and transmitting or re-transmitting the same on electro-magnetic waves on specified frequencies, on a broadcasting network so as to make it available for access by multiple users by connecting their receiving devices to the network, and includes the management and operation of any of the following:

i. Terrestrial television service;

ii. Terrestrial radio service;

iii. Satellite television service;

iv. Satellite radio service;

v. Cable television channel service;

vi. Community radio service;

vii. Such other content broadcasting services as may be prescribed by the Central Government.

(q)"Content Code" means broadcasting content certification and regulation rules as prescribed under secion 4(3) of this Bill;

(r)"content produced in India" means a television or radio programme, excluding transmission of sporting events and compilations thereof, advertisements, and continuity announcements, which is produced—

(i) by a broadcasting service licensee;

(ii) by a person who is a citizen of, and permanently resident in India;

(iii) by a juristic person, the majority of the directors, shareholders or members of whom are citizens of, and permanently resident in India;

(iv) in a co-production in which persons referred to in subparagraphs (i), (ii) or (iii) have at least a fifty percent financial interest;

(v) by persons referred to in subparagraphs (i), (ii), (iii) or (iv), in circumstances where the prescribed number of key personnel who are involved in the production of the television programme, are citizens of, and permanently resident in India; or

(vi) by persons referred to in subparagraphs (i), (ii), (iii) or (iv), in circumstances where the prescribed percentage of the production costs are incurred in India;

(s)"Decoder" means an equipment for decoding an encrypted channel to facilitate its intelligible reception;

(t)" Digital Addressable System" means a mechanism or electronic device or more than one electronic devices put in an integrated system through which digital broadcasting signals of a service provider can be sent in an encrypted or unencrypted form, which can be decoded by a mechanism or device or devices at the premises of the subscriber within the limits of authorisation made, on the choice and request of such subscriber, by the service provider to the subscriber;

(u)"Direct-To-Home Broadcasting Service" means a service for multi channel distribution of programmes direct to subscriber's premises by uplinking to a satellite system specified for the purpose by the Competent Authority;

(v)"Downlinking" with reference to satellite broadcast or DTH Broadcasting service means reception of programmes transmitted from a satellite to an earth station or a receiving device;

(w)"Encrypted" means treated electronically or otherwise for the purpose of preventing intelligible reception by unauthorized persons;

(x)"Frequency" means frequency of electro-magnetic waves used for transmission of broadcasting service;

(y)"Foreign satellite broadcasting service' means a broadcasting service provided by using a satellite, up linked from a foreign country and receivable in India;

(z)"Free-to-air broadcasting service" means a non encrypted broadcasting service made available for reception by receiving apparatus commonly available to the public without requiring payment of a subscription fee;

(aa)"interconnected undertakings" shall have the same meaning as assigned to it in the Monopolies and Restrictive Trade Practices Act, 1969

(ba)"License" means a license issued for any of the broadcasting services by the relevant Licensing Authority prescribed by the Central Government under this Act;

(ca)"Licensing Authority" means an officer of the Central Government or the Authority or the State Government, so notified by the Central Government in respect of any of the broadcasting services and for such limits of jurisdiction as may be determined by the Central Government.

(da)"Licensed service" means a broadcasting service licensed by the Licencing Authority;

(ea)"live" in relation to broadcasting of an event, or series of events, has the meaning generally accepted within the broadcasting industry.

(fa)"Local cable operator" means any person who manages and operates or is responsible for the management and operation of a cable television network to provide a cable television service to multiple subscribers in a particular area

(ga)"Local Delivery service" means a service for multi-channel downlinking and distribution of television programmes by a land based transmission system using wired cable or wireless cable or a combination of both for simultaneous reception either by multiple subscribers directly or through one or more local cable operators

(ha)"Member" means a Whole-time Member of the Authority referred to in section 13 and includes the Chairperson;

(ia)"Multi-System Cable Television Network" means a system for multi-channel downlinking and distribution of television programmes by a land based transmission system using wired cable or wireless cable or a combination of both for simultaneous reception either by multiple subscribers directly or through one or more local cable operators

(ja)"Multi System Operator (MSO)" means any person who manages and operates a multisystem cable television network to provide a cable television service to multiple subscribers, which may or may not include other value added services including telecommunications and Internet.

(ka) "Network operator" means any person who provides a broadcasting network service.

(la)"News and Current Affairs Channel" means a channel that broadcasts programs containing reports and discussions on current events, ideas, individuals and institutions dealing with political, social, economic and such other subjects as are of general interest to the public at large, but does not include a channel that exclusively broadcasts scientific, cultural, educational or entertainment programs including news relating thereto.

(ma)" Non Prime Band" shall be interpreted in relation to Prime Band

(na)"Notification" means a notification published in the official Gazette or posted on the official web site of the Ministry of Information & Broadcasting or of the Authority or of the Council, as the case may be, and the expression "notified" to be construed accordingly;

(oa) " Person" as mentioned in the definitions of Cable operator, Local Cable Operator and Multi-System Operator means

ii) An individual who is a citizen of India;

iii) An association of individuals or body of individuals, whether

incorporated or not, whose members are citizens of India;

iv) A company as defined in section 3 of the Companies Act, 1956 (1 of 1956) with such eligibility conditions as may be specified by the Central Government or the Authority;

(pa)"Prescribed" means prescribed by rules notified under this Act;

(qa)"Prasar Bharti" means the Corporation known as the Prasar Bharati

(Broadcasting Corporation of India) established under subsection (1) of section 3 of the Prasar Bharti (Broadcasting Corporation of India) Act,1990;

(ra)"Prime Band" constitutes frequencies relating to channel falling in band 1 (Channels 2 to 4 ranging from 47 to 68 MHz) and Band III (Channels 5 to 12 ranging from 174 to 230 MHz)

(sa)"Private communication" means:

(i) A communication between two or more persons that is of a private or

domestic nature;

(ii) An internal communication of a business, government agency or other

organization for the purpose of the operation of the business, agency or

organization; and

(iii) Communication in such other circumstances as may be prescribed.

(ta) " Program" in relation to broadcasting service, means:

(i) Any matter the purpose of which is related to entertain, educate or inform public or

(ii) Any advertising or sponsorship matter, whether or not of a commercial kind; But does not include any matter that is wholly related to or connected with any private communication.

(ua) "Public service broadcaster" means Prasar Bharati or any other entity which may be notified as public service broadcaster by Central Government

(va)"Public Service Broadcasting" means the broadcasting of content that is socially , economically and culturally relevant and is in public interest and welfare

(wa)"Public Service Broadcasting Channel" means a radio or television channel of Public Service Broadcaster i.e Prasar Bharati or any other Channel so notified by the Central Government on the recommendations of the Public Service Broadcasting Council

(xa)"Public Service Broadcasting Council' means an autonomous body constituted as per section 30 of this Act

(ya)"Public Service Broadcasting Obligation Fund" refers to the fund created as per provisions of subsection (4) of section 14 of this Act.

(za)" Public Service Broadcasting Obligation" shall mean obligations supposed to be discharged by a broadcasting service provider as per provisions of section 13 of this Act

(ab)"Registered channel" means a broadcasting channel registered under this Act

(bb) "Regulations" means regulations made by the Authority or by the Council under this Act;

(cb)"Satellite television service" means a television broadcasting service provided by using a satellite, and received with or without the help of a local delivery system but does not include Direct-to-Home delivery service;

Explanation: Decision of the Authority whether a particular service falls in the category of a satellite broadcasting service or a Direct-to-Home delivery serviceshall be final.

(db)"Satellite radio service" means a radio broadcasting service provided by using a satellite and directly receivable through receiver sets by multiple subscribers in India;

(eb) "Service provider" means provider of a broadcasting service;

(fb) "sporting events of national importance" means such national or international sporting events; held in India or abroad, as may be notified by the Central Government in the Official Gazette to be of national importance;

(gb)"Subscriber" of a service means a person who receives the service at a place indicated by him without further transmitting it to any other person;

(hb)"Subscription fee" means any form of consideration given by subscriber;

(ib)"Terrestrial television service" means a television broadcasting service provided over the air by using a land based transmitter and directly received through receiver sets by the public but does not include a local delivery service;

Explanation: Decision of the Authority whether a particular service falls in the category of a terrestrial television service or a local delivery service shall be final;

(jb)"Terrestrial radio service" means a radio broadcasting service provided over the air by using a land-based transmitter and directly received through receiver sets by the public;

(kb)"Whole-time Member" means a Whole-time Member of the Authority appointed under section 13;

(lb)"Wireless cable" means a land based wireless transmission system used for multi-point multi-channel distribution of programmes on frequencies designated for the purpose by the Competent Authority;

(mb)"Uplinking" with reference to satellite broadcast or Direct-to-Home service means uplinking of programme transmission from an earth station or a transmitting device to the satellite;

(nb)"Year" means the financial year.

CHAPTER 2

REGULATION OF BROADCASTING SERVICES

3. Broadcasting services not without license: (1) No person shall, after the commencement of this Act, provide any broadcasting service, or broadcast any program or channel, without obtaining a license for such service or permission for such program or registration of such channel, in accordance with the policy guidelines prescribed under this Act for regulating such broadcasting service, program or channel.

Provided that the cable operators registered under the Cable Television Networks (Regulation) Act, 1995 may continue to provide cable services in accordance with the conditions laid down in section 49 of this Act;

Provided further that the permissions issued, license agreements signed with private operators, and registration of channels done, by the Central Government, from time to time under respective guidelines listed under sub-section (3) of this section, read with Indian Telegraph Act, 1885, prior to the commencement of this Act shall be deemed to be licenses issued under the provisions of this Act from the respective dates of issue of such permission or signing of such license agreement, or registration of such television channel, and shall be valid till the date of expiry of the original permission or license agreement or registration, as the case may be, notwithstanding anything contained in this Act or any other law for the time being in force.

Provided further that the Central Government or the Authority may make appropriate modifications, additions and deletions in the terms and conditions of such permissions or licences or registrations or any agreements already executed as mentioned in the second proviso to bring them in conformity with the provisions of this Bill or any Rules or Regulations or Guidelines issued thereunder

Provided further that the Central Government may, by notification, exempt Prasar Bharti or any other Public service Broadcasting Channel, as may be specified, from all or any of the provisions of this Act.

Provided further that the Government may, by notification, exempt such noncommercial establishments under common ownership from obtaining a license for a

Local Delivery Service without using wireless cable, for the purpose of providing such service for the exclusive use of their members subject to such conditions and restrictions as may be specified.

4. Registration of channels and compliance with the Content Code:

(1) Every service provider shall register his television or radio channel with the Authority in the manner prescribed.

(2) The Authority may refuse to register a channel, if it is of the considered opinion that the content of the channel is likely to threaten the security and integrity of the State or threaten peace and harmony or public order in the whole or a part of the country, or threaten relations with foreign countries

Provided that no such order of refusal shall be issued without giving a reasonable opportunity to the applicant company or the service provider of being heard.

(3) No service provider shall provide any broadcasting content that is not in conformity with the broadcasting content certification and regulation rules, hereafter referred to as 'the Content Code', as may be prescribed by the Government under this Act Provided that till such time as the Content code is notified under this Act, all service providers shall adhere to the Programme Code and the Advertising Code prescribed under the Cable Television Network Rules 1994.

. Central Government to exercise certain powers in a situation of external threat or war involving India :

(i)The Central Government may at any time, if it appears necessary or expedient to do so in public interest , in respect of a broadcasting service , in a situation of external threat or war involving India, direct the service provider to stop broadcasting its service or transmit in its broadcasting service such programmes or announcements in such manner as may be considered necessary. The service provider shall immediately comply with all such directions failing which the Central Government may direct the Licencing Authority to suspend or revoke its licence.

(ii) A copy of every direction issued under this section shall be laid before each house f Parliament

6. Central Government to exercise certain powers in exceptional circumstances:

(i) The Central Government may under exceptional circumstances, if it appears necessary or expedient to do so in public interest, in respect of any broadcasting service, which is considered prejudicial to relations with a foreign country, public order, or internal security , direct the service provider to stop broadcasting its service or transmit in its broadcasting service such programmes or announcements in such manner as may be considered necessary. The service provider shall immediately comply with all such directions failing which the Central Government may direct the Licencing Authority to suspend its licence

(ii)An appeal against any such order or direction under subsection (i)shall lie to the High court.

(iii) A copy of every direction issued under this section shall be laid before each house of Parliament

7 Mandatory sharing of Sports Broadcasting signals with Prasar Bharti :

(l)For the purpose of ensuring the widest availability of broadcast signals for viewing in India, no content rights owner or holder and no television or radio broadcasting service provider shall carry a live or delayed live television broadcast on any cable or Direct-to-Home network or radio commentary broadcast on its Amplitude Modulation (AM) and Frequency Modulation (FM) channels in India of sporting events of national importance, unless it simultaneously offers the same live or delayed live broadcasting signal, without its advertisements, to the Prasar Bharati to enable it to re-transmit the same on its terrestrial networks and Direct-to-Home networks in such manner and on such terms and conditions as may be specified.

Provided that if a content rights owner or holder is not generating any radio commentary of the event, then Prasar Bharati shall have the right to produce the radio commentary for transmission on its Amplitude Modulation (AM) and Frequency Modulation (FM) channels subject to the condition that the revenue derived from such broadcast shall be shared on a 50:50 basis after exclusion of production cost

(2) The terms and conditions under sub-section (1) shall also provide that the advertisement revenue sharing between the content rights owner or holder and the Prasar Bharati shall be in the ratio of not less than 75:25 in case of television coverage and 50:50 in case of radio coverage.

(3) The Central Government may specify a percentage of the revenue received by the Prasar Bharati under sub-section (2), which shall be utilised by the Prasar Bharati for broadcasting other sporting events.

8. Compulsory transmission of Public Service Broadcasting channels:

(1) Every cable operator shall re-transmit,-

(i) channels operated by or on behalf of Parliament in the manner and name as may be specified by the Central Government by notification in the Official Gazette;

(ii)at least two Doordarshan terrestrial channels and one regional language channel of a State in the Prime band, in satellite mode on frequencies other than those carrying terrestrial frequencies.

(2) The channels referred to in sub-section (1) shall be re-transmitted without any deletion or alteration of any programme transmitted on such channels.

(3) The Central Government may, by notification in the Official Gazette, specify the name of every Doordarshan channel and any other public service broadcasting channel to be retransmitted by cable operators in their cable service as also the number of channels to be carried in the non-prime band and the manner of reception and retransmission of such channels.

(4) The Central Government may specify the number and names of channels to be mandatorily carried by other categories of Broadcasting Network service Providers and the manner of reception and retransmission of such channels.

9. Introduction of digital addressable systems (DASs) in broadcasting network services:

(1) Where the Central Government is satisfied that it is necessary in public interest to do so, it may, by notification, make it obligatory for every broadcasting network service provider in the country to transmit or re-transmit content of any or all channels provided by him, through a digital addressable system with effect from such date as may be specified in the notification.

(2) With a view to ensuring that the broadcasting network service providers comply with the obligation under sub-section (1), the Central Government may, by notification, prescribe a transitional scheme for introduction of digital addressable systems (DASs) by service providers, with effect from such date as may be specified in the notification, and different dates may be specified for different types of service providers in different States, cities, towns or areas, which may, inter alia, provide for the following:

(a) Policy guidelines, transitional arrangements and the time frame within which the service providers in different areas shall complete the process of providing the DASs to all their viewers,

(b) Obligations of the broadcasters in terms of declaration of prices of their registered channels, commercial arrangements with their distributors and networks service providers etc.

(c) Obligations of the Multi-service Operators (MSOs) and Local Cable

Operators (LCOs) who introduce DASs in terms of their supply, maintenance, quality of service standards, subscriber management system etc.

(d) Obligations of the MSOs and LCOs who continue for the time being with the existing non-addressable systems in terms of declaration of the available number, names and prices of channels, maintenance of subscriber registers and furnishing periodical information etc.

(e) Rights and obligations of the viewers in terms of getting quality of service, options to choose channels, making payments for the DASs and monthly subscriptions for the channels, proper upkeep and use of DASs etc.

(f) Powers and functions of the Authority in terms of regulation of, and adjudication on, the commercial arrangements among various service providers, prescribing quality of service standards, enforcement of license conditions and other obligations under the scheme on the service providers and the viewers etc.

(g) Such other terms and conditions of the scheme as are considered necessary and desirable for ensuring the successful transition from the existing technology to the digital addressable systems within the time frame

prescribed under sub-section (1).

(3) Notwithstanding anything contained in sub-sections (1) and (2) or any other law for the time being in force, the Central Government shall have the power, for reasons to be recorded in writing, to postpone or advance any specified date or dates, or by notification, modify, suspend or revoke a notification already issued or any other order or direction issued by it or the Authority

Provided that any order issued or action taken by the Central Government or the Authority or by any other person in pursuance of the earlier notification or order shall, unless specified otherwise, be deemed to be valid and continue to be in operation as if the earlier notification had never been modified, suspended or revoked, as the case may be.

10. Powers and functions of the Central Government: The Central Government shall have the authority to -

i) Prescribe policy guidelines and procedures for the grant, refusal or revocation of licenses/ registration for all types of broadcasting services;

ii) Designate and notify such officers of the Central Government, State Governments or the Authority as may be considered necessary, as the Licensing Authorities to grant, refuse or revoke licenses/ registration in respect of such broadcasting services and for such limits of jurisdiction as may be prescribed;

iii) Prescribe the terms and conditions of licenses / registration to service

providers and procedures to ensure their compliance by the service providers;

iv) Prescribe license fees and processing fees for grant of licenses / permissions / registration for different types of broadcasting services;

v) Prescribe policy guidelines, including transitional arrangements, to facilitate the introduction of digital addressable systems in broadcasting services throughout the country in a time-bound manner;

vi) Prescribe guidelines and norms to evaluate and certify broadcasting content and the terms and conditions of broadcasting different categories of content by the service-providers;

vii) Prescribe policy guidelines and institutional arrangements for self-regulation of broadcasting content by the service providers in conformity with the prescribed norms;

viii) Prescribe guidelines and institutional arrangements for complaint / grievance redressal against violations of the prescribed norms of broadcasting content code by service providers;

ix) Prescribe policy guidelines to facilitate competition and promote efficiency in the operation of broadcasting services so as to facilitate growth in such services;

x) Prescribe policy guidelines laying down terms and conditions for mandatory sharing of broadcasting signals with prasar Bharati relating to sporting events of national importance

xi) Prescribe a percentage of revenue received by Prasar Bharati under subsection (3) of section 7, which shall be utilized by the Prasar Bharati for broadcasting other sporting events

xii) Prescribe such eligibility conditions and restrictions on ownership as

mentioned in section 12

xiii) Prescribe limits on Public service Broadcasting obligations as mentioned in section 13

xiv) Exercise, or authorize other existing institutions to exercise, any or all the powers and perform any or all the functions of the new institutions, pending their creation and operationalisation.

11. Validation of the guidelines already issued:

(1)The following guidelines issued and amended by the Central Government from time to time before coming into force of this Act, shall be deemed to have been issued under this Act:

(i) Uplinking Guidelines of 2000

(ii) FM Radio Policy for private agencies of 2000 (Phase 1)

(iii) DTH Policy Guidelines of 2001

(iv) SNG/DSNG Use Guidelines of 2002

(v) Community Radio Policy of 2002

(vi) Revision of Uplinking Policy Guidelines of March 2003

(vii) Revision of Uplinking Policy Guidelines of August 2003

(viii) FM Radio Policy Phase 2 of July 2005

(ix) Downlinking Guidelines of November 2005

(x) Consolidated Uplinking Guidelines of December 2005

(2) Notwithstanding anything contained in any judgement , decree or order of any court, tribunal or other authority, any action taken by the Central Government or the Prasar Bharati in pursuance of the Guidelines referred to in sub-section (1) shall be deemed to be and to have always been for all purposes in accordance with the law, as if the Guidelines had been validly in force at all material times and notwithstanding anything as aforesaid and without prejudice to the generality of the foregoing provisions, no legal proceeding shall be maintained or continued in any court for the enforcement of any direction given by any court or any decree or order which would not have been so given had the Guidelines been validly in force at all material times.

12. Restrictions on accumulation of interest:

(1) The Central Government shall have the authority to prescribe such eligibility conditions and restrictions with regard to accumulation of interest at national, state or local level in the broadcast segments of the media by the print or other media as may be considered necessary from time to time, to prevent monopolies across different segments of the media as well as within the broadcast segments, to ensure plurality and diversity of news and views.

(2) No content broadcasting service provider together with its interconnected undertakings shall have more than the prescribed share of paid up equity or have any other financing or commercial arrangement that may give it management control over the financial, management or editorial policies of any broadcasting network service provider.

Provided that this condition will not be applicable in cases where a content

broadcasting service provider requires a teleport or such other infrastructure for captive use to make its content available to other broadcasting network service providers.

(3) No broadcasting network service provider together with its interconnected undertakings shall have more than the prescribed share of paid up equity or have any other financing or commercial arrangement that may give it management control over the financial, management or editorial policies of any content broadcasting service provider.

(4) No content broadcasting service provider together with its interconnected undertakings shall have more than the prescribed share of the total number of channels in a city or a state subject to a prescribed overall ceiling for the whole country.

(5) The restrictions as required under subsections (1) to (4) above shall be laid down by the Central Government in consultation with the Authority, on the basis of a review to be conducted every 3 years by the Authority.

Provided that till such a review is done by the Authority and restrictions revised by the Government the prescribed share under subsection(2) and (3) shall be taken as 20% and the overall ceiling on the total number of channels under subsection(4) as 15%.

Provided further that in a subsequent review the Central Government shall not reduce the prescribed share to a level below that prescribed under first proviso Provided further that any broadcasting service provider, in breach of the restrictions as provided under the first proviso of this subsection , shall submit his compliance plan to the Government within two months and shall come into compliance within one year of the coming into force of this Act.

13. Public Service Broadcasting Obligations: (1) Every broadcasting service provider shall discharge such public service broadcasting obligations as the Central Government may prescribe from time to time in accordance with the limits indicated below:

(a) The share of content produced in India shall be as prescribed by the Central Government and shall not be less than 15% of the total content of a channel broadcast during every week.

(b) The share of public service/social messaging through advertisements and such other promotional materials/messages shall be as notified by Central Government from time to time and not more than 10% of the total commercial time of a channel broadcast during every week.

(c) The share of public service/socially relevant program content shall be as

notified by Central Government from time to time and not more than 10% of the total program content of a channel broadcast during every week.

Provided that the Central Government may provide a time frame to comply with any one or more of the obligations as mentioned above,

Provided further that Central Government may lay down policy Guidelines to either exempt or to allow partial compliance or the permissible manner of compliance with respect to an individual broadcaster or certain categories of broadcasters.

(2) In the event of failure to comply with the public service obligation, every content-broadcasting service provider shall be liable to pay such amount to the Authority , as may be calculated by the Authority in the manner prescribed by the Central Government towards its public service obligation.

(3) (i)Public Service Broadcasting Council as constituted under the Act shall discharge the responsibility of ensuring compliance of public service broadcasting obligations by broadcasters and shall suggest to the Authority the amount of penalty to be paid by a broadcaster for non-compliance of its obligations as laid down under subsection (1)

(ii) Public Service Broadcasting Council will also lay down regulations from time to time as to what will constitute public service/socially relevant programming or messaging and how its share is to be calculated.

(4) The amount of penalty paid shall be deposited in a fund to be called the " public service broadcasting obligation fund".

CHAPTER 3

BROADCASTING REGULATORY AUTHORITY OF INDIA

14. Establishment and incorporation of the Authority: (1) With effect from such date, as the Central Government may by notification appoint in this behalf, there shall be established for the purposes of this Act an Authority, to be known as the Broadcast Regulatory Authority of India.

(2) The Authority shall be a body corporate by the name aforesaid, having

perpetual succession and a common seal with power to acquire, hold and dispose of property, both movable and immovable, and to contract, and shall by the said name sue and be sued.

(3) The Authority shall consist of one Chairperson and not more than six wholetime Members . One third of the Members shall be Women.

(4) The head office of the Authority shall be New Delhi.

15. Appointment of Chairperson and Members:

(1) The Chairperson and Members of the Authority shall be appointed by the Central Government on the recommendations of a Committee consisting of the Chairman of the Council of States (Rajya Sabha), the Speaker of the House of the People (Lok Sabha) and the Leader of the opposition in the House of the People (Lok Sabha)). The quorum for making this recommendation shall be two (2) in case the post of Leader of Opposition is vacant.

(2) The Central Government shall intimate the vacancies to the Committee and also provide a list of names of eligible applicants for consideration. The Committee shall be free to consider any other eligible names as it deems fit.

(3) If the Committee fails to arrive at a consensus within 30 days of submission of the list of eligible applicants or in three sittings, whichever is earlier, the matter will be placed before the President of India for a decision..

(4)The whole-time Chairperson and six whole-time members of the Authority shall be so appointed as to include one each from amongst eminent persons who have special knowledge of and professional experience of at least 25 years in, the fields of

(a) Television, Radio, Cinema, Advertising, Audio-Visuals, Fine Arts etc.;

(b) Journalism, Mass Communication, Literature, Social Sciences etc.;

(c) Finance, Commerce, Audit, Accountancy etc.;

(d) Electronics, Telecommunication, Information Technology etc;.

(e) Consumer Affairs, Social Work/Service, Civil Society Organizations etc.;

(f) Law, Judiciary etc.;

(g) Public Administration, Management etc.;

(5) The recommendations made by the Committee constituted under subsection(1) shall be binding for the purposes of appointment under this section.

16. Term of office, conditions of service etc. of the Chairman and other members:

(1) Before appointing any person as the Chairperson or a whole-time member, the Central Government shall satisfy itself that the person does not have any such financial or other interest as is likely to affect prejudicially his functions as such member.

(2) The Chairperson and other whole-time members shall hold office for a term of six years from the date on which they enter upon their offices or till they attain the age of sixty-five years, whichever is earlier.But one-third of the Members shall retire on the expiration of every second year.

(3) As soon as may be after the establishment of the Authority, the Central Government may, by order, make such provision as it thinks fit for curtailing the term of office of some of the Members then appointed in order that one third of the Members holding office shall retire in every second year thereafter

(4) The Chairperson or a member shall not be eligible for a second term but a member will be eligible for appointment as Chairperson of the Authority for the remaining part of his term.

(5) Where before the expiry of the term of office of a person holding the office of Chairman, or any other Member, a vacancy arises, for any reason whatsoever, such vacancy shall be deemed to be a casual vacancy and the person appointed to fill such vacancy shall hold office for the unexpired period of the term for which his predecessor in office would have held office if such vacancy had not arisen.

(6) The Chairperson or a whole-time member shall not take up any commercial employment in the organizations that fall within the operational jurisdiction of the Authority, after demitting office within a period of one year without the prior permission of the Central Government.

(7) The salary and allowances payable to and other conditions of service of the Chairperson and other whole-time members shall be such as may be prescribed.

(8) A person having commercial employment or interest, direct or indirect, in any broadcasting services provider, newspaper, advertising or programme producing agency shall not be eligible for appointment or continuation as Chairperson or a whole-time member.

17. Powers of the Chairperson: The Chairperson shall have powers of general superintendence and direction in the conduct of the affairs of the Authority and he shall, in addition to presiding over the meetings of the Authority, exercise such powers of the Authority, and shall discharge such functions of the Authority, as may be prescribed.

18. Removal, suspension or resignation of Chairperson and members: (1) The Central Government may remove from office or suspend the Chairperson or any member of the Authority who:

(a) Ceases to be a citizen of India; or

(b) Is adjudged an insolvent; or

(c) Is convicted or any offence involving moral turpitude; or

(d) Is, in the opinion of the Central Government, unfit to continue in office by reason of infirmity or body or mind; or

(e) Engages during his term of office in any paid employment outside the

duties of his office;

(f) Acquires such financial or other interest as is likely to affect prejudicially his functions as a Chairperson or member;

(g) Abuses his position so as to render his continuance in office prejudicial to public interest.

(2) The Chairperson or any other member may resign his office by giving notice thereof in writing to the Central Government and on such resignation being accepted, the Chairperson or the member shall be deemed to have vacated his office.

19. Meetings of the Authority or its committees:

(1) The Authority may constitute committees of the Authority for specific purposes, and make regulations for the transaction of business at the meetings of the Authority as well as its committees

(2) The Authority or its committee shall meet at such time and place and shall observe such procedure in regard to the transaction of business at its meetings as may be provided by regulations.

(3) The Chairperson shall preside at the meetings of the Authority or its committee, and if for any reason he is unable to attend any meeting, any other wholetime member elected by the members present at such meeting, shall preside at the meetings.

(4) A member shall be deemed to have vacated his office if he absents himself for three consecutive meetings of the Authority without the leave of the Chairperson.

(5) All questions which come up before any meeting of the Authority shall be decided by a majority of the votes of the members present and voting and, in the event of an equality of votes, the Chairperson, or in his absence, the person presiding, shall have and exercise a second or casting vote.

20. Vacancies not to invalidate proceedings:

No act or proceedings of the Authority shall be invalid merely by reason of-

(a) Any vacancy in, or any defect in the constitution of, the Authority; or

(b) Any defect in the appointment of a person acting as a member; or

(c) Any irregularity in the procedure of the Authority not affecting the merits of the case.

21. Regional offices of the Authority:

The Authority may, with the prior approval of the Central Government set up Regional Offices at Ahmedabad, Bangalore, Bhopal, Chennai, Delhi, Guwahati, Kolkata, Lucknow, Mumbai, Patna and such other regional offices at places to be notified by the Govt., and to perform such functions and with such jurisdictions as may be prescribed. At each such Regional Offices there shall be one Regional Director to be appointed by the Central Government to discharge the functions delegated to him by the Authority.

22. Secretary and other officers and employees of the Authority:

(1) Secretary of the Authority shall be the Chief Executive Officer of the Authority. Subject to the provisions of section 17 of the Act, the Secretary shall exercise such powers and discharge such functions of the Authority as may be delegated to him by the Authority.

(2) The Central Government shall make available to the Authority, a panel of not less than three officers of the rank of the Additional Secretary to the Government of India, and the Authority may select one of them and recommend his appointment as Secretary of the Authority to the Government.

(3) The Central Government shall make available a panel of not less than three officers of the rank of Joint Secretary to the Government of India for each of the ten Regional Offices, and the Authority may select one from each panel and recommend his/her appointment to the Government. As and when more regional offices are opened, the Authority may seek officers of the rank of Joint Secretary or Director to the Government of India, as the case may be, for appointment as their Regional Directors.

(4) The Authority may appoint such officers and other employees, as it considers necessary for the efficient discharge of its functions under this Act in the manner as provided by the regulations.

(5) The salary and allowances payable to and other conditions of service of the officers and other employees of the Authority shall be such as may be determined by regulations.

23. Powers and functions of the Authority:

(1) Authority shall exercise the following powers and functions:

(a) Notify the terms and conditions of licenses for various categories of service providers, in accordance with the policy guidelines prescribed by the Government;

(b) Recommend to the Central Government, guidelines or norms oramendments of prescribed guidelines or norms, in the light of its experience in the discharge of its functions, as well as on such other issues as may be referred to it by the Government;

(c) Grant registration to TV and Radio channels as provided under Section 4 of the Bill;

(d) Lay-down the standards of quality of service to be provided by the service providers and conduct the periodical survey of such service provided by the service providers so as to protect interest of the consumers of broadcasting service;

(e) Notify detailed regulations to implement the policy guidelines prescribed by Government and take all necessary legal and administrative actions to ensure their compliance by the service providers

(f) Formulate and determine conditions for fair, equitable and non discriminatory access to broadcasting services

(g) Consider and publish its findings for wider public debate on issues of public importance relating to broadcasting services and their program content;

(h) Facilitate competition and promote efficiency in the operation of broadcasting services so as to facilitate growth in such services;

(i) Advise the Central Government in the matters relating to the development of broadcasting technology and any other matter relatable to broadcasting industry in general;

(j) Evolve codes and practices in respect of such other services which are neither licensed nor registered under this Act as may be notified by the Central Government from time to time and lay down obligations on services providers for such codes and practices in a manner as may be prescribed;

(k) Hear appeals against the orders and directions of the Licensing Authorities

(l) Adjudicate on disputes between two or more Licensing Authorities or between a licensing authority and one or more service providers under jurisdiction of other licensing authorities, or between two or more service providers under jurisdiction of more than one licensing authority

(m)Certify content in respect of such categories of programs or advertisements or promotional materials as require certification before broadcast, as may be prescribed in the Content Code;

(n) Adjudicate between licensing authorities or consumers or complainants and the service providers in respect of violations of the Content Code, and impose penalties in accordance with prescribed norms;

(o) Perform such other functions including such administrative and financial functions as may be entrusted to it by the Central Government or as may be necessary to carry out the provisions of this Act.

(2) The Authority may, for the discharge of its functions under sub-section (1) of this section, issue such directions from time to time to the service providers, as it

may consider necessary.

(3) The Authority may by general or special order, delegate to its Chairperson or a Member or Secretary or Regional officers or any other officer of the Authority or to any "Authorized Officer", subject to such conditions and limitations, if any, as may be specified therein, such of its powers and duties under this Act as it may deem fit.

24. Powers and functions of the Licensing Authorities:

(1) The Licensing Authorities shall exercise all or any of the following powers and functions with respect only to the service provider licenced by it

(a) Grant, refuse or revoke licenses / registration in respect of such broadcasting services and for such limits of jurisdiction as may be prescribed;

(b) Inspect, enquire or supervise, or direct an "authorized officer" to inspect, enquire or supervise all or any of the service providers to ensure compliance with the terms and conditions of their respective licenses

(c) Ensure technical compatibility and effective inter-connection between service providers

(d) Arbitrate between service providers in respect of commercial arrangement mandated by the Central Government or the Authority for sharing their revenue derived from providing broadcasting services;

(e) Ensure effective compliance of such public service broadcasting obligations as may be prescribed for its licensees;

(f) Perform such other functions including such administrative and financial functions as may be entrusted to it by the Central Government or as may be necessary to carry out the provisions of this Act.

(g) Adjudicate between consumers and service providers, in respect of complaints and disputes regarding the quality or standards of service and payments by the consumers.

(h) Impose in accordance with prescribed norms, all or any of the penalties, individually or in combination, in case of breach of any terms and conditions of the license / permission / registration, after providing an opportunity to the concerned service provider of being heard

Provided that the violations of the Content Code shall be punishable only by the Authority, and the licensing authority shall have the power to enforce compliance with such punishment by the service provider.

25. Powers and functions of the 'Authorized Officers': Subject to such directions as may be given from time to time by the Central Government or the Authority, every authorized officer shall have the following powers:

(i) To inspect, search and seize equipment etc. under section 26 of this Act.

(ii) To prosecute, on a written complaint by the concerned Licensing Authority, such licensed service providers or other persons as are found to have committed offences under the Act.

(iii) To co-ordinate with the Licensing Authorities to ensure that the terms and conditions of the licenses are not violated by any service provider

(iv) To receive and enquire into complaints from consumer groups or individual consumers or others regarding content or quality of service and report to the Licensing Authority for appropriate action.

(v) Any other powers and functions as may be delegated to him by the Authority as deemed necessary.

26. Seizure and confiscation of certain equipment:

(1) If any authorized officer has reason to believe, or is directed by the Licensing Authority or the Authority or the Central Government, as the case may be, that the provisions of sub-section (1) of section 3, with respect to requirement of licences for broadcasting services ; or subsection (1) of section 4 with respect to registration of channels ; or of section 5 with respect to directions of the Central Government in case of external threat or war; or section 6 with respect to directions of the Central Government in case of exceptional circumstances , of this Act have been or are being contravened by any person, he may seize the equipment being used by such person for operating such unlicensed service or broadcasting such unregistered channel or program or for failure to comply with the directions under section 5 or 6 of the Act.

Provided that the authorized officer shall not retain such equipment for a period exceeding 30 days from the date of its seizure without the approval of the District Judge, within the local limits of whose jurisdiction such seizure has been made.

(2) The equipment so seized under sub-section (1) above shall be liable to confiscation unless the person operating such service or channel complies with the provisions of the Act within a period of sixty days from the date of such seizure.

(3) The District Judge shall not pass any order adjudicating confiscation unless the person operating such service or channel has been given a reasonable opportunity in writing to make his representation against the proposed confiscation.

27. Finance, Accounts and Audit: (1) The proceeds of the license / registration / permission fees in respect of broadcasting services shall be credited to the Consolidated Fund of India.

(2) The Central Government may for enabling the Authority to discharge its functions efficiently, after due appropriation made by Parliament by law in this behalf, pay to the Authority in each financial year such sums of money as the Government considers necessary by way of grants-in-aid.

(3) The Authority shall have its own fund and all the receipts of the Authority shall be credited to the fund and all payments by the Authority shall be made there from. All money belonging to the fund shall be deposited in one or more Scheduled Banks in such manner as the Authority may decide and Authority may spend such sums as it thinks fit for performing its function under this Act.

(4) The Authority shall prepare, in such form and at such time each year as may be prescribed, a budget in respect of the financial year next ensuing showing-

(a) The expenditure which is proposed to be met from the internal resource of the Authority; and

(b) The sums required from the Central Government to meet other expenses, And copies thereof shall be forwarded to the Central Government.

(5) The Authority shall maintain proper accounts and other relevant records and prepare an annual statement of accounts in such form and in such manner as may be prescribed.

(6) The accounts of the Authority shall be audited by the Comptroller and Auditor General of India at such intervals as may be specified by him and any expenditure incurred in connection with such audit shall be payable by the Authority to the Comptroller and Auditor General. Provided the matters relating to the adjudication by the Authority, manner and number of issue of licenses and quantum of license fee, levied by the Authority or the nature and quantum of penalties imposed by the Authority on any service provider, shall lie outside the purview of such Audit.

(7) The Comptroller and Auditor General of India and any person appointed by him in connection with the audit of the accounts of the Authority shall have the same rights and privileges and authority in connection with such audit as the Comptroller and Auditor General has in connection with the audit of Government accounts and, in particular, shall have the right to demand the production of books, accounts, connected vouchers and other documents and papers and to inspect any of the offices of the Authority.

(8) The accounts of the Authority as certified by the Comptroller and Auditor General of India or any other person appointed by him in this behalf together with the audit report thereon shall be forwarded annually to the Central Government and that Government shall cause the same to be laid before each House of Parliament.

(9) The Authority shall, after the end of each financial year, shall submit to the Central Government a report on their activities during the preceding financial year and containing such information relating to the proceedings and policy of the Authority, as the Government may prescribe from time to time.

(10) The Central Government shall cause such report to be laid before each House of Parliament.

28. Furnishing of returns, etc. to the Central Government: (1) The Authority shall furnish to the Central Government at such time and in such form and manner as may be prescribed or as the Central Government may direct, such returns and statements and such particulars in regard to any proposed or existing program for the promotion and development of the broadcasting services, as the Central Government may, from time to time, require.

(2) The Authority shall prepare once every year in such form and at such time as may be prescribed, an annual summary of its activities during the previous year and copies of the report shall be forwarded to the Central Government.

(3) A copy of the report received under sub-section (2) shall be laid, as soon as may be after it is received, before each House of Parliament.

29. Power of the Authority to make regulations:

(1) The Authority may, by notification, make regulations not inconsistent with this Act and the rules made thereunder, for enabling it to perform its functions under this Act.

(2) Without prejudice to the generality of the foregoing power, such regulations may provide for all or any of the following matters, namely: -

(a) The manner of appointment of officers and other employees of the Authority under sub-section (4) of section 22;

(b) The salary and allowances payable to and other conditions of service of the officers and other employees of the Authority under subsection (5) of section 22;

(c) The terms and conditions, fees and procedure to be followed for granting licenses /registration under clause (a) of sub-section (1) of section 23;

(d) The times and places at which meetings of the Authority and its committees may be held and, the procedure to be followed in regard to the transaction of the business at such meetings under sub-section

(l) and sub-section (2) of section 19;

(e) The technical and other quality standards and the reasonable quality of reception under clause (d) of sub-section (1) of section 23;

(f) The places and types and quantity of equipment to be provided, free of cost, by the licensee service provider for monitoring of content and the quality of technical standards of service, and the manner in which such monitoring may be carried out by the licensing authorities or authorised officers under clause (e) of sub-section (1)of section 23.

(g) The delegation of powers and functions to the Chairman, members and other officers of the Authority under sub-section (3) of section 23;

(h) The documentary record and transmission schedule to be maintained by the licensees under sub-section (1) of section 51;

(i) The manner in which broadcasters shall establish and operate the system of self-certification of broadcasting content under sub-section (vii) of section 10;

(j) Any other matter in respect of which provision is, in the opinion of the Authority, necessary for the performance of its functions under this Act.

Provided that the regulations under clauses (a), (b) and (c) shall be made with the prior approval of the Central Government.

CHAPTER 4
PUBLIC SERVICE BROADCASTING COUNCIL

30. Establishment of Public Service Broadcasting Council, term of office of members thereof.—

1) There shall be established, by notification a Council, to be known as the Public Service Broadcasting Council

(2) The Broadcasting Council shall consist of—

(i) a President and five other members to be appointed by the Central

Government from amongst persons of eminence in public life, media and civil society organisations; and one representative of Prasar Bharati

(ii) at least two persons in the Council should be women

(3) The President of the Broadcasting Council shall be a whole-time member and every other member shall be a part-time member and the President or the part-time member shall hold office as such for a term of three years from the date on which he enters upon his office.

(4) The President of the Broadcasting Council shall be entitled to such salary and allowances and shall be subject to such conditions of service in respect of leave, pension (if any), provident fund and other matters as may be prescribed:

Provided that the salary and allowances and the conditions of service shall not be varied to the disadvantage of the President of the Broadcasting Council after his appointment.

(5) The other members of the Broadcasting shall be entitled to such allowances as may be prescribed.

31. Powers and functions of the Public Service Broadcasting Council.— (1) The Public Service Broadcasting Council shall exercise the following powers and functions:

(ii) Ensure effective compliance of public service broadcasting obligations cast upon broadcasting service providers as per the provisions of this Act, and in the event of failure of a licensed service provider to meet such obligations, suggest to the Authority the amount of penalty to be levied and collected as per guidelines laid down by Central Government;

(iii) make recommendations to the Central Government on whether a broadcasting channel deserves to be categorized as a public service broadcasting channel

(iv) institute national awards for public service broadcasting

(v) define from time to time as to what will constitute public service /socially relevant programming or messaging

(vi) produce or organize the production of benchmark quality content, public service messages and programmes that private television can use to fulfill its public service broadcasting regulations

(vii) create and administer mechanisms to provide free airtime for public service content created or funded by civil society groups and NGOs etc, which may also include starting a public service broadcasting channel

(viii) support formal training courses, workshops, seminars, discussions, research in Public Service Broadcasting for content producers, media watchers, critics and those working in the social sector

32. Powers of the President: The President shall have powers of general

superintendence and direction in the conduct of the affairs of the Council and he shall, in addition to presiding over the meetings of the Council, exercise such powers of the Council, and shall discharge such functions of the Council, as may be prescribed.

33. Removal or resignation of President and members:

(1) The Central Government may remove from office the President or any member of the Council who:

(a) Ceases to be a citizen of India; or

(b) Is adjudged an insolvent; or

(c) Is convicted or any offence involving moral turpitude; or

(d) Is, in the opinion of the Central Government, unfit to continue in office by reason of infirmity or body or mind; or

(e) Acquires such financial or other interest as is likely to affect prejudicially his functions as a Chairperson or member;

(f) Abuses his position so as to render his continuance in office prejudicial to public interest.

(2) The President or any other member may resign his office by giving notice thereof in writing to the Central Government and on such resignation being accepted, the President or the member shall be deemed to have vacated his office.

34. Meetings of the Council or its committees:

(1) The Council may constitute committees of the Council for specific purposes, and make regulations for the transaction of business at the meetings of the Council as well as its committees

(2) The Council or its committee shall meet at such time and place and shall

observe such procedure in regard to the transaction of business at its meetings as may be provided by regulations.

(3) The President shall preside at the meetings of the Council or its committee, and if for any reason he is unable to attend any meeting, any other member elected by the members present at such meeting, shall preside at the meetings.

(4) A member shall be deemed to have vacated his office if he absents himself for three consecutive meetings of the Council without the leave of the President.

(5) All questions which come up before any meeting of the Council shall be

decided by a majority of the votes of the members present and voting and, in the event of an equality of votes, the President, or in his absence, the person presiding, shall have and exercise a second or casting vote.

35. Vacancies not to invalidate proceedings: No act or proceedings of the Council shall be invalid merely by reason of-

(a) Any vacancy in, or any defect in the constitution of, the Council; or

(b) Any defect in the appointment of a person acting as a member; or

(c) Any irregularity in the procedure of the Council not affecting the merits of the case.

36. Secretary and other officers and employees of the Council: (1) Secretary of the Council shall be the Chief Executive Officer of the Council. Subject to the provisions of section 32 of the Act, the Secretary shall exercise such powers and discharge such functions of the Council as may be delegated to him by the Council.

(2) The Central Government shall make available to the Council, a panel of not less than three officers of the rank of the Joint Secretary to the Government of India, and the Council may select one of them and recommend his appointment as Secretary of the Council to the Government.

(4) The Council may appoint such officers and other employees, as it considers necessary for the efficient discharge of its functions under this Act in the manner as provided by the regulations.

(5) The salary and allowances payable to and other conditions of service of the officers and other employees of the Council shall be such as may be determined by regulations.

37. Finance, Accounts and Audit:

(1) The Central Government may for enabling the Council to discharge its functions efficiently, after due appropriation made by Parliament by law in this behalf, pay to the Council in each financial year such sums of money as the Government considers necessary by way of grants-in-aid.

(2) The Council shall have its own fund and all the receipts of the Council shall be credited to the fund. All money belonging to the fund shall be deposited in one or more Scheduled Banks in such manner as the Council may decide and Council may spend such sums as it thinks fit for performing its function under this Act.

(3) The Council shall be able to collect any amount or donation or grant from any government or non government body as a contribution towards public service broadcasting obligation fund.

(4) The Council shall prepare, in such form and at such time each year as may be prescribed, a budget in respect of the financial year next ensuing showing-

(a)The expenditure which is proposed to be met from the internal resource of the Council; and

(b) The expenditure which is proposed to be met from public service broadcasting obligation fund

(c)The sums required from the Central Government to meet other expenses, and copies thereof shall be forwarded to the Central Government.

(5) The Council shall maintain proper accounts and other relevant records and prepare an annual statement of accounts in such form and in such manner as may

be prescribed.

(6) The accounts of the Council shall be audited by the Comptroller and Auditor General of India at such intervals as may be specified by him and any expenditure incurred in connection with such audit shall be payable by the Council to the Comptroller and Auditor General.

(7) The Comptroller and Auditor General of India and any person appointed by him in connection with the audit of the accounts of the Council shall have the same rights and privileges and authority in connection with such audit as the Comptroller and Auditor General has in connection with the audit of Government accounts and, in particular, shall have the right to demand the production of books, accounts, connected vouchers and other documents and papers and to inspect the offices of the Council.

(8) The accounts of the Council as certified by the Comptroller and Auditor General of India or any other person appointed by him in this behalf together with the audit report thereon shall be forwarded annually to the Central Government and that Government shall cause the same to be laid before each House of Parliament.

(9) The Council shall, after the end of each financial year, submit to the Central Government a report on its activities during the preceding financial year and containing such information relating to the proceedings and policy of the Council, as the Government may prescribe from time to time.

(10) The Central Government shall cause such report to be laid before each House of Parliament.

38. Furnishing of returns, etc. to the Central Government:

(1) The Council shall furnish to the Central Government at such time and in such form and manner as may be prescribed or as the Central Government may direct, such returns and statements and such particulars in regard to any proposed or existing program for the promotion and development of the public service broadcasting, as the Central Government may, from time to time, require.

(2) The Council shall prepare once every year in such form and at such time as may be prescribed, an annual summary of its activities during the previous year and copies of the report shall be forwarded to the Central Government.

(3) A copy of the report received under sub-section (2) shall be laid, as soon as may be after it is received, before each House of Parliament.

39. Power of the Council to make regulations:

(1) The Council may, by notification, make regulations not inconsistent with this

Act and the rules or guidelines issued thereunder, for enabling it to perform its functions under this Act.

(2) Without prejudice to the generality of the foregoing power, such regulations may provide for all or any of the following matters, namely: -

(a) The manner of appointment of officers and other employees of the Council ;

(b) The salary and allowances payable to and other conditions of service of the officers and other employees of the Council

(c) The times and places at which meetings of the Council may be held and, the procedure to be followed in regard to the transaction of the business at such meetings

(d) The delegation of powers and functions to the President, members and other officers of the Council

(e) The documentary record to be maintained by the licensees

(f) The manner in which broadcasters shall establish and operate the system of selfcertification of public service/ socially relevant programming or messaging (g) Constitution of public serice/socially relevant programming or messaging and calculation of its share

(h) Any other matter in respect of which provision is, in the opinion of the Council, necessary for the performance of its functions under this Act.

Provided that the regulations under clauses (a)&(b) above shall be made with the prior approval of the Central Government

CHAPTER 5

OFFENCES, PENALTIES AND APPEALS

40. Punishment for offences under this Act:

(1) A person who in contravention of the provisions of this Act, provides, distributes or receives any broadcasting service which is not licensed under sub-section (1) of section 3 or broadcasts a channel which is not registered under sub-section (1) of section 4, or abets or assists transmission or distribution of such service or content, as the case may be, in any manner shall be guilty of committing an offence of illegal broadcasting, and on conviction, shall be punishable with imprisonment which may extend up to three years, or with fine which may extend up to rupees twenty five Lakhs or both, and for subsequent offence and conviction such imprisonment may extend to five years or fine up to rupees fifty Lakhs, or with both.

Provided that unauthorized decoding or receiving of a program that is not permitted or of a channel that is not registered or dealing in or distribution of equipment for the purpose shall also constitute an offence of illegal broadcasting and shall be dealt with accordingly.

(2) Whoever contravenes the provisions of sections 5 of this Act shall be punishable:

(a) For the first offence, with imprisonment for a term which may extend upto three years or with fine which may extend to rupees twenty five lakhs or with both,

(b) For every subsequent offence, with imprisonment for a term which may extend to five years and with fine which may extend to rupees fifty lakhs or with both.

(3) Whoever contravenes the provisions of sections 6 of this Act shall be punishable:

(a) For the first offence, with imprisonment for a term which may extend to two years or with fine which may extend to rupees ten lakhs or with both,

(b) For every subsequent offence, with imprisonment for a term which may extend to five years and with fine which may extend to rupees twenty-five lakhs

41. Offences by companies: (1) Where an offence under this Act has been committed by a company, every person who, at the time the offence was committed, was in charge of, and was responsible to, the company for the conduct of the business of the company, as well as the company, shall be deemed to be guilty of the offence and shall be liable to be proceeded against and punished accordingly;

Provided that nothing contained in this sub-section shall render any such person liable for such punishment, if he proves that the offence was committed without his knowledge or that he had exercised all due diligence to prevent the commission of such offence.

(2) Notwithstanding anything contained in sub-section (1), where an offence under this Act has been committed by a company and it is proved that it has been committed with the consent or connivance of, or is attributable to the negligence on the part of ay director, manager, secretary or other officer of the company, such director, manager, secretary or other officer shall also be deemed to be guilty of that offence and shall be liable to be proceeded against and punished accordingly.

Explanation: For the purpose of this section,

(a) "Company" means any body corporate and includes a firm or other association of individuals; and

(b) "Director" in relation to a firm, means a partner in the firm.

42. Cognizance of offences: (1) No court shall take cognizance of any offence punishable under this Act except upon a complaint made in writing by any authorized officer.

(2) No Court inferior to that of a Chief Metropolitan Magistrate or a Chief Judicial Magistrate of First Class shall try any offence punishable under this Act.

43. The Authority to prescribe penalties for violations of license conditions etc.:

Subject to the provisions of subsection (ii),the Authority may prescribe the penalties to be imposed for violation of various terms and conditions of the license / permission / registration subject to the condition that such penalties shall not exceed a fine of rupees fifty lakhs, besides suspension or revocation of such license / permission / registration, subject further to the condition that no penalty shall be imposed unless and until a reasonable opportunity has been given to the service provider to explain its position.

(ii) . The Authority may specify penalties to be imposed, including suspension or revocation of licence , permission or registration, for violation of various terms and conditions as may be specified under section 7, subject to the condition that amount of a pecuniary penalty shall not exceed one crore rupees: Provided that no penalty shall be imposed without giving a reasonable opportunity to the service provider:

Provided further that no act or omission on the part of any person after the 11 th November, 2005 and before the date of promulgation of the Sports Broadcasting Signals (Mandatory Sharing with Prasar Bharati) Ordinance, 2007(Ord 4 of 2007), shall be subjected to penalties.

44. The Licensing Authorities to impose penalties:

(1) Subject to the provisions of section 31 of this Act, every licensing authority shall have the power to impose any of the following penalties, individually or in combination, in respect of licences issued by it, in case of breach of any terms and conditions of the license or permission or registration, as the case may be, namely:

(i) Direct the licensee to broadcast a correction or an apology or not to repeat a programme; and/or

(ii) Impose a fine which may extend up to rupees five lakhs in case of cable operators and to twenty five lakhs in case of others

(iii) Suspend the license for a specified period; or

(iv) Curtail the period of the license; or

(v) Revoke the license.

Provided that no such penalty shall be imposed without giving a reasonable opportunity to the concerned service provider of being heard in person or through a legal representative.

Provided that the violations of the Content Code shall be punishable only by the Authority, and the licensing authority shall have the power to enforce compliance with such punishment by the service provider.

(2) Pending disposal of the case, the Licensing Authority may, if it considers it expedient or desirable in public interest to do so, direct the concerned service provider to stop the repeat broadcast or broadcasts of a particular program or portion thereof which is under investigation or enquiry, and the service provider shall immediately comply with such a direction Provided that no such interim direction shall be issued without giving a reasonable opportunity, as far as practical, to the concerned service provider of being heard in person or through a legal repre-

sentative.

45. Appeals against the orders of the Licensing Authorities:

An aggrieved person may prefer an appeal against an order or direction of any of the Licensing Authorities to the Authority within a period of thirty days of such an order or direction. Provided that the Authority may entertain the appeal after expiry of the said period of 30 days if it is satisfied that the appellant was prevented by sufficient cause from preferring the appeal in time.

46. Appeals against the orders of the Authority:

An aggrieved person may prefer an appeal against the order or direction of the Authority before the Film Certification Appellate Tribunal (FCAT) in respect of cases of violations of the Content Code, and before the Telecom Disputes Settlement and Appellate Tribunal (TDSAT) in respect of cases of all other violations of the terms and conditions of license within a period of 30 days of such an order or direction. Provided that the Tribunal may entertain the appeal after expiry of the said period of 30 days if it is satisfied that the appellant was prevented by sufficient cause from preferring the appeal in time.

47. Appeals before the Supreme Court:

(1) Notwithstanding anything contained in the Code of Civil Procedure or in any other law, an appeal by either party to the dispute shall lie against any order, not being an interlocutory order, of the TDSAT or FCAT, as the case may be, to the Supreme Court on one or more of the grounds specified in Section 100 of that Code.

(2) No appeal shall lie against any decision or order made by the TDSAT or FCAT, as the case may be, with the consent of the parties.

(3) Every appeal under this section shall be preferred within a period of 90 days from the date of the decision or order appealed against, Provided that the Supreme Court may entertain the appeal after expiry of the said period of 90 days if it is satisfied that the appellant was prevented by sufficient cause from preferring the appeal in time.

48. Transfer of pending cases to the Authority:

(1) On the date to be notified by the Central Government, after the establishment of the Authority, all proceedings pending before the Telecom Regulatory Authority of India (TRAI) shall be deemed to be pending before the Authority and shall be disposed off in accordance with the provisions of this Act.

(2) On the date to be notified by the Central Government, after the establishment of

the Authority, all proceedings pending before the Ministry of Information and Broadcasting, Government of India shall be deemed to be pending before the Authority and shall be disposed of in accordance with the provisions of this Act.

49. Civil Court not to have jurisdiction:

No Civil Court shall have jurisdiction to entertain any suit or proceedings in respect of any matter which the Authority or the Licensing Authority, as the case may be, is empowered by or under this Act to determine and no injunction shall be granted by any civil court or other authority in respect of any action taken or to be taken in pursuance of any power conferred by and under this Act.

CHAPTER 6

MISCELLEANOUS

50. Power of the Central Government to issue directions:

(1) The Central Government may, from time to time, issue to the Authority such directions as it may deem necessary in the interest of the sovereignty and integrity of India, the security of the State, friendly relations with foreign countries, public order.

(2) Without prejudice to the foregoing provisions, the Authority shall, in

exercise of its powers or the performance of its functions, be bound by such directions on questions of policy as the Central Government may give in writing to it from time to time

Provided that the Authority shall, as far as practicable, be given an opportunity to express its views before any such direction is given under this sub-section.

(3) The decision of the Central Government whether a question is one of policy or not shall be final.

51. The Authority to follow principles of natural justice:

(1) The Authority shall not be bound by the procedure laid down by the Code of Civil Procedure, 1908, but shall be guided by the principles of natural justice and, subject to the other provisions of this Act and of any rules, the Authority shall have powers to regulate its own procedure including the fixing of places and times of its enquiry.

(2) The Authority shall have, for the purposes of discharging its functions under this Act, the same powers as are vested in a civil court under the Code of Civil Procedure, 1908, while trying a suit, in respect of the following matters, namely: -

(a) Summoning and enforcing the attendance of any person and examining him on oath;

(b) Requiring the discovery and production of documents;

(c) Receiving evidence on affidavits;

(d) Issuing commissions for the examination of witnesses or documents;

(e) Requisitioning any public record or document or a copy of such record or document, from any office;

(f) Reviewing its decisions;

(g) Dismissing an application for default or deciding it, ex-party;

(h) Setting aside any order of dismissal of any application for default or any other passed by it, ex-party;

(i) Any other matter, which may be prescribed.

52. Service providers to maintain records:

(1) Every service provider shall maintain such documentary records and transmission schedules as may be specified in the policy guidelines, notified under this Act and allow inspections of the facilities and such documentary records and transmission schedules by any person authorized by the Authority.

(2) The Authority may call for any information from the service provider, which is necessary for transparency and ascertaining the true ownership of the serviceNprovider.

(3) The Authority or any officer authorized by the Authority shall have power to inspect and obtain information wherever necessary, from programme producers, distributors and advertising agents.

(4) For effective enforcement of restrictions on holding of licenses, as provided under section 10, the Authority or any officer authorized by the Authority for that purpose, shall have all the powers of an inspecting officer as provided under Section 209-A of the Companies Act, 1956.

(5) It shall be the duty of every service provider to carry out the directions of the Authority given under this section.

(6) If default is made by a service provider in complying with the provisions of sub-section (5), the Authority may take such action as provided under section 32 (1) after providing him an opportunity of being heard.

53. Members and employees of the Authority to be public servants:

The Chairman, every member, every officer or other employee of the Authority, shall be deemed to be a public servant within the meaning of section 21 of the Indian Penal Code.

54. Protection of action taken in good faith: No suit or other legal proceeding shall lie against the Government, Authority, or any Member or Officer or other employee thereof for anything which is in, good faith done or intended to be done in pursuance of this Act or of any rules or regulations made there under.

55. Exemption from tax on wealth and income:

Notwithstanding anything contained in the Wealth Tax Act, 1957, the Income Tax Act, 1961, or any other enactment for the time being in force relating to wealth, income, profit or gains, the Authority shall not be liable to pay wealth tax, income tax, or any other tax in respect of their wealth, income, profit or gains derived.

56. This Act to have over-riding effect:

(1) This Act shall have overriding effect over provisions of any other law for the time being in force and shall be given effect to, notwithstanding anything contained in any other law for the time being in force and notwithstanding any rights claimed under contract or created under any other law for the time being in force.

(2) Notwithstanding anything contained in section 31 or section 37 of the Indian Copyright Act, 1957, where one or more persons have made complaints in respect of a work which has been published or performed in public or which has already been broadcast or whose licensed reproductions have already been made available in public, licenses shall be granted to all such complainants under sub-section (1) of section 31 of the Indian Copyright Act 1957.

57. Power of the Central Government to make rules:

(1) The Central Government may, by notification, makes rules for carrying out provisions of this Act.

(2) In particular and without prejudice to the generality of the foregoing power, such rules may provide for all or any of the following matters, namely: -

(a) To determine other circumstances for communication under sub-clause

(c) of clause (ii) of section 2;

(b) To notify the sporting events and to lay down the procedure to be followed for enabling their being shared with Prasar Bharti under section 6;

(c) The policy guidelines, designate licensing authorities, specify terms and conditions, and procedures for grant of the licenses/ permissions/ registration to the service provider under clauses (i) to (iv) of section 9;

(d) To lay down a time frame for change over to digital addressable networks for broadcasting content, and commercial and technical arrangements during the transition phase under clause (v) of section 9;

(e) The lay down the Content Code and procedures to be followed for content certification by the service providers, adjudication of complaints against content certification and appeals against imposition of penalties, under clauses (vi) to (viii) of section 9;

(f) The norms of public service broadcasting obligations, rates and procedures for levying and collection of fees, and setting up institutional arrangement and norms for managing and operating the public service broadcasting obligation fund under clauses (x) and (xi) of section 9;

(g) The eligibility conditions and restrictions to prevent accumulation of interest in licensed services and restrictions on controlling interest in print media and electronic media as well as within different segments of the electronic media under section 10;

(h) The salaries and allowances payable and other conditions of service of the Chairperson and whole-time members under sub-section (5) of section 14;

(i) The places where the Regional Offices may be set up and the functions to be performed by such offices under section 19;

(j) The form in which and the time at which in each year the Authority shall prepare a budget under sub-section (4) of section 25;

(k) The form and the manner in which the annual statement of accounts shall be prepared under sub-section (5) of section 25;

(l) The information relating to the proceedings and policy of the Authority to be contained in a report to be submitted by the Authority under sub-section (9) of section 25;

(m) Any other matter which is required to be or may be prescribed.

58. Rules and regulations to be laid before Parliament:

Every rule and every regulation made under this Act shall be laid, as soon as may be after it is made, before each House of Parliament, while it is in session for a total period of thirty days which may be comprised in one session or in two or more successive sessions, and if, before the expiry of the session immediately following the session or the successive sessions aforesaid, both Houses agree in making any modification in, the rule or regulation, or both Houses agree that the rule or regulation should not be made, the rule or regulation shall thereafter have effect only in such modified form or be of no effect, as the case may be; so, however, that any such modification or annulment shall be without prejudice to the validity of anything previously done under that rule or regulation.

59. Application of certain laws:

The provisions of this Act shall be in addition to the provisions of the Indian Telegraph Act, 1885 and Indian Wireless Telegraphy Act, 1933 and, in particular, nothing in this Act shall affect any jurisdiction, powers and functions required to be exercised or performed by the Telegraph Authority in relation to any area falling within the jurisdiction of such Authority.

60. Power to remove difficulties:

(1) If any difficulty arises in giving effect to the provisions of this Act, the Central Government may, by other published in the Official Gazette, make such provisions, not inconsistent with the provisions of this Act, as it may deem necessary, for the removal of the difficulty.

Provided that no such order shall be made after the expiry of a period of three years from the commencement of this Act.

(2) Every order made under this section shall be laid, as soon as may be after it is made before each House of Parliament.

61. Repeal and saving:

(1)(i) The Cable Television Networks (Regulation) Act 1995 is hereby repealed.

(ii) Notwithstanding such repeal any cable operator registered under that Act as on the date of repeal, may continue to provide his services, provided he makes an application to the Authority for the grant of a license for any of the broadcasting network services within six months from the date of the commencement of this Act or where he has made such an application, till the disposal of such application, whichever is later.

(iii) The Authority may on receipt of an application under sub-section (2) grant a license for any of the broadcasting network services subject to fulfillment of such eligibility and other terms and conditions as may be prescribed.

(iv) The cable operators operating under sub-section (2) above shall continue to be regulated as if the Cable Television Networks (Regulation) Act, 1995 has not been repealed during the interregnum i.e. the period from the commencement of this Act and disposal of his application for the license or a period of six months, whichever is later.

(v) Notwithstanding such repeal, all cable operators registered under that Act as on the date of repeal, shall continue to comply with the provisions of the Program Code under Rule 6 and the Advertising Code under Rule 7 of the Cable Television Networks Rules, 1994 prescribed under that Act, till the said Codes are replaced by the new guidelines and norms (the Content Code) provided for under sub-section (vi) of section 9 of this Act.

(2) The Sports Broadcasting Signals (Mandatory Sharing with Prasar Bharati)Act, 2007 Is hereby repealed.Notwithstanding the repeal of the Sports Broadcasting Signals (Mandatory Sharing with Prasar Bharati) Act,2007, anything done or any action taken under the said Act shall be deemed to have been done or taken under the corresponding provisions of this Act.

(2)

GUIDELINES for implementation of Prime Minister's New 15 Point Programme for the Welfare of Minorities

The Hon'ble President, in his address to the Joint Session of Parliament on February 25, 2005, had announced that the Government would recast the 15 Point Programme for the Welfare of Minorities with a view to incorporate programme specific interventions. Prime Minister, in his address on the occasion ofIndependence Day, 2005, announced inter-alia that "We will also revise and revamp the 15 Point Programme for Minorities. The new 15 Point Programme will have definite goals which are to be achieved in a specific time frame". In pursuance of these commitments, the earlier programme has been revised as the Prime Minister's New 15 Point Programme for the Welfare of Minorities. A copy of the programme is enclosed.

2. **The objectives of the programme** are as follows:-

a) Enhancing opportunities for education.

b) Ensuring an equitable share for minorities in economic activities and employment, through existing and new schemes, enhanced credit support for self-employment,and recruitment to State and Central Government jobs.

c) Improving the conditions of living of minorities by ensuring an appropriate share for them in infrastructure development schemes.

d) Prevention and control of communal disharmony and violence.

3. An important aim of the new programme is to ensure that the benefits of various government schemes for the underprivileged reach the disadvantaged sections of the minority communities. The underprivileged among the minorities are, of course, included in the target groups of various government schemes. But in order to ensure that the benefits of these schemes flow equitably to minorities, the new programme envisages location of a certain proportion of development projects in

minority concentration areas. It also provides that, wherever possible, 15% of targets and outlays under various schemes should be earmarked for minorities.

4. The emphasis of the programme on the maintenance of communal peace and harmony, through appropriate measures, and ensuring a reasonable representation of minorities in government, including the public sector, remains as emphatic as ever and these continue to be important constituents of the new programme.

5. The programme does not envisage any change or relaxation of any criteria, norms or eligibility conditions in any scheme for minorities. These would continue to be as provided for in the original schemes included in the programme.

6. The term 'substantial minority population' in the 15 Point Programme applies to such districts/sub-district units where at least 25% of the total population of that unit belongs to minority communities.

7. (a) The target group of the programme consists of the eligible sections among the minorities notified under Section 2 (c) of the National Commission for Minorities Act, 1992, viz, Muslims, Christians, Sikhs, Buddhists and Zoroastrians (Parsis).

(b) In States, where one of the minority communities notified under Section 2 (c) of the National Commission for Minorities Act, 1992 is, in fact, in majority, the earmarking of physical/financial targets under different schemes will be only for the other notified minorities. These states are Jammu & Kashmir, Punjab, Meghalaya, Sikkim, Mizoram and Nagaland. Lakshadweep is the only Union Territory in this group.

8. The new programme will be implemented by Central Ministries / Departments concerned through State Governments / Union Territories. Each Ministry/Department concerned shall appoint a nodal officer, not below the rank of a Joint Secretary to Government of India, for this programme. The Ministry of Minority Affairs shall be the nodal Ministry for this programme.

9. **Physical Targets and Financial Outlays:**

Considering the complexity of the programme and its wide reach, wherever possible, Ministries/Departments concerned will earmark 15 percent of the physical targets and financial outlays for minorities. These will be distributed between States/UTs on the basis of the proportion of Below Poverty Line (BPL) population of minorities in a particular State/Union Territory to the total BPL population of minorities in the country, subject to the following:-

(a) (i) For schemes applicable exclusively to rural areas, only the ratio relevant to the BPL minority population in rural areas would be considered.

(ii) For schemes applicable exclusively to urban areas, only the ratio relevant to the

BPL minority population of urban areas would be considered.

(iii) For others, where such differentiation is not possible, the total would be considered.

(b) For States/UT referred to in para 7 (b), the earmarking will only be for the BPL minorities, other than that in majority.

10. The schemes amenable to such earmarking are the following:-

Point No. (A) Enhancing opportunities for Education

(1) Equitable availability of ICDS Services Integrated Child Development Services (ICDS) Scheme by providing services through Anganwadi Centres

(2) Improving access to School Education Sarva Shiksha Abhiyan, Kasturba Gandhi Balika Vidyalaya Scheme, and other similar Government schemes.

Point No. (B) Equitable Share in Economic Activities and Employment

(7) Self-Employment and Wage Employment for the poor

(a) Swarnjayanti Gram Swarojgar Yojana (SGSY)

(b) Swarn Jayanti Shahari Rojgar Yojana (SJSRY)

(c) Sampurna Grameen Rozgar Yojana (SGRY)

(8) Upgradation of skills through technical training New Industrial training Institutes (ITI) and upgradation of existing ITI.

(9) Enhanced credit support for economic activities

(b) Bank credit under priority sector lending.

Point No. (C) Improving the conditions of living of minorities

(11) Equitable share in rural housing scheme Indira Awaas Yojana (IAY)

(12) Improvement in condition of slums inhabited by minority communities

Integrated Housing & Slum Development Programme (IHSDP) and Jawaharlal Nehru National Urban Renewal Mission (JNNURM)

11. **Implementation, Monitoring and Reporting** –

A. **Ministry/Department Level:**

Ministries/Departments implementing the schemes, included in the programme shall continue to implement and monitor these schemes with reference to the physical targets and financial outlays. They are expected to review the progress of the programme on a monthly basis and report the progress of implementation, in respect of the schemes under this programme, on a quarterly basis, by the fifteenth day of next quarter, to the Ministry of Minority Affairs.

B. **State/UT Level:**

(i) States/UTs are expected to constitute a State Level Committee for Implementation of the Prime Minister's New 15 Point Programme for the Welfare of Minorities headed by the Chief Secretary with members consisting of the Secretaries and Heads of Departments implementing the schemes under the 15 Point Programme, representatives from the Panchayati Raj Institutions/Autonomous District Councils, three representatives from reputed non-governmental institutions dealing with minorities and three such other members considered appropriate by the state government/UT administration. The Department dealing with Minorities of the State/UT may be made the nodal department for monitoring the 15 Point

Programme. The Committee should meet at least once every quarter and the Department dealing with Minorities of the State/UT may send a quarterly progress reports to the Ministry of Minority Affairs by the 15th day of the next quarter.

(ii) **District Level:**

Similarly, at the district level, a District Level Committee for Implementation of the Prime Minister's New 15 Point Programme for the Welfare of Minorities may be constituted headed by the Collector/Deputy Commissioner of the district, with District level officers of the departments implementing the programme, representatives from the Panchayati Raj Institutions/Autonomous District Councils, and three representatives from reputed institutions dealing with minorities. The District Level Committee shall report progress of implementation to the Department dealing with Minorities of the state government/UT administration for placing it before the State Level Committee.

C. **Central Level:**

(i) At the central level, the progress of implementation, with reference to targets, will be monitored once in six months by a Committee of Secretaries (COS), and a report will be submitted to the Union Cabinet. The Ministry of Minority Affairs shall be the nodal Ministry to prepare reports in this regard for placing before the COS and the Union Cabinet once in six months. All

Ministries/Departments concerned with this programme shall submit quarterly reports to the Ministry of Minority Affairs by the 15th day of the next quarter.

(ii) There shall be a Review Committee for the Prime Minister's New 15 Point Programme for the Welfare of the Minorities headed by Secretary, Ministry of Minority Affairs, with nodal officers from all the Ministries/Department concerned which shall meet at least once every quarter to review the progress, obtain feedback and resolve problems and provide clarifications, as might be needed.

Prime Minister's New 15 Point Programme for the Welfare of Minorities

(A) Enhancing opportunities for Education

(1) Equitable availability of ICDS Services

The Integrated Child Development Services (ICDS) Scheme isaimed at holistic development of children and pregnant/lactating mothers from disadvantaged sections, by providing services through Anganwadi Centres such as supplementary nutrition, immunization, health check-up, referral services, pre-school and nonformal education. A certain percentage of the ICDS projects and Anganwadi Centres will be located in blocks/villages with a substantial population of minority communities to ensure that the benefits of this scheme are equitably available to such communities also.

(2) Improving access to School Education

Under the Sarva Shiksha Abhiyan, the Kasturba Gandhi Balika Vidyalaya Scheme, and other similar Government schemes, it will be ensured that a certain percentage of all such schools are located in villages/localities having a substantial population of minority communities.

(3) Greater resources for teaching Urdu

Central assistance will be provided for recruitment and posting of Urdu language teachers in primary and upper primary schools that serve a population in which at least one-fourth belong to that language group.

(4) Modernizing Madarsa Education

The Central Plan Scheme of Area Intensive and Madarsa Modernization Programme provides basic educational infrastructure in areas of concentration of educationally backward minorities and resources for the modernization of Madarsa education. Keeping in view the importance of addressing this need, this programme will be substantially strengthened and implemented effectively.

(5) Scholarships for meritorious students from minority communities

Schemes for pre-matric and post- matric scholarships for students from minority communities will be formulated and implemented.

(6) Improving educational infrastructure through the Maulana Azad Education Foundation

The Government shall provide all possible assistance to Maulana Azad Education Foundation (MAEF) to strengthen and enable it to expand its activities more effectively.

(B) Equitable Share in Economic Activities and Employment

(7) Self-Employment and Wage Employment for the poor

(a) The Swarnjayanti Gram Swarojgar Yojana (SGSY), the primary self-employment programme for rural areas, has the objective of bringing assisted poor rural families above the poverty line by providing them income generating assets through a mix of bank credit and Governmental subsidy. A certain percentage of the physical and financial targets under the SGSY will be earmarked for beneficiaries belonging to the minority communities living below the poverty line in rural areas.

(b) The Swarn Jayanti Shahari Rojgar Yojana (SJSRY) consists of two major components namely, the Urban Self-Employment Programme (USEP) and the Urban Wage Employment Programme (UWEP). A certain percentage of the physical and financial targets under USEP and UWEP will be earmarked to benefit people below the poverty line from the minority communities.

(c) The Sampurna Grameen Rozgar Yojana (SGRY) is aimed at providing additional wage employment in rural areas alongside the creation of durable community, social and economic infrastructure. Since the National Rural Employment Guarantee Programme (NREGP) has been launched in 200 districts, and SGRY has been merged with NREGP in these districts, in the remaining districts, a certain percentage of the allocation under SGRY will be earmarked for beneficiaries belonging to the minority communities living below the poverty line till these districts are taken up under NREGP. Simultaneously, a certain percentage of the allocation will be earmarked for the creation of infrastructure in such villages, which have a substantial population of minorities.

(8) Upgradation of skills through technical training

A very large proportion of the population of minority communities is engaged in low-level technical work or earns its living as handicraftsmen. Provision of technical training to such people would upgrade their skills and earning capability. Therefore, a certain proportion of all new ITIs will be located in areas predominantly inhabited by minority communities and a proportion of existing ITIs to be upgraded to 'Centres of Excellence' will be selected on the same basis.

(9) Enhanced credit support for economic activities

(a)The National Minorities Development & Finance Corporation (NMDFC) was set up in 1994 with the objective of promoting economic development activities among the minority communities. The Government is committed to strengthen the NMDFC by providing it greater equity support to enable it to fully achieve its objectives.

(b) Bank credit is essential for creation and sustenance of selfemployment

initiatives. A target of 40% of net bank credit for priority sector lending has been fixed for domestic banks. The priority sector includes, inter alia, agricultural loans, loans to small-scale industries & small business, loans to retail trade, professional and self-employed persons, education loans, housing loans and micro-credit. It will be ensured that an appropriate percentage of the priority sector lending in all categories is targeted for the minority communities.

(10) Recruitment to State and Central Services

(a) In the recruitment of police personnel, State Governments will be advised to give special consideration to minorities. For this purpose, the composition of selection committees should be representative.

(b) The Central Government will take similar action in the recruitment of personnel to the Central police forces.

(c) Large scale employment opportunities are provided by the Railways, nationalized banks and public sector enterprises. In these cases also, the concerned departments will ensure that special consideration is given to recruitment from minority communities.

(d) An exclusive scheme will be launched for candidates belonging to minority communities to provide coaching in government institutions as well as private coaching institutes with credibility.

(C) Improving the conditions of living of minorities

(11) Equitable share in rural housing scheme

The Indira Awaas Yojana (IAY) provides financial assistance for shelter to the rural poor living below the poverty line. A certain percentage of the physical and financial targets under IAY will be earmarked for poor beneficiaries from minority communities living in rural

(12) Improvement in condition of slums inhabited by minority communities

Under the schemes of Integrated Housing & Slum Development Programme (IHSDP) and Jawaharlal Nehru National Urban Renewal Mission (JNNURM), the Central Government provides assistance to States/UTs for development of urban slums through provision of physical amenities and basic services. It would be ensured that the benefits of these programmes flow equitably to members of the minority communities and to cities/slums, predominantly inhabited by minority communities.

(D) Prevention & Control of Communal Riots

(13) Prevention of communal incidents

In the areas, which have been identified as communally sensitive and riot prone, district and police officials of the highest known efficiency, impartiality and secular record must be posted. In such areas and even elsewhere, the prevention of communal tension should be one of the primary duties of the district magistrate and superintendent of police. Their performances in this regard should be an important factor in determining their promotion prospects.

(14) Prosecution for communal offences

Severe action should be taken against all those who incite communal tension or take part in violence. Special court or courts specifically earmarked to try communal offences should be set up so that offenders are brought to book speedily.

(15) Rehabilitation of victims of communal riots

Victims of communal riots should be given immediate relief and provided prompt and adequate financial assistance for their rehabilitation.

(3)

GOVERNMENT OF INDIA, MINISTRY OF AGRICULTURE

NATIONAL COMMISSION ON FARMERS

SERVING FARMERS AND SAVING FARMING

Fifth and Final Report, 4 October 2006

Jai Kisan : Revised Draft National Policy for Farmers

The first draft of this policy was presented to the Union Minister for Agriculture and Food on 13 April 2006. Since then, the draft policy has been discussed widely throughout the country with the principal stakeholders. Based on their inputs, the present revised draft has been prepared. NCF requests that this draft, after being examined by the Government of India, may be put up, with such changes as deemed appropriate, to the National Development Council (NDC) for consideration and adoption. After obtaining the NDC concurrence, the draft policy may be

placed before the Parliament for consideration. The final policy statement may be adopted on August 15, 2007 which marks the 60th anniversary of what Jawaharlal Nehru said, "India's Tryst with Destiny". We are confident that if our hardworking farm women and men are assisted on the lines proposed in this draft policy statement, they will ensure a glorious destiny for the country in the field of agriculture and food security.

M S Swaminathan

(Chair)

R B Singh Y C Nanda

(Member) (Member)

Atul Sinha Atul Kumar Anjan

(Member-Secretary) (Member-Part time)

Jagadish Pradhan R L Pitale

(Member-Part time) (Member-Part time)

Chanda Nimbkar

(Member-Part time)

JAI KISAN

REVISED NATIONAL POLICY FOR FARMERS*

1.1 **Why a National Policy for Farmers?**

To those who are hungry, God is Bread – Mahatma Gandhi, 1946

Everything else can wait, but not agriculture – Jawaharlal Nehru, 1947

A majority of the hungry live in rural India and also depend on agriculture for their livelihood; accelerated agricultural progress is therefore essential for their income and their food. The two statements above hence constitute the guiding principles of this policy

1.1.1 Many steps have been taken since 1947 to strengthen agricultural research, education and extension as well as to produce essential inputs like seeds, fertilizer and electricity. Also, both mega and minor irrigation projects have been developed. An integrated programme of agricultural development was initiated in the early 1960s to help farmers benefit from irrigation facilities. Nevertheless food shortages continued partly because of a fast growth in population arising from advances in preventive and curative

medicine. Import of foodgrains increased year after year and touched a level of 10 million tonnes in 1966, largely under the PL 480 programme of the United States of America. Fortunately, our scientists, with the help of international partners, developed high- yielding varieties / hybrids of wheat, rice, maize, *jowar* and *bajra*. These were introduced to farmers through the High Yielding Varieties Programme in 1966. A major breakthrough in productivity and production occurred in wheat in 1968 and resulted in a special stamp titled, "Wheat Revolution" being released by then Prime Minister, Smt Indira Gandhi. Since then the progress of agricultural production was steady and the growth rate in food production remained above the level of population growth. This came to be known as the "Green Revolution Era". This era was characterized by synergy among technology, services, public policy and farmers' enthusiasm and hence was christened "Green Revolution Symphony". Unfortunately during the past ten years, production and productivity have remained stagnant or even tended to go down. The reasons for this situation are well known and there is now considerable effort to reverse the decline and get our agriculture moving forward once again.

1.1.2 Several policies for agriculture have been developed by the Government of India from time to time, the last one being in the year 2002. The decline in the growth of agriculture has now led to a climate of despair among farmer families, policy makers and the general public. Some areas in the States of Maharashtra, Andhra,

Karnataka and Kerala have been affected by a serious agrarian crisis, leading occasionally to farmers' suicides. The time has therefore come when we should focus more on the economic well-being of the women and men feeding the nation than just on production. It is clear that the human dimension must be the principal determinant of agricultural policies and not just production in physical terms. The aim of this Policy is to stimulate attitudes and action which will result in assessing agricultural progress in terms of the net income of farm families rather than just in million tonnes of farm commodities produced, and which will help to place faces before figures.

(* First draft was submitted to Government on April 13, 2006. It has been widely discussed throughout the country since and the revised draft is based on extensive consultations and comments)

1.2 Silver lining in the Dark Cloud

1.2.1 Fortunately, several significant initiatives have been taken during the last 2 years to reverse the downward trend in agricultural production and to find permanent solutions to the agrarian crisis. Some of the important new initiatives are:

i) Bharat Nirman or a New Deal for Rural India

ii) National Rural Employment Guarantee Programme

iii) National Horticulture Mission

iv) Expansion of agricultural credit

v) Lowering of interest rates

vi) National Rainfed Area Authority

vii) National Fisheries Development Board

viii) Changes in the Agriculture Produce Marketing Committee (APMC) Act, to make it farmer-friendly

ix) Integrated Food Law

x) Warehouse Receipt Act, making warehouse receipts a negotiable instrument, thereby helping to prevent distress sales

xi) Knowledge connectivity through 100,000 rural Common Service Centres (CSC)

1.2.2 The above programmes will make a positive impact on the well-being of farmer families if they are given a pro-nature, pro-poor, pro-women and pro-livelihood orientation.

1.2.3 The time is therefore opportune for revitalizing our agricultural progress by making agrarian prosperity and food security and sovereignty the bottom line for government policies and priorities in agriculture and rural development. Given adequate investment and pro-small farmer public policies, we can reverse the decline and restore confidence in our agricultural capability. During the VI Five Year Plan (1980- 85), the growth rate in agriculture was 5.7% as against a GDP growth rate of 5.5%. This was partly because of the allocation of 12.5% of the VI Plan budget for irrigation.

1.2.4 The growth rate of agriculture was about 2% during the IX Plan period and is slated to decline to 1.8% per annum during the X Plan1. The consequent declining share of agriculture in the total GDP without adequate shift of population dependent on agriculture has worsened the already adverse per capita farm income to per capita nonfarm income ratio. A major problem confronting the rural areas is the lack of employment opportunities. During 1993-94 – 1999-2000, the growth of jobs in the farm sector was only 0.2%. While all efforts are needed to increase jobs in the farm sector by switching over to more labour intensive crops and practices to the extent feasible, and increased investment in irrigation, watershed development, wasteland development, land reclamation etc, greater focus has to be for accelerated development of the rural non-farm sector and development of clusters around towns/market centres. A growing farm sector, better rural infrastructure particularly rural connectivity, power, regular bus service, easy availability of credit and availability of trained manpower could help in development of rural non-farm sector and creation of more job opportunities.

1.3 Draft National Policy for Farmers

Ten Major Goals

• To improve the economic viability of farming by ensuring that farmers earn a "**minimum net income**", and ensure that agricultural progress is measured, by the advance made in improving that income.

• To mainstream the human and gender dimension in all farm policies and

programmes and give explicit attention to sustainable rural livelihoods.

• To complete the unfinished agenda in land reforms and to initiate comprehensive asset and aquarian reforms.

• To develop and introduce a social security system and support services for

farmers.• To protect and improve the land, water, biodiversity and climate resources essential for sustained advances in the productivity, profitability and stability of major farming systems by creating an economic stake in conservation.

• To foster community-centred food, water and energy security systems in rural India and to ensure nutrition security at the level of every child, woman and man.

• To introduce measures which can help to attract and retain youth in farming by making it both intellectually stimulating and economically rewarding, by conferring the power and economy of scale to small and marginal farmers both in the production and post-harvest phases of farming.

• To strengthen the biosecurity of crops, farm animals, fish and forest trees for safeguarding both the work and income security of farmer families, and the health and trade security of the nation.

• To restructure agricultural curriculum and pedagogic methodologies for enabling every farm and home science graduate to become an entrepreneur and to make agricultural education gender sensitive.

• To make India a global outsourcing hub in the production and supply of the inputs needed for sustainable agriculture, and products and processes developed through biotechnology and Information and Communication Technology.

1.3.1 Definition

For the purpose of this Policy, the term "farmers" will refer to both men and women, and include landless agricultural labourers, sharecroppers, tenants, small, marginal and sub-marginal cultivators, farmers with larger holdings, fishers, livestock and poultry rearers, pastoralists, small plantation farmers, as well as rural and tribal families engaged in a wide variety of farming related occupations such as apiculture, sericulture and vermiculture. The term will include tribal families sometimes engaged in shifting cultivation and in the collection and use of nontimber forest products. Farm and Home Science Graduates earning their livelihoods from crop and animal husbandry, fisheries and agro-forestry will have their rightful place in the world of farmers and farming. The gender-specific needs of women in each category will also be recognized.

1.4 Asset Reform

1.4.1 The purpose of asset reform is to ensure that every man and woman in villages either possesses or has access to a productive asset like land, livestock, fishpond, homestead farm or income through an enterprise, or a market driven skill, so that household nutrition security is safeguarded, and children are able to go to school.

1.4.2 Land

1.4.2.1 The ownership of land is highly skewed with over 60% of the rural households owning less than one hectare. Farmers owning over one hectare comprise about 28% of rural families. The landless population amounts to 11.24% of rural households. These data relate to 1991-92 and it is obvious that by now there would have been further fragmentation of holdings leading to a much larger incidence of very small operational holdings.

1.4.2.2 The first and foremost task of the National Policy for Farmers would be in the area of land reform with particular reference to tenancy laws, land leasing, distribution of ceiling surplus land and wasteland, providing adequate access to common property and wasteland resources, and the consolidation of holdings. The Mohan Dharia Committee recommendations on Wasteland Development should be implemented since it will be more appropriate to refer to wastelands as wasted lands. Following the conferment of land rights to women under the Hindu Succession Amendment Act (2005), the provision of appropriate support services to women farmers has become urgent. *Joint Pattas* for both houses and agricultural land are essential for women to get access to credit with alternative collateral till the *pattas* are issued. The Land Acquisition Act needs review and revision, with particular reference to the formula for calculating compensation.

1.4.2.3 Prime farmland must be conserved for agriculture and should not be diverted for non-agricultural purposes and for programmes like the Special Economic Zone. Such special programmes should be assigned wastelands and/or land affected by salinity and other abiotic stresses that reduce the biological potential of land for the purpose of farming. Every State should constitute a Land Zonation Team consisting of soil scientists, agronomists and remote sensing specialists to earmark soils with a low biological potential for farming such as wastelands, lands affected by salinity, acidity, etc., for industrial activities and construction. It is in our national interest that agriculture and industry both prosper in a mutually reinforcing manner.

Land for the Landless

1.4.2.4 The ownership of a small plot of land will help the family improve household income and nutrition security. Wherever feasible, landless labour households should be provided with at least 1 acre per household, which will give them space for home gardens and animal rearing. The allotment of such land should be in the name of the woman or in the joint names of both husband and wife. Tamil Nadu's recent example of allocation of land to the landless deserves to be studied and emulated throughout the country.

1.4.3 Water

1.4.3.1 Water is a public good and social resource and not private property. Priority should be given to evolving just and equitable mechanisms to give access to water and to include local people in management of water resources. Women must have a significant role in both access and management, as water users and managers. Irrigation water at the right time and in adequate quantities is now becoming a serious constraint in achieving both higher productivity and stability of farming in many parts of the country. *Jal Swaraj or self-sufficiency in irrigation water availability is the need of the hour*. Though the total rainfall in our country is satisfactory, its distribution is highly skewed, with most of the rainfall occurring in 100 hours in a year. It is also important to note that the majority of farmers depend on groundwater for irrigating their crops. This resource, in which farmers have invested their hard-earned savings, is today increasingly depleted with groundwater tables declining. Therefore rainwater harvesting and aquifer recharge have become essential for ensuring the stability of supply. A nationally debated and accepted strategy for bringing 10 million hectares of new area under irrigation under the Bharat Nirman programme should be developed. Only dialogue and consensus building can reconcile different viewpoints regarding the development of large-scale water projects.

1.4.3.2 There is considerable scope for improving the efficiency of water use. It has been calculated that even a 10% increase in the present level of water use efficiency in irrigated projects may help to provide crop life saving irrigation in large areas. Higher efficiency can be achieved by generating synergy among water, variety, nutrients (macro and micro) and farm implements. The concept of maximizing yield and income per unit of water should become internalized in all crop production programmes.

1.4.3.3 Water quality also needs attention since water often gets polluted at source with fertilizers, pesticide residues and toxic chemicals. For example, the problem of arsenic poisoning in ground water continues because people residing in regions blessed with abundant surface water such as West Bengal increasingly depend on the groundwater for drinking and irrigation purposes. This dependency can be removed by making available other safe drinking water options. Effective management of surface water including rivers, canals, water bodies, lakes, ponds and rainwater can reduce groundwater dependency.

1.4.3.4 Besides problems relating to adequacy and quality, there are serious issues concerning equity in water distribution. The privatization of water supply distribution is fraught with dangers and could lead to water conflicts in local communities.

1.4.3.5 **The following steps are needed for supply augmentation and demand man-**

agement:

i) Rainwater harvesting and aquifer recharge should be mandatory and farmers must be provided with financial assistance to invest in the replenishment of their renewable resource. This is the imperative need for conservation farming.

ii) All existing wells and ponds should be renovated.

iii) Demand management through improved irrigation practices, including sprinkler and drip irrigation, should receive priority attention.

iv) A Water Literacy movement should be launched and regulations should be developed for the sustainable use of ground water.

v) The conjunctive use of rain, river, ground, sea, and treated sewage water should become the principal method for the effective use of available water resources and for increasing income per every drop of water.

vi) In water scarce areas, the land use system should place emphasis on the cultivation of high value – low water requiring crops, such as pulses and oilseeds.

vii) **A Pani Panchayat** in every village can help in getting the available water distributed on an equitable basis.

viii) Where large scale dislocation of families living in the areas which will be submerged as a result of the construction of large dams or linking of rivers is likely, the Gram Sabhas of the affected villages should be involved in the preparation of rehabilitation plans. This should be done at the time the large dam or other steps like the interlinking of rivers are on the drawing board.

1.4.3.6 Water Users' Associations may be encouraged to gain expertise in maximizing the benefits of the available water. The National Rainfed Area Authority could help in promoting scientific water harvesting, sustainable and equitable use and the introduction of efficient methods of water use. There should be symbiotic interaction between the National Rainfed Area Authority, the National Horticulture Mission, the Technology Missions in oilseeds and pulses and the National Rural Employment Guarantee Programme.

1.4.3.7 Monsoon behaviour is often erratic. In drought prone areas, a **Drought Code** may be introduced which details the action needed to minimize the impact of an adverse monsoon and maximize the benefits of a good season. Similarly, in areas prone to heavy rainfall, a **Flood Code** may be introduced which will again mitigate distress and help convert the flood-free season into a major agricultural production period. In the arid areas of Rajasthan, a **Good Weather Code** may be introduced for taking advantage of occasional heavy rainfall for strengthening the ecological infrastructure essential for sustainable livestock production, drinking water security and sand dune stabilization. The National Rainfed Area Authority could provide technical leadership in the integrated preparation and application of Drought, Flood and Good Weather Codes.

1.4.4 Livestock

1.4.4.1 Livestock, including poultry, is the second major land-based livelihood, contributing 26% of the agricultural GDP in 2004-05. It is clear that livestock and livelihoods are very intimately related in our country and that crop-livestock integrated farming is the pathway to farmers' well being.

1.4.4.2 The ownership of livestock is much more egalitarian since resource poor farmer families own a majority of cattle, buffalo, sheep and goats. Women play a critical role in the care and management of livestock, but may not have ownership rights, and hence the cooperative model of production should be encouraged. The major constraints experienced by such families relate to fodder, feed, healthcare and remunerative price. There is an urgent need for establishing **Livestock Feed and Fodder Corporations at the State Level** for ensuring availability of quality fodder and feed. Such a Corporation should be a facilitating body for providing seeds and planting material of improved varieties to Self-help Groups (SHGs) for local level production. The productivity of our livestock is low and can be easily improved through better nutrition and healthcare. Agriclinics operated by veterinary and farm science graduates will be very helpful to enhance the income of livestock owners through higher productivity. At the same time, croplivestock integrated farming systems should be promoted since this will not only help improve income and household nutritional security, but also facilitate organic farming.Livestock insurance also needs revamping and should be made accessible to small livestock owners.

1.4.4.3 A **National Livestock Development Council** may be established to give integrated attention to all aspects of this important sector, such as breeding policy, feed and fodder, healthcare through Para-veterinary professionals, marketing, value addition, biomass utilization (skin, bones and blood) and efficient use of animal energy, forexample, through improved bullock carts. 1.4.4.4 In the case of poultry, the following steps are needed:

i) **Quarantine and testing facilities at all ports of entry should be established and strengthened** as such safeguards are absolutely necessary for the health and survival of the poultry industry and for the protection of lives and livelihoods.

ii) A 100% quarantine of all imported birds for a minimum period of six weeks should be enforced as done in other countries.

iii) Testing for safety and efficacy of imported poultry vaccines before they are allowed to be marketed as is done in the case of human vaccines, should be made compulsory.

iv) Poultry rearing should be recognized as an agricultural activity and appropriate support should be provided to backyard poultry farmers to establish Small Holders' Poultry Estates.

1.4.5 Fisheries

1.4.5.1 Both coastal and inland fisheries provide employment and livelihoods to millions of families. There is considerable scope for improving the income of fisher families on an environmentally sustainable basis by introducing Integrated Coastal Zone Management and scientific fish rearing, harvesting and processing. In the area of public policy, there is need for well-planned **Aquarian Reforms** in order to provide landless labour families access to village ponds and other water bodies in the public domain for aquaculture.

1.4.5.2 The establishment of a **National Fisheries Development Board** (NFDB) is a welcome step. The guiding principles for the NFDB should be ecology, economics, gender equity and employment generation. Such a Board should have representatives of fisher communities engaged in the capture and culture aspects of fish farming. It should set up an interdisciplinary Task Force for preparing guidelines for aquarian reforms. In addition, resolution of conflicts in areas such as the following deserves urgent attention from the NFDB:

i) Conflicts between mechanized and artesinal fishing enterprises.

ii) Conflicts between aquaculturists and agriculturists as well as local population over salt water entering into the aquifer, and pollution caused by intensive systems of aquaculture.

iii) Lack of well-defined policies for the allocation of ponds and reservoirs to landless labour and *dalit* families for practising modern aquaculture based on composite fish farming.

iv) Concerns of environmentalists in the areas of sea weed farming and introduction of exotic carps and other alien invasive species.

1.4.5.3 Aquarian reforms should enable resource poor fisher and labour families to earn their livelihood from capture and culture fisheries in a sustainable manner. Other aspects of policy that need attention are:

i) "**Fish for All Training and Capacity Building Centres**" which can impart training to fisher families in all aspects of the capture/culture–consumption chain.

ii) Quality literacy to safeguard the harvested fish from *Salmonella* and other infections capable of producing mycotoxins.

iii) Mother Ships, which can ensure hygienic handling of the catch in mid-ocean.

iv) Small-size dredgers for ensuring the efficiency of fish landing centres.

v) Centralized services to support the decentralized capture and culture fisheries sectors.

vi) Special attention to the training needs of fisher women who handle the harvested catch.

vii) Inland aquaculture, including the culture of ornamental fish and air breathing fish, for additional income by providing necessary space in ponds and reservoirs

viii) Artificial coral reefs to compensate for the loss of natural coral reefs to revive the fish catch.

ix) Integrated Coastal Zone Management Policy should pay concurrent attention to the management of about 10 km of land surface and 10 km of sea surface from the shoreline to ensure that land-based occupations do not cause damage to ocean fisheries as a result of release of effluents and other pollutants.

x) The coastal communities can also be enabled to raise bioshields comprising mangroves, *casuarina, salicornia, atriplex* and other halophytic plants, to safeguard the lives and livelihoods of coastal fisher and farm families in the event of cyclonic storms and seawater inundation, as for example like the one caused b **tsunami of December 26, 2004.**

xi) The National Aquaculture Authority and the NFDB should work together, s that capture fisheries and aquaculture become mutually reinforcing in improvin the economic well-being of fisher families and the nutritional well-being of consumers. In all structures, the special needs and concerns of women should be included and they be given representation.

xii) Fisher families can be trained to take up additional income-earning activities lik poultry farming, fish pickle preparation, agar production, pearl oyster culture an other enterprises.

1.4.5.4 There is also need for a dynamic policy for the management and econom use of the Exclusive Economics Zone (EEZ) extending to nearly 2 million sq km of sea surface, which amounts to two-thirds of the land surface available to India. Th can be a priority task of the NFDB.

1.4.6 Bioresources

1.4.6.1 Bioresources refer to the abundant wealth of flora and fauna including soil microflora and microfauna, which after land and water forms the third important natural resource available to farmers. The aim of the policy is to conserve as well as enhance these resources, to provide equitable access and lead to sustainable use with equitable sharing of benefits. Two major legislations are now in place to achieve some of the above aims.

1.4.6.2 The Plant Variety Protection and Farmers' Rights Act (PVPFR) was enacted in 2001. The Act recognizes the multiple roles of farmers as cultivators, conservers and breeders. Detailed guidelines should be developed for ensuring that the rights of farmers in their various roles are safeguarded. For example, most farmers who are cultivators are entitled to "Plant Back Rights". This implies that they can keep their own seeds and also enter into limited exchange in their vicinity. Farmers as breeders have the same rights as professional breeders and they can enter their varieties for registration and protection.Farmers as conservers are entitled to recognition and reward from both the National Gene Fund and the National Biodiversity Fund. Quite often, the conserved material of great value is the contribution of a community and not an individual. **Therefore the procedures adopted should be such that community contributions can be recognized and suitably rewarded**. The Gene and Biodiversity Funds should be used exclusively for recognizing and rewarding the contributions of tribal and rural women and men and for supporting the revitalization of the *in situ* on-farm conservation traditions of such communities.

1.4.6.3 Breeders should be required to indicate in the pedigree of the variety for which they are seeking protection, the names of the landraces and the areas from where they were collected, while submitting their application for registration.

1.4.6.4 The provisions in the Biodiversity Act (2002) for prior informed consent and benefit sharing are equally important for tribal and rural women and men. Invariably, much of the conservation work has been and is being done by women. Therefore the recognition procedures should take into account gender roles in the conservation and enhancement of bioresources. The gender mainstreaming of the implementation procedures of both the Acts is important. A gender audit provision may be introduced in the operation of both the Gene and Biodiversity Funds.

1.4.6.5 The following should be promoted:

i) Documentation of Traditional Knowledge (TK) should be done through Community Biodiversity Registers with the involvement of women, who hold much of this knowledge.

ii) Tribal and rural women and men should get support in revitalising their *in situ* on-farm conservation traditions.

iii) Participatory breeding procedures involving scientists and local conservers would be particularly helpful in improving the productivity of landraces.

iv) Genetic engineers working in public good institutions should perform the role of pre-breeding, i.e., development of novel genetic combinations for important economic traits, such as resistance to biotic and abiotic stresses. They should then work with farmers in participatory breeding programmes, so that genetic efficiency and genetic diversity can be integrated in an effective manner.

v) Genetic homogeneity enhances genetic vulnerability to pests and diseases, so the integration of pre-breeding and participatory breeding would help insulate small farmers from the risks of pest epidemics.

vi) A **genetic and legal literacy** movement must be launched in areas rich in agro biodiversity such as the North East, Western and Eastern Ghats and the Arid Zone.

vii) **Genome Clubs** can be organized in rural schools and colleges for imparting an understanding of the importance of genetic resources conservation.

viii) Legal literacy would help tribal and rural families understand the provisions of the PVPFR and Biodiversity Acts with reference to their entitlements.

ix) Farm and tribal families should be trained in methods of preventing gene erosion.

x) Coastal biodiversity, including coral reefs and sea grass beds is also in urgent need of conservation.

xi) Traditional methods of conservation like Sacred Groves need to be supported and encouraged.

xii) Herbal Biovalleys can be organized in the Western Ghats, Eastern Ghats, Vindhyas and Himalayan region for the conservation and sustainable use of medicinal plants. In such Biovalleys, young farm women and men could be assisted through a form of venture capital and other support to take to the conservation, selection and multiplication of medicinal plants of value to health security.

xiii) A nationwide programme needs to be launched for the *ex situ* and *in situ* conservation of plant genetic resources at the field/farmer level. Farmer level Gene/Seed banks need to be set up in areas where traditional varieties are in danger of extinction. Some State Governments are promoting a "Seed Exchange Programme" under which farmers are given hybrid rice in exchange for their traditional rice varieties. There is need to ensure that in this process, the traditional rice gene pool is not lost. Participatory management of National Parks, Biosphere Reserves and Gene Sanctuaries should be promoted.

1.4.7 Animal Genetic Resources

1.4.7.1 The burden of conservation of genetic resources cannot be allowed to fall on the largely impoverished communities which maintain animal genetic diversity. A system of rewards and incentives must be developed to enable and motivate people to conserve their breeds under the Biodiversity Act. The Biodiversity Fund should be used for such purposes. Livestock keepers' inherent rights to continue to use and develop their own breeding stock and breeding practices should be acknowledged. The government must recognise these rights, acknowledge livestock keepers' contribution to the national economy, and adapt its policies and legal frameworks accordingly. This is particularly important to pre-empt attempts to use the intellectual property system to obtain control over animal resources which are an important component of the country's food and livelihood security systems.

1.4.7.2 Apart from conserving genetic diversity and acknowledging the vital role of livestock keepers, there is a need to document the indigenous knowledge of pastoral communities about animal maintenance and breeding. Community-based conservation and development of indigenous livestock breeds and species should be encouraged, with a special focus on both hot and cold arid and semiarid areas where the genetic diversity and associated indigenous knowledge are particularly well developed. State Farms could be used to promote *in situ* conservation of animal breeds, even those that are amenable to *ex situ* conservation. Grazing lands must be earmarked to enable the conservation of animal genetic resources. Documentation of special traits should be done in the context of the new biology and new nutritional needs or for other economic traits like hide/ leather quality. Offshore Quarantine Centres should be developed for screening germplasm for resistance to serious diseases like the H5N1 strain of avian influenza virus.

1.4.7.3 In Brazil and other Latin American countries as well as in Africa, there is a demand for Indian breeds of cattle and buffaloes. Animal Science Graduates and SHGs may be encouraged to maintain pedigree animals of these breeds for the purpose of developing export opportunities. However, export of all biological material including animals should be done in strict accordance with the provisions of the Biodiversity Act.

1.5 Support Services

1.5.1 Science and Technology

1.5.1.1 Science and Technology are the drivers of change in farm operations and output. New technologies, which can help enhance productivity per unit of land and water, are needed for overcoming the prevailing technology fatigue. Frontier technologies like biotechnology, information and communication technology (ICT), renewable energy technologies, space applications and nanotechnology provide opportunities for launching an "evergreen revolution" capable of improving productivity in perpetuity without ecological harm. Similarly, the use of remote sensing technology can help identify borewell sites on farmers' fields. In order to ensure social inclusion in access to new technologies, public investment in socially relevant agricultural research should be stepped up under the umbrella of the National Agricultural Research System (NARS), which comprises large numbers of ICAR institutions, State Agricultural Universities, All India Coordinated Research Projects and National Bureaus. NGO and private sector R & D institutions should also be included under the NARS umbrella.

1.5.1.2 The research strategy should be pro-nature and pro-small farmer. For example, in the case of Bt cotton, public good institutions should concentrate on developing varieties rather than hybrids, so that farmers can keep their own seeds. Even now 80% of the seeds used in agriculture come from farmer-seed systems. Community managed Seed Villages and Seed Technology Training Centres are needed, with women playing the major role because of their traditional knowledge of seeds and seed management, especially in tribal communities. Scientific literacy and removing doubts and fears about the risks and benefits associated with biotechnology and other new technologies can be done by one woman and man selected by each Panchayat and trained with the help of agricultural / animal sciences universities. They will serve as Farm Science Managers in their respective villages.

1.5.1.3 The safe and responsible use of recombinant DNA technology or genetic engineering will need credibie and capable regulatory mechanisms. A National Biotechnology Regulatory Authority should be set up for this purpose, with farmers' representatives on it. It should be autonomous and professionally-led so that risks and benefits can be assessed objectively.

The bottom line for any biotechnology regulatory policy should be:

i) The safety of the environment

ii) The well-being of farming families

iii) The ecological and economic sustainability of farming systems

iv) The health and nutrition security of consumers

v) Safeguarding of home and external trade, and

vi) The biosecurity of the nation.

1.5.1.4 There is urgent need for stepping up breeding crop varieties, particularly fruits and vegetables, for processing quality. Also, research on breeding crops for high yield in an environmentally safe manner needs strengthening.

1.5.1.5 Organic farming requires greater scientific inputs than chemical farming. Hence, this area of research needs high-level multidisciplinary attention. Farmers feel the need for technological guidance, but research work based on careful field experiments is currently inadequate. Crop-livestock-cum-fish integrated production systems offer scope for the adoption of the principles and methods of organic farming.

1.5.1.6 In intensively cultivated mono-crop areas, crop diversification may be beneficial from the points of view of ecology, economics and employment generation. **However, steps to ensure effective market support for the alternative crops must accompany any advice on crop diversification.** In planning for crop diversification, particularly from food to non-food crops, such as for the production of biofuels, the food security of the nation should be kept in view.

1.5.1.7 Intellectual Property Rights (IPR) policies should make provision for compulsory licensing of rights in the cases of research products and processes of value to resource-poor farming families. In all cases of health and food security, social inclusion should be the guiding factor in the development of IPR.

1.5.2 Agricultural Biosecurity

1.5.2.1 Agricultural Biosecurity covering crops, trees and farm and aquatic animals is of great importance since it relates both to the work and income security of 70% of the population, and food and trade security of the nation. The **National Agricultural Biosecurity System (NABS)** should have the following aims:

i) Safeguard the income and livelihood security of farmer families, as well as the food, health and trade security of the nation, through effective and integrated surveillance, vigilance, prevention and control mechanisms designed to protect the productivity and safety of crops, farm animals, fishes and forest trees.

ii) Enhance national and local level capacity in initiating proactive measures in the areas of monitoring, early warning, education, research, control and international co-operation

iii) Introduce an integrated biosecurity package comprising regulatory measures, education, improved sanitary and phytosanitary measures and social mobilization.

iv) Organize a coordinated **National Agricultural Biosecurity Programme** on a hub and spokes model, with effective home and regional quarantine facilities capable of insulating the major agro-ecological and farming systems zones of the country from invasive alien species of pests, pathogens and weeds as well as from the introduction and release of GMOs.

1.5.2.2 The NABS should have the following three mutually reinforcing components:

i) **National Agricultural Biosecurity Council (NABC),** chaired by the Union Minister for Agriculture, to serve as the apex policymaking and coordinating body

ii) **National Centre for Agricultural Biosecurity (NCAB),** with four wings dealing with crops, farm animals, living aquatic resources and agriculturally important micro-organisms. It should be concerned with analysis, aversion and management of risks, as well as the operation of an early warning system. The NCAB will provide the Secretariat for the NABC.

iii) **National Agricultural Biosecurity Network (NABN):** The NCAB will also serve as the coordinating and facilitating center for a National Agricultural Biosecurity Network designed to facilitate scientific partnerships among the existing institutions in the public, private, academic and civil society sectors engaged in biomonitoring, biosafety, quarantine and other biosecurity programmes to maximize the benefits available to scientific expertise and institutional strengths.

1.5.3 **Agro-meteorology**

1.5.3.1 The national capacity in short, medium and long-term weather forecasting is quite considerable. Generic information about weather has to be turned into location- specific land use advice, based on cropping patterns and water availability. Panchayat level Farm Science Managers, trained to give appropriate land use suggestions, can use the Agro-meteorological Advisories issued by Indian Agromet Advisory Service Centre, Pune. There should be a **National Land Use Advisory Service** that gives proactive advice to help farm families plan their sowing based on anticipated meterological and marketing factors. In the case of marine fisheries, data available on wave heights and location of fish shoals should be transmitted to the fishermen before they move into the sea. An integrated internet-FM or HAM radio service would be very helpful to fishermen on the high seas.

1.5.4 Climate Change

1.5.4.1 Climate change leading to adverse changes in temperature, precipitation and sea level is no longer just a theoretical possibility. Most experts agree that we are already beginning to experience the impact of global warming as evident from the melting of glaciers and Antarctic and Arctic ice caps. Coastal storms and cyclones are also increasing in frequency and intensity. Droughts and floods are likely to be more frequent.

Although climate change is a product of the unsustainable consumption of non-renewable forms of energy by industrialized countries, the harmful impact of climate change will be felt more by poor nations, and the poor in all nations, due to their limited coping capacity. Proactive measures to reduce the vulnerability to climate change have to be developed. Based on computer simulation models, contingency plans and alternative land and water use strategies will have to be developed for each major agro-climatic zone. In drought Band flood prone areas, experienced farm women and men can be trained as "Climate Managers", in the art of managing drought, flood and aberrant monsoons.

1.5.5 Inputs and Services

i) **Seeds**: Good quality seeds and disease free planting material, including in vitro cultured propagules, are essential for crop productivity and security. Hybrids are now becoming available in many crops. Women SHGs can produce hybrid seeds on contract for seed companies, with proper technical guidance and training in seed technology. In the case of new varieties, foundation seeds could be provided to SHGs. Mutually beneficial farmer-seed company partnerships can be fostered. Agricultural Universities should organize courses on Seed Technology and Business and mainstream business principles in all applied courses.

ii) **Soil Health: Soil Health Enhancement holds the key to raising small farm productivity**.

Every farm family should be issued with a Soil Health Passbook, which contains integrated information on the physics, chemistry and microbiology of the soils on their farm. More laboratories to detect specific micronutrient deficiencies in soils are urgently needed. Soil organic matter control will have to be increased by incorporating crop residues in the soil. Proper technical advice on the reclamation of wastelands and on improving their biological potential should be available. Pricing policies should promote a balanced and efficient use of fertilizers.

iii) **Pesticides:** The triple alliance of pests, pathogens and weeds causes crop losses ranging from 10 to 30 per cent every year. The development, introduction and diffusion of environmentally safe and effective pesticides should be given priority. There is need for incorporating the use of chemical pesticides in an Integrated Pest Management (IPM) system. Farmers need training in crop care and IPM. Suitable quality control, safety evaluation and other regulatory systems should be strengthened. The sale of spurious and substandard pesticides should be prevented. Botanic pesticides should be promoted. In each block, breeders, farmers, pesticide manufacturers and extension personnel could form a Crop Care Consortium.

iv) **Implements**: Small farmers need implements for timely sowing, management of weeds and improved post-harvest technology. This need is particularly great in hill areas. Women especially need women-friendly implements / tools which can reduce drudgery, save time and enhance output and can be handled comfortably. Farm graduates can provide tractors and other larger farm implements on a custom-hire basis by organizing Agri-business Centres.

v) **Vaccines and Sero-diagnostics**: Major gaps in the facilities presently available will have to be filled in the case of important animal diseases. Biotechnology research in the area of vaccine development needs to be stepped up. Public-private partnerships should be encouraged in this area.

vi) **Fish Seed and Feed**: Good quality and disease-free fish seed holds the key to successful inland aquaculture. SHGs could be trained in induced breeding and fish seed production. Feed at affordable prices is another requirement. Fish farmers' cooperatives could organize the production of both feed and seed, with technical assistance from the National Fisheries Development Board.

vii) **Animal Feed**: Inadequate nutrition is the primary cause of low milk yield in dairy animals; where both under-nutrition and malnutrition can be seen. Annual milk production in the country can reach over hundred million tones if the nutritional requirements of cows and buffaloes are met. Here both conventional and non-conventional approaches are needed. Many of the cellulosic wastes can be converted into good animal feed through appropriate treatment and enrichment. Planting of nutrition rich fodder plants should receive high priority. Established technologies such as baling and ensiling, need to be disseminated widely.

viii) Other essential support services needed for higher farm animal productivity are: establishing genetic evaluation systems for indigenous breeds as well as crosses, so that selection can lead to genetic improvement of production characteristics; upgrading of breed through artificial insemination; cross breeding suited to the farmers' resources; and improved processing and marketing. The livestock sector has to become sanitary and phytosanitary compliant. A cadre of Para-veterinarians will have to be trained. They will help promote early detection and treatment of diseases and other veterinary services.

ix) The Wildlife Protection Act, 1972, should permit the right of farmers to protect their crops by killing wild boars and *nilgai*, whenever there is no other option for saving crops.

x) Free grazing of cattle during the *rabi* season is a major bottleneck to farmers for the taking of a second crop and should be curtailed by the Gram Panchayat.

xi) **Support Services for Women:** Women suffer from a multiple burden on their time due to their home making, child rearing, and income earning responsibilities. When they work the whole day in fields and forests, they need appropriate support services like crèches and child care centres. Adequate nutrition is also important. A **Gram Panchayat Mahila Fund** should be established to enable SHGs and other women's groups to undertake community activities that help to meet essential gender-specific needs. The feminisation of agriculture, due to male out-migration, needs specific attention with reference to gender-sensitive farm and credit policies. All research, development and extension programmes in agriculture, and all services must be engendered

1.5.6 Credit and Insurance

1.5.6.1 The need is to improve the outreach and efficiency of the rural banking system. The financial services must reach all its users effectively; the credit must be in time, in required quantities and at appropriate interest rate. The interest rate should be as low as possible. It should be possible to bring about a reduction in transaction cost by eliminating all forms of waste and inefficiency in the operation of the banking system. The inefficiencies of the delivery system should not be loaded on the interest charged. The delivery system has to be proactive and should respond to the financial needs of clients in the rural areas. The banking system needs to explore the large unmet credit potential needed to raise agriculture to higher thresholds, and for the growth of rural and agri-business enterprises and employment.

1.5.6.2 The State has a responsibility towards improving the credit absorptive capacity of the farmers and to support the banking system by creating favourable environment for expanding and deepening of financial services.

1.5.6.3 NABARD as the leader of agriculture and rural credit should ensure,

convergence between credit availability and credit absorptive capacity of the farmers and other rural borrowers, and an efficient credit delivery system. NABARD should actively involve itself in institution building and provide backup support through research and development initiatives. NABARD should function like a National Bank for Farmers. There is a need for a fresh look at its mandate, role and business model after about years of its establishment and vastly changed circumstances.

1.5.6.4 The Reserve Bank and Government of India have to broadly assign the roles and responsibilities to different agencies in the multi-agency system and ensure implementation of their policies and programmes. There is a **need for an Agriculture Credit Policy.** The credit cooperatives have an important position in the rural financial system and priority should be given to the implementation of the recommendations of the Vaidyanathan Committee.

1.5.6.5 Agriculture is a high-risk economic activity. Credit without insurance is an added risk factor. Farmers need user-friendly insurance instruments covering production, right from sowing to post-harvest operations and also to cover the market risks for all crops throughout the country, in order to insulate them from financial distress and in the process make agriculture financially viable. Satellite imagery and agro-climatic analyses can play a significant role in evaluating the extent of crop losses and thus speed up the process of settling claims.

1.5.6.6 There is a need for both credit and insurance literacy in villages. *Gyan Chaupals* can help in this task.

1.5.6.7 Women need special attention because of their lack of land title/collateral. Kisan Credit Cards should be issued to women speedily with joint *pattas* to house / agricultural land as collateral. Till then, indemnity bonds/guarantees should be accepted from husband, male relatives and prominent local figures.

1.5.6.8 Drought prone areas should have a 4-5 year repayment cycle for crop loans, taking into account the management of risk.

1.5.7 Cooperatives

1.5.7.1 Besides their role in production, cooperatives have an important role to play in banking, marketing, agro-processing and other agri-businesses, to protect the farmers from the vagaries of existing imperfections in the supply of inputs, production, value addition and marketing. Cooperatives are basically economic enterprises [not an extended arm of the State]. They require entrepreneurial approach, gather competitive edge through suitable enterprise focus and form suitable strategic alliances with private and public sector units. The need is to find means and measures by which farmers can obtain greater control of the market channels and improve their chances of profit.

1.5.7.2 The policy and legal framework under which cooperatives are functioning need to be reviewed so as to create an enabling environment for them to attain autonomy and run their operations in business-like fashion without rigid controls and regulations imposed by the State laws. They have to become voluntary, member-driven, autonomous and largely self-regulating organisations working on the principles of self-help. The management of the cooperatives needs to be professionalized with clear demarcation of functions of the elected members and the professional managers. The audit and accounting systems have to be improved and made transparent so as to give greater confidence to all those who are associated with them.

1.5.7.3 With economic liberalization and market competitiveness, cooperatives would require much larger capital and other financial resources. The changes in legal framework and regulatory system would help gain greater access to capital/financial resources.

1.5.8 Extension, Training and Knowledge Connectivity

1.5.8.1 There is a growing gap between scientific know-how and field level do-how. This knowledge deficit should be overcome speedily in order to enhance the productivity and profitability of small farms and launch a Small Farm Management Revolution. Postharvest technology wings must be added to Krishi Vigyan Kendras urgently and lab to land demonstrations in the area of post-harvest technology, agro-processing and value addition to primary products must be taken up to provide skilled jobs in villages to landless labour families. In addition to the retraining and retooling of existing extension personnel, there is a need to promote farmer to farmer learning. For this purpose, Farm Schools may be established in the fields of outstanding farmers and awardees of nationally recognized awards for farmers. Farmer-to-farmer learning can speed up the process of technological upgrading of crop and animal husbandry, fisheries and agroforestry. Farm Schools can also be set up in the fields of eminent horticulturists including those who are raising organic vegetables and fruits and tissue culture propagated planting material.

1.5.8.2 The help of ICT should be harnessed by establishing a *Gyan Chaupal* in every village. The Common Service Centre (CSC) programme of the Department of Information Technology (DIT), Government of India, should aim at social inclusion in the use of this important technology. The structure of the ICT based knowledge system will be as follows:

i) **Block level**: Village Resource Centre (VRC) established with the help of the Indian Space Research Organisation.

ii) **Village level**: *Gyan Chaupals* established with the help of the CSC Programme of the D I T.

iii) **Last mile and the last person connectivity**: This can be accomplished

through either internet – community radio or internet – mobile phone synergy.

1.5.8.3 Empowering rural women and men with the right information at the right time and place is essential for improving the efficiency and economics of small scale agriculture. Mass media, particularly the radio, television and local language newspapers, have an important role to play in this area.

1.5.9 Social Security

1.5.9.1 Coverage of farmers, particularly small and marginal farmers and landless agricultural workers, under a comprehensive National Social Security Scheme is essential for ensuring livelihood security. Such a scheme should take care of expenses upto a ceiling for hospitalization in case of illness of a family member, maternity, life insurance and old age pension. This should also include protection from occupational hazards. In addition, the subsistence allowance for fisher families during the "closed season" period should be at least Rs.1500 per month. The Government should take necessary action to have such a comprehensive scheme in place for the farmers in unorganized sector in order to ensure the livelihood security of farm families. At the very minimum, the recommendations of the Arjun Sengupta Commission for Enterprises in the Unorganised Sector may be suitably adapted to the needs of farmer families.

1.5.10 Assured and Remunerative Marketing Opportunities

1.5.10.1 Assured and remunerative marketing opportunities hold the key to continued progress in enhancing farm productivity and profitability. The Union Ministry of Agriculture has already initiated several significant market reforms. The State Governments will have to undertake such reforms speedily in order to provide more options to the farmers for selling their produce, allowing the private sector, including the cooperatives, to develop markets, promote direct sales to consumers and remove bottlenecks and scope for corruption and harassment. What farmers seek is greater protection from market fluctuations. Important steps needed are:

i) The Minimum Support Price (MSP) mechanism has to be developed, protected and implemented effectively across the country. MSP of crops needs to keep pace with the rising input costs.

ii) The Market Intervention Scheme (MIS) should respond speedily to exigencies especially in the case of sensitive crops in the rainfed areas.

iii) The establishment of Community Foodgrain Banks would help in the

marketing of underutilized crops and thereby generate an economic stake in the conservation of agro-biodiversity.

iv) Indian farmers can produce a wide range of health foods and herbal medicines and market them under strict quality control and certification procedures.

v) The Public Distribution System (PDS) **should be universal** and should undertake the task of enlarging the food security basket by storing and selling nutritious millets and other underutilized crops.

1.5.10.2 Farmers require authentic advice based on meteorological, marketing and management information for land use decisions and investments. Restructured Land Use Boards supported by a team of technical experts/agencies should render this service. Infrastructure support has to be put in place to minimize post-harvest losses and enable agro-processing and value addition at the village level itself to increase jobs and income. The collective strength of farmers has to be built up by encouraging farmers' organizations and other entities like cooperatives and small farmers' estates so that they can get a fair deal and enjoy the economies and power of scale. Farmers, particularly the small and marginal ones, need pledge loans to be able to avoid distress sale and sell their produce when the price is favourable. Constraints in improving the negotiability of warehouse receipts also need to be removed.

1.5.10.3 There is need for an Indian Trade Organisation (ITO), that will safeguard the interests of farmer families by establishing a Livelihood Security Box to ensure fair trade. The Livelihood Security Box should have provision to impose quantitative restrictions on imports and or/increases in import tariffs, under conditions where imports of certain commodities will be detrimental to the work and income security of large numbers of farming families. It should be emphasized that **there is no level playing field between the capital, subsidy and technology driven mass production agriculture** of the industrialized countries, and the "**production by masses"** agriculture of India characterized by weak support services, heavy debt and "resource and technology poverty". An **Indian Single Market** will also help to promote farmer-friendly home markets. The bottom line of our trade policies in agriculture should be the economic wellbeing and livelihood security of agricultural families. Nothing should be done that will destroy job opportunities in rural India.

1.5.10.4 In relation to commodities that are exported, it will be essential to conform to WTO regulations. At present, such commodities constitute about 7% of total agricultural production in the country. Quality and trade literacy programmes have to be launched across the country.

1.5.10.5 Farmers' Associations and SHGs should be helped to export on competitive terms by spreading awareness of the opportunities available for external agricultural trade. The agri-export zones should be further strengthened and should become places where farmers will get the best possible price for their produce. The future of Indian agriculture will depend upon the efficiency and seriousness with which pro-farmer marketing systems are put in place.

1.5.10.6 The twin goals of ensuring justice to farmers in terms of a remunerative price for their produce, and to consumers in terms of a fair and affordable price for staples (65% of consumers are also farmers) can be achieved through the following integrated strategy:

i) The MSP and procurement operations are two separate initiatives and should be operated as such. The Government needs to ensure that both the farmers (who also constitute the majority of consumers) and the urban consumers get a fair deal. Due care should be taken of the cost escalation after the announcement of the MSP in its operationalisation. The Government should procure the staple grains needed for the PDS at the price private traders are willing to pay to farmers. Thus, the procurement prices could be higher than the MSP and would reflect market conditions. The MSP needs to be protected in all the regions across the country.

ii) The food security basket should be widened to include the crops of the dry farming areas like ***bajra, jowar, ragi,*** **minor millets** and **pulses**. The PDS should include **these nutritious cereals and pulses purchased at a**

reasonable MSP. This will be a win-win situation both for the dryland farmer and the consumer. **We will witness neither a second green revolution nor much progress in dryland farming unless farmers get assured and remunerative prices for their produce.**

iii) Both universal PDS and enforcing MSP throughout the country for the selected crops are essential for imparting dynamism to agriculture.

1.5.10.7 The Commission on Agricultural Costs and Prices (CACP) should be an autonomous statutory organization with its primary mandate being the recommendation of remunerative prices for the principal agricultural commodities of both dry-farming and irrigated areas. The MSP should be at least 50% more than the weighted average cost of production. The "net take home income" of farmers should be comparable to those of civil servants. The CACP should become an important policy instrument for

safeguarding the survival of farmers and farming. Suggestions for crop diversification should be preceded by assured market linkages. The Membership of the CACP should include a few practising farm women and men. The terms of reference and status of the CACP need review and appropriate revision.

1.6 Curriculum Reform

1.6.1 Agricultural / Animal Sciences Universities

1.6.1.1 The goal of these universities should be "**every scholar an entrepreneur**". This will call for integrating business management principles with major applied courses. Also, the Farm Universities should engender their curricula in a manner that the relative roles of women and men in farming are recognized and they are equally empowered technologically. The Home Science Colleges of Universities should be restructured as **College of Human Sciences** with both male and female scholars mastering disciplines like nutrition and post-harvest technology. A network of **Regional Institutes on Food Safety and Security** needs to be set up to promote safe handling of food and a quality literacy movement in villages. This will also help to strengthen our capacity to deal with sanitary and phytosanitary measures and Codex Alimentarius standards of food safety.

1.6.1.2 A system for according recognition to Farm Graduates to provide extension and other services by recognizing them as **Registered Farm Practitioners** should be developed. An **All India Agricultural Council** on the model of the Medical and Veterinary Councils is required to give such accreditation, which will also be an oversight mechanism to ensure the quality and credibility of the services provided by farm practitioners. A few **Centres of Excellence in Agriculture** (Crop and Animal Husbandry, Fishery and Forestry) on the model of the IITs and IIMs, should be established to enhance competitiveness of the graduates. Taking into account the new opportunities opened up by ICT, new **pedagogic methodologies** should be introduced for promoting a learning revolution among our students. University centres should also establish employment and business advisory services and a special **one-stop window** for generating awareness on self-employment opportunities.

1.7 Special Categories of Farmers

1.7.1 Tribal Farmers

1.7.1.1 Scheduled Tribes account for 8.6% of the total population of the country. A majority of tribal communities across the country are dependent on forests and animal husbandry for their livelihoods. These include cultivation (shifting cultivation in many cases), collection of fuel, fodder and a range of non-timber forest produce. Tribal farmers are among the most disadvantaged category of farmers.

1.7.1.2 These communities have customary norms for ownership of the forest areas and also have community-based mechanisms for protection and rejuvenation. At the same time, the responsibility for the protection and conservation of forests area has been under the control and administration of the State Forest Departments. There has been no systematic effort to demarcate areas that are used and managed by forest dwelling communities, or to provide legal rights and titles to these communities. The relation between the Forest Department and forest dwelling communities has largely been one of conflict and confrontation, with the latter being labelled 'encroachers'. Forest communities are often forced to eke out their livelihoods through a pattern of bribes and fines. Attempts towards Joint Forest Management have been successful in some States but are dispersed and have not generally been gender sensitive.

1.7.1.3 Large development projects, including dams and mines, have encroached upon vast tracts of forest areas and displaced several thousand forest dwelling communities who are still struggling to survive in the absence of human-centred rehabilitation efforts. In most instances, in the absence of land titles, their very existence is not acknowledged.

1.7.1.4 Management of forest areas in the country will have to balance the demands for ecological conservation with protecting the livelihoods of forest dwelling communities. The following steps will be helpful in this respect:

i) A clear statement of rights relating to what has traditionally been the domain of forest dwellers (both tribal and non-tribal) including lands traditionally occupied and resources traditionally used.

ii) A clear process by which legitimate land rightholders can be identified and recorded, and conversely, by which recent encroachers, and others who have been taking advantage of forest dwellers for vested interest, can be identified and removed.

iii) Explicit provisions to ensure conservation, including priority to provisions of wildlife/biodiversity/forest laws which are meant to ensure conservation, with special focus on protected areas and threatened species.

iv) Strengthening changes in institutional structures to enable more participatory processes in decision-making.

v) Explicit provisions that enable forest-dwelling communities to say 'no' to, or seek changes in, 'development' projects that are impinging on their lands and resources.

vi) Provisions for regular and open processes of dialogue, consultation, and sharing of information, involving communities, NGOs, officials, and others.

vii) Clear monitoring provisions that enable a constant check on whether the rights are being honoured or not, as also whether the exercise of rights is respecting conservation parameters.

1.7.1.5 An important area of conflict between people and protected areas is the problem of compensation for damage caused to livestock, crop or life by animals. States must review the provisions and procedures for compensation for human life, livestock and crop damage. Compensation must be paid to affected families who continue to live within the reserves also. The joint forest management programme in the vicinity of the reserves must be revamped so that people living on the fringes can be given management decisions and rights over the produce of forests; this will help to enhance the productivity of the resources as well.

1.7.1.6 Other issues are:

i) Vesting of land in the community, absence of alienable rights with the farmers and the problems in creation of charge/mortgage on land in certain tribal areas constrain flow of institutional credit. The need is to develop innovative methods of collateral substitution and documentation procedures to overcome the difficulties.

i) Tribal families have conserved rich agro-biodiversity. Many traditional crops are now disappearing. Both dying crops and dying wisdom will have to be saved by creating an economic stake in conservation.

.7.2 Pastoralists

.7.2.1 The Draft Scheduled Tribes (Recognition of Forest Rights) Bill, 2005 envisages, "rights of use or entitlements such as grazing in forests and traditional seasonal resource access of nomadic or pastoralist communities". This Act is yet to be passed by Parliament. Many of the Joint Forest Management Committees are designed to provide opportunities to tribal families and pastoralists for access to non-timber forest products. The following steps are needed to ensure the livelihood rights of pastoralists:

) Restoration of traditional grazing rights and camping rights in forest areas

including wildlife sanctuaries and national parks, and also those areas earmarked for grazing purpose in village common lands.

i) Formalizing entitlements (including issue of permanent grazing cards) for traditional pastoralists / herders maintaining native animal breeds to enable free access to notified or demarcated grazing sites and migration routes.

ii) Whenever a tree planting programme is to be implemented, alternative grazing land and drinking water resources for animals should be allotted by the concerned authorities. It should be mandatory for the implementing agency before initiating afforestation to seek prior consent from forest dependent communities including pastoralists. Rotational system of grazing should be encouraged instead of complete closing of forest zones for tree plantation purpose.

v) In-depth documentation and characterization of indigenous livestock breeds should be carried out to recognize and protect the IPR of the local communities / individuals conserving these livestock breeds.

) Pastoralists should be involved in all local natural resource management programmes, including village forest committees.

i) Common land assigned to Forest Departments and unutilized or encroached land should be retrieved and brought under the control of village level committees or grassroots institutions for pasture development.

1.7.3 Other Categories:

1.7.3.1 Besides the above two groups, there are several small groups with distinct and special needs such as small plantation farmers, island farmers and urban farmers.

Plantation Labour

1.7.3.2 A large number of small farmers are engaged in the cultivation of plantation crops like tea, coffee, rubber, cardamom, pepper and vanilla. Price fluctuation and competition from products imported from abroad are among the major problems facing them. A Price Stabilization Fund will help insulate them from the vagaries of the market.

Island Farmers

1.7.3.3 The farming and fisher families in Andaman and Nicobar Islands and the Lakshadweep group of Islands need special attention including technology, training, techno-infrastructure and trade. Island agriculture also has the problem of transport costs, particularly for perishable commodities like fish which may have to be sold in the main land. Ancient tribes in the Andaman and Nicobar Islands have rich traditional knowledge and wisdom. Steps should be taken to recognize and reward their indigenous knowledge in the areas of biodiversity conservation and traditional healthcare. The islands are also ideal for horticulture including coconut plantation, but have special health problems. Therefore both the National Horticulture Mission and National Rural Health Mission should pay particular attention to the needs of island farmers and fishermen. The creation

of mangrove and non-mangrove based bioshields should be initiated to safeguard the lives and livelihoods of island populations in the event of sea level rise due to global warming and calamities like tsunami.

Urban Farmers

1.7.3.4 Urban home gardens could make a substantial contribution to improving nutrition security through the cultivation and consumption of vegetables and fruits. Home nutrition gardens could be designed for low income groups in such a manner as to provide horticultural remedies to major nutritional maladies. Support services in the form of good seeds and planting material and safe plant protection techniques will be needed. Urban slums need particular attention from the point of view of combating malnutrition through nutrition gardens.

1.8 Special Categories of Farming

1.8.1 Organic Farming

The organic farming movement in India suffers from lack of adequate institutional support in the areas of research, extension and marketing. Organic farming requires more scientific support than chemical farming. Krishi Vigyan Kendras should be equipped to provide training in organic agriculture. Internationally accepted certification procedures also need strengthening and must be farmer-friendly and affordable. Organic farming zones could be identified, like some of the hill areas and islands where currently chemical fertilizer use is very low, and for medicinal plants where the use of chemical pesticides and fertilizers is not advisable. Food safety and quality specifications should conform to the Codex Alimentarius standards since there are occasional reports of heavy metals being present in organic foods. Subsidies or loans similar to those given to farmers to buy chemical fertilizers / pesticides should be available for organic manures like farm yard manure, compost and biofertilizers and biopesticides also. Farmers engaged in organic farming should be linked to niche markets where they will obtain a premium price, in order to compensate for any loss in yield. Farm graduates may be supported for establishing agri-clinics and agribusiness centers for organic farming.

1.8.2 Green Agriculture

Green Agriculture involving integrated pest management, integrated nutrient supply, scientifice water management, integrated natural resources management and improved in organic farming, green agriculture permits the safe and minimal use of mineral fertilizers and chemical pesticides as well as crop varieties developed by genetic modification. Green agriculture products also should have distinct labelling as in the case of organic farming.

1.8.2 Genetically Modified (GM) crops

The establishment of a professionally-led National Biotechnology Regulatory Authority will help the assessment of risk and benefits associated with GM crops in a credible and transparent manner. It is important that priority is given in genetic modification to the incorporation of genes, which can help impart resistance to drought, salinity and other stresses. Water use efficiency as well as improvement of both nutritive and processing quality should also be accorded priority in the research agenda. The village-level Farm Science Managers to be trained in each Panchayat could be introduced to the agronomic management procedures in respect of GM crop varieties, such as the cultivation of a refuge of the old variety in order to prevent the loss of resistance in the GM variety caused by mutations in the pests and pathogens.

1.8.4 Protected (Greenhouse) Agriculture

With the rapid growth of horticulture, there is opportunity for green house cultivation of vegetables, fruits and flowers supported by economic methods of water and fertilizer use such as fertigation. Support may be given to farm and home science graduates to take to green house horticulture under the agribusiness programme and the National Horticulture Mission. Low cost green houses along with micro-irrigation and fertigation techniques may be popularized in areas where evaporation exceeds precipitation during several months in a year. Suitable support should be given for such technologies, which can help to increase income in water deficit areas.

1.9 Special Regions

1.9.1 Distress Hotspots

Several steps have already been taken to mitigate agrarian distress and it is

important that special attention is paid to such areas from the point of view of spreading low risk and low external input sustainable agricultural practices. Opportunity for remunerative marketing is a must. It is also important that in such areas, knowledge connectivity and social support systems are strengthened.

1.9.2 Megabiodiversity areas

Biodiversity rich areas occur in Western and Eastern Ghats and the eastern Himalayan region. Local communities should be involved in the conservation of megabiodiversity areas and their contributions should be appropriately recognized and rewarded. Steps should also be taken to enable local communities in megabiodiversity areas to convert bioresources into economic wealth in a sustainable manner. A movement for 'Biodiversity for Biohappiness', may be launched with the help of local research and educational institutions.

1.9.3 Islands

The Andaman and Nicobar Islands and the Lakshadweep Group of Islands offer great potential for improving the income of farmer families. Greater attention is needed to plantation crops and coconut, rainwater harvesting and agro-processing facilities. The coastal ecosystems rich in mangroves and coral reefs should be protected. The youth in such islands can be trained in the science and art of natural resources conservation and enhancement. Mixed cropping and crop-livestock integrated farming systems are ideal for such islands. The Lakshadweep group of islands can also be the home for offshore quarantine facilities.

1.10 Farmers of the future

1.10.1 The slow growth of opportunities in the non-farm employment sector has led to the proliferation of tiny and economically non-viable holdings. **Increase in small**

farm productivity and creating multiple livelihood opportunities through croplivestock integrated farming systems as well as agro-processing and value addition to biomass have become urgent tasks for increasing farmers' income. Methods of providing the power of scale to small farmers will have to be developed and popularized on a win-win basis for all concerned to enhance yield and income. Women can participate in such group activities only if they are given dignity of recognition as owners and farmers. The following are some of the methods that small and marginal farmers could consider for gaining in efficiency and economy:

i) **Cooperative Farming and Service Cooperatives** – In the early 5-year Plan periods, there was much emphasis on cooperative farming. This did not take off due to both socio-cultural and policy hurdles. It is clear that small farm families will benefit from cooperation, even if they do not form cooperative societies. Service cooperatives have been successful in the case of the dairy industry. Marketing cooperatives are generally successful since members cooperate on the basis of enlightened self-interest. Other forms of service cooperatives are slowly emerging, but the pace needs to be accelerated. For example, there is scope for Irrigation Water Cooperatives which can operate community tube-wells and lift irrigation. Cooperative farming will be ideal for small and marginal farmers since the cooperative can provide centralized services like tractors and other farm equipment as well as threshing and drying machines, to support small scale decentralized production. This will bring down the cost of production and enhance the quality of produce and thereby of income. Instead of denying small farmers the many opportunities provided by cooperatives, the emphasis should be on the introduction of appropriate reforms to make cooperatives small farmer-friendly and efficient.

ii) **Group Farming by Self-help Groups** – So far, SHGs have been mainly organized for supporting micro-enterprises operated by women with the help of microcredit. With the growing diminution in the size of operational holdings, it will be useful to promote the SHGs at the production end of the farming enterprise by encouraging groups to lease farmland. This will be particularly helpful in the case of "Green Agriculture". The SHGs will, however, become sustainable only if they have backward linkages with technology and credit and forward linkages with processing and marketing organizations. Also microcredit banks operated by the SHGs should be helped to become Sustainable Livelihood Banks.

iii) **Small Holders' Estates** – The formation of Small Holders' Estates, for example in cotton, horticulture, medicinal plants, poultry and aquaculture will help promote group cooperation among farmers living in a village or watershed or the command area of an irrigation project. Improving productivity, reducing the cost of production and entering into marketing contracts with textile mills, food processing industries, pharmaceutical companies, and fish marketing agencies will be some of the advantages. Such Small Farmers' Estates can also manufacture products under brand names and enhance income security so that group insurance becomes feasible. Agri-clinics and Agribusiness Centres could be linked to such Estates.

iv) **Contract Farming** – Symbiotic contracts which confer benefits to both producers and purchasers, will be ideal for ensuring assured and remunerative marketing opportunities. At the moment, the Central and State Governments through organizations like Food Corporation of India (FCI), National Agricultural Cooperative Marketing Federation of India (NAFED, etc., ensure the operation of the MSP announced by the Government. Contract cultivation based on a well-defined Code of Conduct will be helpful to small producers in getting good quality input, a fair price and prompt payment for their produce.

A Code of Conduct for Contract Farming will have to be developed for major groups of farm commodities such as vegetables, fruits, flowers, medicinal plants, tuber crops, pulses, oilseeds, sugarcane, cereals and cotton. A farmer should not be alienated from his/her land under any circumstance. **Available evidence indicates that direct contract between the producer and purchaser with the government, as third party for intervention in the case of legal disputes is more advantageous to small farmers than indirect contract through intermediary agencies.** At the State level, a Monitoring Committee comprising farmers and appropriate officials may be set up to ensure the spread of a non-exploitative pattern of contract cultivation.

v) **Farmers' Companies** – Private Limited Companies, registered under the Companies (Amendment) Act, 2002, are now coming into existence in the area of seed production and the production of biofertilizers, biopesticides and other forms of biological software essential for sustainable agriculture. Small farmers and SHGs should be associated in such companies as stakeholders and not just as shareholders.

vi) **State Farms** – In the 1950s, there was considerable emphasis on the development of large State Farms on the model of the farms promoted by the former Soviet Union. Most such farms are now being used for purposes other than the production of food crops. The land available with State Farms could be made available to women SHGs for the production of say, hybrid and improved seeds of crop and fodder plants, vegetables, fruits and flowers. Also, State Farms could be used for developing **Living Heritage Gene Banks** of the germplasm of local breeds of cattle, sheep and poultry in order to preserve our animal genetic wealth.

1.11 Attracting Youth

Youth will be attracted to take to farming as a profession only if farming becomes economically rewarding and intellectually stimulating. This is where new technologies like biotechnology, information and communication technology, renewable energy technologies, space technology etc., can help. Educated youth should be helped through a form of Venture Capital Fund, low interest loans and allotment of wasteland for setting up agri-clinics and production-cum-processing centres to undertake outsourcing jobs both from within and outside the country, enabling India to emerge as a major agricultural outsourcing hub. Eco-agriculture is knowledge intensive and hence there is need to ensure that large numbers of educated young men and women take to farming and farm related enterprises as their vocation. This is an area where symbiotic partnerships between young entrepreneurs and the private sector will be beneficial.

1.12 Public Policies for Sustainable Livelihoods

1.12.1 The following policies will ensure **well-being and livelihood security of all included under the category of "farmers":**

i) A **National Land Use Advisory Service** should be immediately established and linked to State and Block Level Land Use Advisory Services on a hub and spokes model. These can be virtual organisations with the capacity to link land use decisions with ecological, meteorological and marketing factors on a location and season specific basis. They should provide proactive advice to farmers on land use. Land use decisions are also water use decisions and hence it is important that the proactive advice is based on both an estimate of likely water availability and the opportunities available for enhancing income per unit of water.

ii) The scope of the MSP programme should be expanded to cover all crops of importance to food and income security for small farmers. Arrangements should be made to ensure MSP at the right time and at the right place, particularly in the areas coming within the scope of the National Rainfed Area Authority. **Also, advice to farmers on crop diversification should be linked to the assurance of MSP. Small farm families should not be exposed to administrative and academic experiments and gambles in the market.**

iii) A Market **Price Stabilisation Fund** should be established jointly by Central and State Governments and financial institutions to protect farmers during periods of violent fluctuations in prices; as, for example, in the case of perishable commodities like onion, potato, tomato.

iv) An **Agriculture Risk Fund** should be set up to insulate farmers from risks arising from recurrent droughts and other weather aberrations.

v) The scope of Agricultural Insurance Policies should become wider and should also cover health insurance, as envisaged under the **Parivar Bima Policy**. Seed Companies should provide insurance in the case of GM crops.

vi) A **Food Guarantee Act** should be formulated and enacted. Farmers, who are also the largest consumer group, will produce more if there is greater consumption and consequently greater demand for farm produce and products. Such an Act that combines the principal features of Food for Work programmes and the National Employment Guarantee Programme would help make food serve the role of currency. Such a procedure will help improve household nutrition security as well as farmers' income.

vii) **A well-defined, pro-farmer and pro-resource poor consumer Food**

Security Policy is an urgent necessity. Food security with home grown foodgrains can alone eradicate widespread rural poverty and malnutrition, since farming is the backbone of the livelihood security system in rural India. This will enable the **Government to remain at the commanding height of the national food security system**. Building a food security system and containing price rise with imported foodgrains may sometimes be a short term necessity, but will be a long term disaster to our farmers and farming.

viii) The time has come for the Government to set up a multi-stakeholder **National Food Security and Sovereignty Board** chaired by the Prime Minister with its membership including the Minister for Agriculture and Food and other concerned Ministers of GoI, the Deputy Chairman of the Planning Commission as well as a few Chief Ministers of food surplus and deficit States, leaders of all national political parties, a few experts including specialists in the gender dimension of agriculture and food security, and mass media representatives. We are confronted with the need to conserve prime farmland and to safeguard the food security requirements of both resource poor farmers and resource poor consumers. The bulk of such resource poor consumers are small or marginal farmers and landless agricultural labour in unirrigated areas. It is these linkages which need to be understood and attended to. The proposed National Food Security and Sovereignty Board can attend to these complex linkages in a holistic manner and provide policy guidelines for developing and implementing a socially and economically sustainable food security programme catering to the interests of all regions of the country and all sections of our population.

ix) Farm families should also be protected from becoming victims of HIV/AIDS and tuberculosis (TB). Anti-retroviral drugs should be made available in villages free of cost. Also the approach to the treatment of HIV/AIDS and TB in villages should be a food cum drug based one. Nutrition support to rural families affected by HIV/AIDS, TB, malaria and leprosy is needed to assist in recovery and restoration to a productive life. There is evidence to suggest that a pure drug based approach alone is not adequate to help economically underprivileged rural women and men recover from diseases involving prolonged treatment. The foodgrains allotted to such a programme can be distributed through the normal channels on the production of a

Food Coupon issued by the appropriate government agencies. For example in the case of HIV/AIDS, the National AIDS Control Organisation (NACO) would be the appropriate agency for the issue of food coupon to children, women and men affected by this debilitating and killing disease. The Food-cum-Drug based approach to healthcare should become an integral part of the National Rural Health Mission.

x) There is need for a **Rural Non-Farm Livelihood Initiative** for rural areas. The initiative could have as its core a more market oriented and professionalised KVIC and a restructured and financially strengthened SFAC and bring all rural non-farm employment programmes together in order to generate convergence and synergy among them. The initiative should be integrated with on-farm employment generation through a pan-GoI programme to establish 'Rural Business Hubs' on the lines of China's Township and Village Enterprise (TVE) programme. A consortium approach involving the different agencies concerned is needed.

xi) An **Indian Trade Organisation** (ITO) should be established to help the Government to operate a Livelihood Security Box and link global policies with local action in a manner beneficial to farmers.

xii) Since agriculture is a State subject, every State Government should set up a **State Farmers' Commission** with an eminent farmer as Chairperson. The membership of the Commission should include all the principal stakeholders in the farming enterprise. Such Commissions should submit an Annual Report to be placed before the respective State Legislature for discussion and decision.

xiii) Agricultural progress should be measured by the growth in the net income of farm families. Along with production growth rates, income growth rates should also be measured and published by the Economics and Statistics Directorate of the Union Ministry of Agriculture.

xiv) Article 243 G of the 11th Schedule of the Constitution (73rd Amendment) Act, 1992 entrusts Panchayats **with responsibility for agriculture including agricultural extension**. They will have to be empowered with the needed information, training and tools for discharging this responsibility. At the moment there are about 2,25,000 panchayats in the country. The problems facing Indian farmers are generally dealt with in an aggregated manner – i.e., taking into consideration the problems of over 100 million farming families as a whole which make them appear formidable. **However, if such problems are disaggregated and dealt with by Gram Sabhas and Panchayats, location-specific problems can be attended to speedily and effectively.** Therefore it is time that the provisions of Article 243 G are implemented, both in letter and spirit.

xv) There are nearly 1.2 million elected women members in panchayats throughout the country. They can play a pivotal role in improving the quality of life in villages and in areas like sanitation, drinking water, child care, early childhood education and nutrition security. They should be empowered to take up such leadership roles in rural transformation through appropriate training and capacity building opportunities. An earmarked Gram Mahila Fund should be available to them for meeting gender-specific needs.

xvi) Mass media (conventional, electronic and the internet) constitute an important pillar of our democratic system of governance. Serious famines do not occur in countries with independent mass media, since they play the role of an early warning system. The green revolution of the 1960s would not have happened, but for the enthusiastic support of the media, particularly radio and language newspapers, which not only spread a message of hope, but also took the latest information on the new technologies to villages. This aroused enormous enthusiasm among farmers resulting in a small Government programme becoming a mass movement. There is need now for spreading messages of hope and information on the agricultural bright spots of the country. In order to assist the mass media with timely and scientifically accurate information on issues relating to agriculture, food security and farmers' welfare, it will be useful to establish a few **Regional Media Resource Centres**, in whose management farmers, media representatives and scientists including extension personnel should play an important part.

xvii) The Ministry and Departments of Agriculture both in the Centre and States may be restructured to become **Ministry / Department of Agriculture and Farmers' Welfare** in order to highlight their critical role in ensuring the income and work security of over 600 million members of India's population. The change of name should be accompanied by structural changes which permit the induction of active farm women and men in senior positions in Government for specific periods and specific tasks.

xviii) We urge the Central and State Governments to consider seriously the question of including Agriculture under the Concurrent List in Schedule VII, Article 246 of the Constitution. Important policy decisions like those relating toprices, credit and trade, are taken by the Government of India (GoI). Also, several pieces of legislation including the Protection of Plant Varieties and Farmers Rights Act, the Biodiversity Act, the Food Bill, etc., are administered by the GoI. GoI provides substantial funds for rural infrastructure development including irrigation, village roads and markets. By placing agriculture on the Concurrent List, serving farmers and saving farming becomes a joint responsibility of the Centre and States, i.e. a truly national endeavour in raising the morale, prestige and economic well being of our farm women and men.

1.13 Matching National Policy with Local Diversity

Indian agriculture is rich in diversity of soils, climate, farming systems, and resource endowments. Hence, a broad national policy will have to be tailored to suit different agro-climatic, socio-economic and socio-cultural factors. The framework for a **National Policy for Farmers** presented in this Report will have to be suitably adapted and elaborated to suit local realities in different parts of the country, particularly with reference to priorities in action points. State level policies can aim to convert national goals into local action. The State Farmers' Commissions could be entrusted with the task of preparing an operational plan for implementing the National Policy for Farmers on a location-specific basis.

1.14 Jai Kisan

Mahatma Gandhi preferred to be known as a farmer, while signing the Visitor's Book of the National Dairy Research Institute at Bangalore in 1927. Let us prove worthy of his trust that India will care for its farmers.

ACKNOWLEDGMENTS

The National Commission on Farmers expressed its gratitude to the Hon'ble Union Minister for Agriculture, Food, Public Distribution and Consumer Affairs, Shri Sharad Pawar, for having taken keen interest in the work of the Commission and for providing overall guidance to its activities. Thanks are also die to the Planning Commission and Ministers for Finance, Rural Development and Panchayati Raj for their valuable suggestions. The National Commission on Farmers would like to sincerely thank the Chief Ministers of various States and their Ministers for their valuable suggestions. Sincere thanks are also die to the senior Officers of the State Governments for the courtesies shown to the NCF teams and for organizing the interaction with farmers and other stakeholders in the States. NCF is grateful to Shrimati Sonia Gandhi, former Chairperson and other members of the National Advisory Council, for the opportunity given for presenting the Recommendation of the NCF to NAC. The Commission would also, in particular, like to thank Shrimati Radha Singh, Secretary, Department of Agriculture & Cooperation, Govt. of India, for assisting the Commission at all stages and making it possible for the Commission to complete its work well within the time allotted to it. The support coming from her senior Officers including Joint Secretary (Policy) in the Department of Agriculture & Cooperation is also gratefully acknowledged. Thanks are due to the various Ministries of the Govt. of India and the National Commission for Women for valuable suggestions.

The entire National Agriculture Research System has actively contributed to the deliberations of the Commission and enriched the quality of its work. Vice Chancellors of the Universities for Agriculture, Animal Husbandry and Fisheries deserve all praise for their support. Private sector R&D institutions have also provided excellent inputs which are appreciated. The National Commission on Farmers is indebted to a large number of farmers, farmers' organizations, leaders of political parties, NGOs and individuals fortheir advice and suggestions, both verbally and in writing. The Commission expresses itssincere thanks to the National Academy of Agricultural Sciences (NAAS) for providing logistical support.NCF acknowledges the valuable technical contributions by Shri S.S. Prasad, and Shri G.C. Pati, former and present Joint Secretary, Ms Mamta Shankar, Director, Ms R.V. Bhavani, OSD to Chairman and Research Officers: Dr.(Ms.) Laxmi Joshi, Dr. Deepak Rathi, Dr. Pavan Kumar Singh, Dr. Ramesh Singh and the sincere work of Research Assistant, Dr. Prabhu Dayal Chaudhary and the secretarial staff of the Commission in the preparation of the Revised Draft National Policy for Farmers.

(4)

Union Budget 2007-08: Finance Minister's speech

Mr. Speaker, Sir

It is my privilege to present the Budget for 2007-08.

I. A MID-TERM REPORT CARD ON THE ECONOMY

2. In November 2006, the UPA Government crossed the midpoint of its term of office. A midterm report card can now be presented. There are many pluses and a few minuses, and I shall deal with both candidly. The biggest plus is that the growth rate of GDP has improved from 7.5 per cent in 2004-05 to 9 per cent (Quick Estimate) in 2005-06 and, according to Advance Estimate, to 9.2 per cent in 2006-07. The average growth rate in the three years of the UPA Government is, therefore, 8.6 per cent. Thanks to this impressive performance, despite the poor start in 2002-03, the growth target set for the Tenth Plan of 8 per cent will be nearly achieved.

3. Manufacturing is the main driver of growth, and this augurs well for the future. In the three years of the UPA Government, the growth rate in manufacturing has accelerated from 8.7 per cent to 9.1 per cent and further to 11.3 per cent. The services sector continues to maintain impressive growth and has recorded, in the three years, a growth rate of 9.6 per cent, 9.8 per cent and 11.2 per cent respectively.

4. On the other hand, the agriculture sector has witnessed sharp ups and downs. Average growth during the Tenth Plan period is estimated at 2.3 per cent, which is below the desired level of 4 per cent a year. About 115 million families are classified as farming families. Furthermore, a country with a large population has to be nearly self-sufficient in essential food items; otherwise supply constraints could upset macro economic stability and growth prospects. Hence, agriculture must top the agenda of the policy makers and must hold the first charge on our resources. In a short while, I shall place before this House a number of proposals in this regard.

Income and Savings

5. To continue with the report card, per capita income in 2005-06, in real terms,

increased by 7.4 per cent, and the savings rate has been estimated at 32.4 per cent and the investment rate at 33.8 per cent. Intuitively, I believe that these high rates have continued in the current year too.

6. The UPA Government has remained committed to economic reforms, fiscal prudence and monetary stability.

7. Revenues are buoyant for the third year in succession. We have garnered additional revenues and, as Honourable Members will notice presently, I have put these revenues to good use to promote inclusive growth, equity and social justice - goals that are at the core of the National Common Minimum Programme (NCMP) and close to the hearts of the UPA, its Chairperson and the Prime Minister.

Outlook on Inflation

8. Until February 2, 2007, bank credit, year on year, had grown by 29.6 per cent. Money supply (M3) had expanded by 21.3 per cent. Foreign exchange reserves stood at US$ 180 billion. While these are concomitant features of high growth, it cannot be denied that these monetary trends have put pressure on prices. Global commodity prices have also exerted pressure on domestic prices. At the same time, supply constraints have emerged in some essential commodities such as wheat, pulses and edible oils.

Consequently, average inflation in 2006-07 is estimated at between 5.2 and 5.4 per cent, which is higher than 4.4 per cent last year. I wish to reiterate Government's concern over inflation. Government has already taken a number of measures on the fiscal, monetary and supply sides to maintain price stability and, if required, will not hesitate to take more measures. When the UPA Government assumed office in 2004, the inflation graph was on the rise; but we succeeded in moderating inflation and we are confident that we can moderate the present inflationary trend too.

II. BHARAT NIRMAN AND THE FLAGSHIP PROGRAMMES

9. Bharat Nirman remains the cornerstone of the Government's policy. I am glad to report that in the current financial year:

? Additional irrigation potential of 2,400,000 hectares, including 900,000 hectares under AIBP, will be created;

? Drinking water has been provided to 55,512 habitations until December 2006 against a target of 73,120 habitations;

? Until December 2006, 12,198 kilometres of rural roads have been completed. The separate window under RIDF will augment funds for the programme by Rs.4,000 crore a year;

? 783,000 rural houses have been constructed up to December 2006 and 914,000 houses are under construction, and the annual target of 1,500,000 houses is likely to be exceeded;

? 19,758 villages have been covered so far under the Rajiv Gandhi Grameen Vidyutikaran Yojana;

? 15,054 villages have been provided with a telephone against the target of 20,000 villages, and the balance will be covered by the end of the year;

Honourable Members will note that Bharat Nirman continues to make impressive progress.

10. The eight flagship programmes of the UPA Government will continue to receive high priority. Presently, I shall refer to these programmes in some detail.

III. HERALDING THE ELEVENTH FIVE YEAR PLAN

11. The year 2007-08 will mark the beginning of the Eleventh Plan. The declared objective is "Faster and More Inclusive Growth". I can state with confidence that, on the eve of the Plan, the economy is in a stronger position than ever before. It therefore behoves us to set higher goals. The Approach Paper to the Eleventh Plan states that the Plan "will aim at putting the economy on a sustainable growth trajectory with a growth rate of approximately 10 per cent by the end of its period." Among the other objectives of the Plan are growth of 4 per cent in the agriculture sector, faster employment creation, reducing disparities across regions and ensuring access to basic physical infrastructure as well as health and education services to all. I have kept these objectives in mind while allocating resources to various sectors.

Gross Budgetary Support

12. Notwithstanding some constraints, I propose to increase substantially the Gross Budgetary Support (GBS) for the Plan. In 2006-07, the GBS was fixed at Rs.172,728 crore and, of this, support to the Central Plan was Rs.131,284 crore. GBS for 2007-08 will be increased to Rs.205,100 crore. Out of this, the Central Plan will receive Rs.154,939 crore.

Allocations for Major Sectors

13. For Bharat Nirman, as against Rs.18,696 crore (including the NER component) in 2006-07, I propose to provide Rs.24,603 crore in 2007-08, which marks an increase of 31.6 per cent.

14. The education and health sectors will also receive substantial funds. In 2007-08,

I propose to enhance the allocation for education by 34.2 per cent to Rs.32,352 crore and for health and family welfare by 21.9 per cent to Rs.15,291 crore.

Sarva Shiksha Abhiyan and Mid-day Meal Scheme

15. In allocating resources, school education must have primacy. Hence, I propose to increase the allocation for school education by about 35 per cent from Rs.17,133 crore in 2006-07 to Rs.23,142 crore in 2007-08.

16. Out of this amount, Sarva Shiksha Abhiyan (SSA) will be provided Rs.10,671 crore. Further, I propose to increase the provision for strengthening teachers training institutions from Rs.162 crore to Rs.450 crore. Next year, we will appoint 200,000 more teachers and construct 500,000 more class rooms.

17. The Mid-day Meal Scheme will be provided Rs.7,324 crore next year. In addition to covering children in primary classes, beginning 2007-08, we propose to cover children in upper primary classes in 3,427 educationally backward blocks.

18. The transfer to Prarambhik Shiksha Kosh will increase from Rs.8,746 crore to Rs.10,393 crore.

19. As more students complete upper primary classes, it is necessary to increase access to secondary education. Schemes for this purpose are under formulation and I propose to double the provision for secondary education from Rs.1,837 crore in 2006-07 to Rs.3,794 crore in 2007-08.

Means-Cum-Merit Scholarships

20. While the SSA has improved the enrolment ratio in schools to 96 per cent, the drop out ratio continues to be high. The critical year appears to be transition from class VIII to class IX. In order to arrest the drop out ratio and encourage student to continue their education beyond class VIII, I propose to introduce a National Means-cum-Merit Scholarship Scheme.

Selection will be made through a national test from among students who hav passed class VIII. Each student will be given Rs.6,000 per year for study in classe IX, X, XI and XII. I propose that 100,000 scholarships may be awarded every yea In order to fund this programme, I intend to create a corpus fund of Rs.750 crore thi year, and add a like amount to the fund every year over the next three years Accordingly, a sum of Rs.750 crore will be placed with the State Bank of India, an the yield from the fund will be used for awarding the scholarships.

Drinking Water and Sanitation

21. 55,512 habitations and 34,000 schools have been provided drinking water supply till December, 2006 under the Rajiv Gandhi Drinking Water Mission. More ambitious targets have been set for 2007-08 to deal with both non-coverage and slippage. I propose to enhance the allocation for the Mission from Rs.4,680 crore in 2006-07 to Rs.5,850 crore in 2007-08.

22. As regards the Total Sanitation Campaign, I propose to increase the provision from Rs.720 crore this year to Rs.954 crore next year.

Health Sector; National Rural Health Mission

23. In the second year of its implementation, the National Rural Health Mission (NRHM) is on schedule to meet its timelines. The institutional integration of all the health schemes at the district and lower levels has been achieved. All districts in the country will complete preparation of District Health Action Plans by March 2007. The major emphasis will be on mother and child care and on the prevention and treatment of communicable diseases such as tuberculosis and malaria. Through Monthly Health Days (MHD) organised at Anganwadi centres, convergence is sought to be achieved among various programmes such as immunization, ante natal care as well as nutrition and sanitation.

24. I am happy to report that 320,000 Associated Social Health Activists (ASHAs) have been recruited and over 200,000 have received orientation training. Besides, 90,000 link workers have been selected by the States. With trained ASHAs in place, I am confident there will be significant improvement in health care in rural areas. The Ayurveda, Yoga & Naturopathy, Unani, Sidha and Homeopathy (AYUSH) systems are also being mainstreamed into the health delivery system at all levels. I propose to increase the allocation for NRHM from Rs.8,207 crore in 2006-07 to Rs.9,947 crore in 2007-08.

HIV/AIDS

25. Government has brought HIV/AIDS out of the closet and promised bold and determined efforts to achieve zero-level growth of the disease. The epidemic will be deemed 'stabilised' if the prevalence rate is less than one per cent of the population. National Aids Control Programme (NACP)-III, starting in 2007-08 and building on NACP-I and NACP-II, will target the high risk groups in all the States.

We will expand access to condoms and ensure universal access to blood screening and safe blood. More hospitals will provide treatment to prevent transmission of HIV/AIDS from mother to child. Support will be given to the protocol on paediatric dosage developed by Indian doctors and launched in November 2006. For the year 2007-08, I propose to step up the provision for the AIDS control programme to Rs.969 crore.

Polio

26. Last year, I had expressed the hope that polio will be eliminated from the country by December 2007. However, there was an outbreak in western Uttar Pradesh in early 2006. The strategy for polio eradication has been revised. The number of polio rounds will be increased, monovalent vaccine will be introduced, and there will be intensive coverage in the 20 high risk districts of Uttar Pradesh and 10 districts of Bihar.

The programme has been integrated into the NRHM. The ASHAs and the Anganwadi workers will visit every household and track every child for the immunization programme. To achieve the goal of eliminating polio, I propose to provide Rs.1,290 crore in 2007-08.

Integrated Child Development Services

27. In the second phase of expansion of the Integrated Child Development Services (ICDS), Government has sanctioned 173 ICDS projects, 107,274 Anganwadi centres and 25,961 mini-Anganwadi centres. Government is committed to expand the scheme in order to cover all habitations and settlements during the Eleventh Plan and to reach out to pregnant women, lactating mothers and all children below the age of six. I propose to increase the allocation for ICDS from Rs.4,087 crore in 2006-07 to Rs.4,761 crore in 2007-08.

National Rural Employment Guarantee Scheme

28. The National Rural Employment Guarantee Scheme (NREGS) was launched on February 2, 2006. The pace of implementation varies from State to State. Since NREGS is a demand-driven scheme carrying a legal guarantee of employment, the budget allocation would have to be supplemented according to need. I therefore propose to make an initial allocation of Rs.12,000 crore (including NER component) for NREGS. I am also happy to announce that NREGS will be expanded from the current level of 200 districts to 330 districts. In addition, I have provided Rs.2,800 crore for Sampoorna Gramin Rozgar Yojana (SGRY) for rural employment in the districts not covered by NREGS.

29. Swaranjayanti Gram Swarozgar Yojana (SGSY) is intended to promote self-employment among the rural poor through Self Help Groups (SHG). I propose to strengthen this programme by increasing the allocation from Rs.1,200 crore in the current year to Rs.1,800 crore (including NER component) next year.

Urban Unemployment

30. The issue of urban unemployment and poverty alleviation is equally critical. Hence, I propose to increase the allocation for Swarna Jayanti Shahari Rojgar Yojana

from Rs.250 crore in 2006-07 to Rs.344 crore next year.

Jawaharlal Nehru National Urban Renewal Mission

31. The Jawaharlal Nehru National Urban Renewal Mission (JNNURM) has evoked a positive response from State Governments. As on date, 538 projects with a total cost of Rs.23,950 crore have been sanctioned in sectors such as water supply, sanitation, transport, road and housing in many cities spread over several States. I propose to enhance the allocation from Rs.4,595 crore in 2006-07 to Rs.4,987 crore 2007-08.

Targeted Public Distribution System and Antyodaya Anna Yojana

32. The issue prices of food grains under the Public Distribution System (PDS) and for the beneficiaries of the Antyodaya Anna Yojana have been retained. A Plan scheme for evaluation, monitoring, management and strengthening of the targeted PDS will be implemented in 2007-08, and this will include computerisation of the PDS and an integrated information system in the Food Corporation of India.

Scheduled Castes and Scheduled Tribes

33. Continuing the practice that was started in 2005-06, a separate statement on the schemes for the welfare of Scheduled Castes (SCs) and Scheduled Tribes (STs) is placed in the Budget documents. The allocation in 2007-08 for SCs and STs has been substantially enhanced. In respect of schemes benefiting only SCs and STs, I have increased the allocation to Rs.3,271 crore. In respect of schemes with at least 20 per cent of the benefits earmarked for SCs and STs, I have increased the allocation to Rs.17,691 crore.

34. SC and ST students studying in M.Phil and PhD courses are supported by the Rajiv Gandhi National Fellowship Programme. I propose to enhance the allocation from Rs.35 crore in 2006-07 to Rs.88 crore in 2007-08.

Post-Matric Scholarships

35. There is a post-matric scholarship programme for SC and ST students. I propose to increase the provision for these scholarships from Rs.440 crore in 2006-07 to Rs.611 crore in 2007-08. I also propose to make a separate provision of Rs.91 crore for similar scholarships to be awarded to students belonging to socially and educationally backward classes.

Minorities

36. Last year, I made a modest contribution of Rs.16.47 crore to the equity of the National Minorities Development and Finance Corporation (NMDFC). Following

the Sachar Committee report, NMDFC would be required to expand its reach and intensify its efforts. Hence, I propose to provide a further sum of Rs.63 crore to the share capital of NMDFC.

37. There are a number of districts with a concentration of minorities. I propose to make a provision of Rs.108 crore for a multi-sector development programme in these districts.

38. Three scholarship programmes are being implemented for students belonging to minority communities. I propose to make the following allocations:
Pre-matric scholarships Rs.72 crore
Post-matric scholarships Rs.90 crore
Merit-cum-Means scholarships at graduate and post-graduate levels Rs.48.60 crore

Women

39. There is growing awareness of gender sensitivities of budgetary allocations. 50 ministries/departments have set up gender budgeting cells. For 2007-08, 27 ministries/departments and 5 Union Territories covering 33 demands for grants have contributed to a statement placed in the budget papers. The outlay for 100 per cent women specific programmes is Rs.8,795 crore and for schemes where at least 30 per cent is for women specific programmes is Rs.22,382 crore. We have made a sincere effort to remove the errors that were pointed out in last year's statement.

North Eastern Region (NER)

40. The total budget allocation in 2007-08 for the North Eastern Region, culled out from allocations under different ministries/ departments, has increased from Rs.12,041 crore in 2006-07 to Rs.14,365 crore in 2007-08. This includes Rs.1,380 crore provided to the Ministry of Development of North Eastern Region (DONER). The new industrial policy for NER, with suitable fiscal incentives, will be in place before March 31, 2007.

Supplement to the GBS

41. I have, so far, outlined the allocations under what may be called Plan 'A' which has a resource basket of Rs.205,100 crore. In consultation with the Planning Commission, I have also drawn up Plan 'B'. Since the Eleventh Plan will begin on April 1, 2007, we recognize that there will be a need to take new initiatives in critical areas. Additional resources will be needed once the proposals are finalised and the pace of expenditure builds up. Therefore, I shall endeavour to find additional resources through better tax administration to the extent of Rs.7,000 crore during the course of the year. I have been advised by the Planning Commission that these additional funds, once voted by this House, will be allocated among sectors such as agricul-

ture, rural development, health, women and child development, urban infrastructure, water resources, etc.

42. I also have Plan 'C'. Under Plan 'C', I propose to tap into resources available outside the Budget and leverage them for the purpose of investment, especially in the infrastructure sector. I shall deal with this subject a little later.

IV. AGRICULTURE

43. I shall now take up our main challenge: agriculture. I may recall the words of Jawaharlal Nehru, who said "Everything else can wait, but not agriculture".

44. The draft National Policy for Farmers submitted by the National Commission on Farmers is under consideration. Meanwhile, I have a number of proposals to improve the economic viability of farming and ensure that farmers earn a minimum net income.

Farm Credit

45. Farm credit continues to grow at a satisfactory pace. The goal of doubling farm credit in three years was achieved in two years. The target of Rs.175,000 crore set for 2006-07 will be exceeded comfortably and is likely to reach Rs.190,000 crore. This year, until December 2006, 53.37 lakh new farmers were brought into the institutional credit system. For 2007-08, I propose to fix a target of Rs.225,000 crore as farm credit and an addition of 50 lakh new farmers to the banking system.

46. The two per cent interest subvention scheme for short-term crop loans will continue in 2007-08, and I am making a provision of Rs.1,677 crore for that purpose.

47. A special plan is being implemented over a period of three years in 31 especially distressed districts in four States of the country involving a total amount of Rs.16,979 crore. Of this, about Rs.12,400 crore will be on water related schemes. In order to provide subsidiary income to the farmer, the special plan includes a scheme for induction of high yielding milch animals and related activities. I propose to provide Rs.153 crore for this scheme.

Agricultural Indebtedness

48. Government had appointed a Committee under Dr. R. Radhakrishna to examine all aspects of agricultural indebtedness. The Committee has held wide ranging consultations across the country and is in the process of finalising its recommendations. Government will act on the report as soon as it is received.

A Mission for Pulses

49. Government is concerned about the stagnation in the production and produc-

tivity of pulses. A critical deficiency is the availability and quality of certified seeds. I therefore propose to expand the Integrated Oilseeds, Oil palm, Pulses and Maize Development programme. There will be a sharper focus on scaling up the production of breeder, foundation and certified seeds. The Indian Institute of Pulses Research (IIPR), Kanpur, the National and State level seeds corporations, agricultural universities, ICAR centres, KRIBHCO, IFFCO and NAFED as well as large private sector companies will be invited to submit plans to scale up the production of seeds. Government will fund the expansion of IIPR, Kanpur, and offer the other producers a capital grant or concessional financing in order to double the production of certified seeds within a period of three years.

Plantation Sector

50. A Special Purpose Tea Fund has been launched for re-plantation and rejuvenation of tea. Government will soon put in place similar financial mechanisms for coffee, rubber, spices, cashew and coconut.

Accelerated Irrigation Benefit Programme

51. The Accelerated Irrigation Benefit Programme (AIBP) has been revamped in order to complete more irrigation projects in the quickest possible time. 35 projects are likely to be completed in 2006-07 and additional irrigation potential of 900,000 hectares will be created. As against an outlay of Rs.7,121 crore in 2006-07, the outlay for 2007-08 will be increased to Rs.11,000 crore. Of this, the grant component to State Governments will be Rs.3,580 crore, an increase from Rs.2,350 crore.

Rainfed Area Development Programme

52. The National Rainfed Area Authority was established a few months ago to coordinate all schemes relating to watershed development and other aspects of land use. I propose to allocate Rs.100 crore for the new Rainfed Area Development Programme.

Water Resources Management: Restoring Water Bodies

53. Honourable Members will recall that, in March 2005, a pilot project to repair, renovate and restore water bodies was launched in 13 States. I am happy to inform the House that the World Bank has signed a loan agreement with Tamil Nadu for Rs.2,182 crore to restore 5,763 water bodies having a command area of 400,000 hectares. An agreement for Andhra Pradesh is expected to be concluded in March 2007 and will cover 3,000 water bodies with a command area of 250,000 hectares. Preparation of similar projects for Karnataka, Orissa and West Bengal are at different stages and at least two more agreements are likely to be concluded before June 2007. I would urge other State Governments to come forward with proposals so that

the whole country can be covered within the next two years.

Ground Water Recharge

54. Depletion of ground water has assumed grave proportions. The Central Ground Water Board has identified 1,065 assessment blocks in the country as 'over-exploited' or 'critical'. Over 80 per cent of these blocks are in 100 districts in seven States. The strategy for ground water recharge is to divert rain water into 'dug wells'. Each structure will cost about Rs.4,000. The requirement is seven million structures, including about two million structures on land belonging to small and marginal farmers. I propose to provide 100 per cent subsidy to small and marginal farmers and 50 per cent subsidy to other farmers. Ministry of Water Resources will finalise the scheme shortly. In anticipation, I intend to transfer a sum of Rs.1,800 crore to NABARD. The amount will be held in escrow and will be disbursed through the lead bank of the district concerned to the beneficiaries.

Training of Farmers

55. With minimum instruction and training, our farmers will easily absorb good water management practices. I therefore propose that the Indian Council of Agricultural Research (ICAR) may set up one teaching-cum-demonstration model of water harvesting in each of 32 selected State Agricultural Universities and ICAR institutes. Each institution will train 100 trainers and 1,000 farmers every year in two-week and one-week programmes respectively. Based on estimates of recurring costs, I intend to provide an interest free loan of Rs.3 crore to each institution to create a corpus fund. The yield from the fund will be used for implementing the training programme. The total cost is estimated at Rs.100 crore.

Extension System

56. The green revolution of the 1960s was brought about by thousands of agricultural extension workers who worked side by side with our farmers under a programme called Training and Visit (T&V). Sadly, the extension system seems to have collapsed. In order to revive extension work, the Ministry of Agriculture will, in consultation with State Governments, draw up a new programme that will replicate T&V with suitable changes.

57. The Agriculture Technology Management Agency (ATMA) that is now in place in 262 districts will be extended to another 300 districts in 2007-08. I propose to enhance the provision for ATMA from Rs.50 crore to Rs.230 crore next year.

Fertiliser subsidies

58. I had budgeted Rs.17,253 crore for fertiliser subsidies in 2006-07. According to Revised Estimates, this will rise to Rs.22,452 crore, and there is a demand for more

money. While fertilisers should indeed be subsidised, we must find an alternative method of delivering the subsidy directly to the farmer. The fertiliser industry has agreed to work with the Department of Fertilisers to conduct a study and find a solution. Based on the report, Government intends to implement a pilot programme in at least one district in each State in 2007-08.

Agricultural Insurance

59. The National Agricultural Insurance Scheme (NAIS) will be continued in its present form for Kharif and Rabi 2007-08. I propose to make a provision of Rs.500 crore for the scheme.

60. Agricultural Insurance Corporation (AIC) has been running a pilot weather insurance scheme since Kharif 2004 and it appears to be a more promising risk mitigation scheme. Hence, Government will ask AIC to start a weather based crop insurance scheme on a pilot basis in two or three States, in consultation with the State Governments concerned, as an alternative to the NAIS. The scheme will be operated on an actuarial basis with an element of subsidy. I intend to allocate Rs.100 crore for this purpose in 2007-08.

National Bank for Agriculture and Rural Development (NABARD)

61. NABARD provides refinance to cooperative institutions. As the volume of farm credit increases and the Vaidyanathan Committee recommendations for reform of rural credit cooperatives are implemented, the demand for refinance will increase. In order to augment its resources, I propose to allow NABARD to issue rural bonds to the extent of Rs.5,000 crore. These bonds will be guaranteed by the Government and will be eligible for suitable tax exemption.

Rural Infrastructure Development Fund

62. The Rural Infrastructure Development Fund (RIDF) continues to sanction and disburse funds to State Governments. In 2006-07, out of a corpus of Rs.10,000 crore, NABARD has so far issued sanctions for Rs.8,440 crore and will achieve its target. Keeping in view the growing demand for these funds, I propose to raise the corpus of RIDF-XIII in 2007-08 to Rs.12,000 crore. I would urge State Governments to use these funds primarily in the distressed districts of the State.

63. A separate window for rural roads under RIDF was opened with Rs.4,000 crore. Against this, projects for Rs.2,311 crore have been sanctioned in 2006-07. I propose to continue the separate window under RIDF-XIII in 2007-08 with a corpus of Rs.4,000 crore.

Social Security

64. One of the commitments made in the NCMP is that Government will introduce a social security scheme for unorganised workers. A committee chaired by Dr. Arjun Sengupta has given its report which is under consideration. Pending a decision, in order to signal the UPA Government's concern for the welfare of unorganised workers, I propose to make a beginning. I propose to extend death and disability insurance cover through Life Insurance Corporation of India (LIC) to rural landless households under a new scheme called 'Aam Admi Bima Yojana' (AABY). According to NSS Report No. 491, the estimate of such households is about 1.5 crore. By end March 2007, 70 lakh households will be covered through existing schemes of the LIC with the support of some State Governments and the social security fund with the LIC. Under AABY, I propose to cover the rural landless households which enjoy no cover at all today, and the number may be actually more than what is indicated in the NSS report. The head of the family or one earning member in the family will be insured. The Central Government will bear 50 per cent of the premium of Rs.200 per year per person and I would urge the State Governments to come forward to bear the other 50 per cent on behalf of the beneficiaries. Taking into account the annual cost to the Central Government, I intend to place a sum of Rs.1,000 crore in a fund that will be maintained by LIC. I propose to finalise the scheme in consultation with State Governments and begin to implement it in 2007-08.

65. Mr. Speaker, Sir, I have devoted the last 15 minutes or so to agriculture. There is no dearth of schemes; there is no dearth of funds. What needs to be done is to deliver the intended outcomes. Saint Tiruvalluvar watches over us and warns:

"Uzhavinar Kai Madangin Illai Vizhaivathoom Vittame Enbarkum Nilai" [If ploughmen keep their hands folded Even sages claiming renunciation cannot find salvation]

V. INVESTMENT

66. All indicators point to an accelerating rate of investment in the economy. For example, gross domestic capital formation (GDCF) in 2005-06 grew by 23.7 per cent over the previous year to Rs.11,47,254 crore. I believe that this trend continues in 2006-07. In April-January, 2006-07, foreign direct investment amounted to US$12.5 billion and outpaced portfolio investment which was US$6.8 billion.

67. Central Public Sector Enterprises (CPSEs) will, through internal and extra budgetary resources, invest Rs.165,053 crore in 2007-08. Government will provide equity support of Rs.16,361 crore and loans of Rs.2,970 crore to CPSEs.

68. Further, in the current year, we have restructured eight CPSEs with a cash infusion of Rs.1,590 crore and non-cash sacrifices of Rs.1,612 crore.

VI. INFRASTRUCTURE

Power

69. Electricity generation has recorded a growth rate of 7.5 per cent in April-December this year. However, as we complete the Tenth Plan, we would have added only 23,163 MW of additional capacity in the five year period including 16,339 MW added in the three years beginning 2004-05. Hence, it is imperative that we take new initiatives.

70. The Ministry of Power has awarded two Ultra Mega Power Projects (UMPP) in Sasan and Mundra. Seven more UMPPs are under process and we are confident that at least two more will be awarded by July, 2007. Other initiatives taken by the Ministry of Power include facilitating setting up of merchant power plants by private developers and private participation in transmission projects.

71. Besides, the Accelerated Power Development and Reforms Project (APDRP) has reduced significantly Aggregate Technical and Commercial (ATC) losses in 213 towns. APDRP is being restructured to cover all district headquarters and towns with a population of more than 50,000. I propose to increase the budgetary support for APDRP from Rs.650 crore in 2006-07 to Rs.800 crore next year.

Rajiv Gandhi Grameen Vidyutikaran Yojana

72. Having regard to the pace of implementation under the Rajiv Gandhi Grameen Vidyutikaran Yojana and the annual target, I propose to increase the allocation from Rs.3,000 crore in 2006-07 to Rs.3,983 crore in 2007-08.

Coal

73. Following the announcement last year, 26 coal blocks with reserves of 8,581 million tonnes and four lignite blocks with reserves of 755 million tonnes have been allotted, up to December 2006, to Government companies and approved end users. The definition of specified end use will be enlarged to include underground coal gasification and coal liquefaction.

National Highways

74. Work on the golden quadrilateral is nearly complete and there is considerable progress in the North-South, East-West corridor project which is expected to be completed by 2009. NHDP-III, NHDP-V and NHDP-VI are in advanced stages of planning or implementation. So far, National Highways Authority of India (NHAI) has given Rs.2,072 crore as viability gap funding but has also received Rs.1,900 crore as negative grant. The private sector investment leveraged under NHDP is Rs.25,366 crore. Under the programme for the North Eastern Region (SARDP-NE),

450 kilometres have been awarded in 2006-07 and the balance will be awarded in 2007-08. I propose to increase the provision for the National Highway Development Programme (NHDP) from Rs.9,945 crore in 2006-07 to Rs.10,667 crore next year.

75. The road-cum-rail bridge at Munger, Bihar, over the Ganga, has been taken up as a national project. Likewise, the road-cum-rail bridge at Bogibeel, Assam, over the Brahmaputra, will be taken up as a national project.

Public Private Partnership and Viability Gap Funding

76. The Public Private Partnership (PPP) model has enabled greater private sector participation in the creation and maintenance of infrastructure. So far, under the viability gap funding scheme, 37 proposals have been received of which 21 proposals have been granted 'in-principle' approval with a total project cost of Rs.9,842 crore and an estimated viability gap funding of Rs.2,521 crore.

The pace is slow, and there is a need to adopt a more aggressive approach for preparing a shelf of bankable projects that can be offered for competitive bidding. Apart from the steps already taken for capacity building and engaging consultants, I intend to set up a revolving fund with a corpus of Rs.100 crore to quicken project preparation. The fund will contribute up to 75 per cent of the preparatory expenditure in the form of interest free loan that will be eventually recovered from the successful bidder. Guidelines for operating the fund will be announced in due course.

VII. INDUSTRY

Petroleum and Natural Gas

77. Energy security is high on the Government's agenda. In the six rounds of New Exploration Licensing Policy (NELP) so far, 162 production sharing contracts have been awarded. Indian and foreign companies have already made an investment of Rs.97,000 crore in exploration. Similarly, after three rounds of bidding, 23 coal bed methane blocks have been awarded for exploration.

Textiles

78. A rejuvenated textile industry is geared to meet the global challenge. 26 parks have been approved so far out of 30 sanctioned under the Scheme for Integrated Textiles Parks (SITP). I propose to increase the provision for these parks from Rs.189 crore in 2006-07 to Rs.425 crore in 2007-08.

79. I am also glad to announce that the Technology Upgradation Fund (TUF) scheme will be continued during the Eleventh Plan. Against a provision of Rs.535

crore in 2006-07, I propose to provide Rs.911 crore in 2007-08. As before, handlooms will be covered under the TUF scheme.

Handlooms

80. A cluster approach for the development of the handloom sector was introduced in 2005-06 and 120 clusters have been selected. 273 new yarn depots have been opened in the current year and the Handloom Mark was launched. Government proposes to take up an additional 100-150 clusters in 2007-08. The 12 schemes that are now implemented will be grouped into five schemes in the Eleventh Plan period. The health insurance scheme has so far covered 300,000 weavers and will be extended to more weavers. The scheme will also be enlarged to include ancillary workers. I propose to enhance the allocation for the sector from Rs.241 crore in 2006-07 to Rs.321 crore next year.

Small and Medium Enterprises

81. Following the credit policy for small and medium enterprises (SME) announced in August 2005, outstanding credit to the SME sector increased from Rs.135,200 crore at end December 2005 to Rs.173,460 crore at end December 2006. While encouraging banks to lend more to the SME sector, I propose to ask banks to have regard to the credit rating acquired by an SME while fixing the interest rate.

Coir Industry

82. Coir is an eco-friendly fibre. The coir industry provides employment to a large number as well as earns valuable foreign exchange. I am happy to announce a scheme for the modernisation and technology upgradation of the coir industry with special emphasis to major coir producing States such as Kerala, Karnataka, Tamil Nadu, Andhra Pradesh and Orissa. I propose to make a provision of Rs.22.50 crore.

VIII. SERVICES SECTOR

Foreign Trade

83. Our merchandise exports crossed the milestone of US$100 billion in 2005-06 and are expected to cross another milestone of US$125 billion by the end of the current fiscal. Foreign trade is growing at a rate more than twice the growth rate of GDP. Government will continue to follow export friendly policies.

Tourism

84. I propose to increase the provision for building tourist infrastructure from Rs.423 crore in 2006-07 to Rs.520 crore in 2007-08.

IX. FINANCIAL SECTOR

Banking

85. In addition to the important legislative measures now before Parliament, Government proposes to take a number of initiatives in banking and insurance.

86. Government proposes to acquire RBI's equity holding in State Bank of India. I have provided a sum of Rs.40,000 crore for this purpose, but the transaction will be deficit neutral to the Government.

87. The Differential Rate of Interest (DRI) scheme provides finance at a rate of 4 per cent to the weaker sections of the community engaged in gainful occupations. I propose to raise the limit of the loan from Rs.6,500 to Rs.15,000 and the limit of the housing loan from Rs.5,000 to Rs.20,000 per beneficiary.

Regional Rural Banks

88. Regional Rural Banks (RRBs) have emerged as the third arm for delivering rural credit, and the sponsor banks have assured me that RRBs are willing to take on greater responsibilities. The Committee on Financial Inclusion, chaired by Dr. C. Rangarajan, has also made certain recommendations concerning RRBs. I, therefore, propose to:

? ask RRBs to undertake an aggressive branch expansion programme and, in 2007-08, open at least one branch in the 80 uncovered districts of the country;

? extend the Securitisation and Reconstruction of Financial Assets and Enforcement of Securitisation of Interest (SARFAESI) Act to loans advanced by RRBs;

? permit RRBs to accept NRE/FCNR deposits; and

? recapitalize, in a phased programme, the RRBs which have a negative net worth.

Housing Loans

89. The National Housing Bank (NHB) will shortly introduce a novel product for senior citizens: a 'reverse mortgage' under which a senior citizen who is the owner of a house can avail of a monthly stream of income against the mortgage of his/her house, while remaining the owner and occupying the house throughout his/her lifetime, without repayment or servicing of the loan.

90. Our people want housing loans. Banks and housing finance companies that lend against mortgages would have greater comfort if the mortgage can be guaranteed through a three way contract among borrower, lender and guarantor. Regula-

tions will be put in place to allow the creation of mortgage guarantee companies.

Insurance

91. On December 6, 2006, Rashtrapatiji launched an exclusive health insurance scheme for senior citizens offered by National Insurance Company. I have asked the other three public sector insurance companies to offer a similar product to senior citizens, and they have agreed to do so in 2007-08.

92. The Micro Financial Sector (Development and Regulation) Bill as well as a comprehensive Bill to amend the insurance laws will be introduced in the Budget Session.

Financial Inclusion

93. Financial inclusion is the process of ensuring access to timely and adequate credit and financial services by vulnerable groups at an affordable cost. The Committee on Financial Inclusion has given an interim report. While we await the final report, Government has decided to implement, immediately, two recommendations. The first is to establish a Financial Inclusion Fund with NABARD for meeting the cost of developmental and promotional interventions. The second is to establish a Financial Inclusion Technology Fund to meet the costs of technology adoption. Each fund will have an overall corpus of Rs.500 crore, with initial funding to be contributed by the Central Government, RBI and NABARD.

Capital Markets

94. The capital market is an important instrument for intermediating financial resources. Recognising the strength of the Indian capital market, the International Organisation of Securities Commissions (IOSCO) has decided to hold its annual conference in Mumbai in April 2007. In line with measures announced every year to strengthen the market, I propose to:

? make PAN the sole identification number for all participants in the securities market with an alpha-numeric prefix or suffix to distinguish a particular kind of account;

? take forward the idea of Self Regulating Organisations (SRO) for different market participants under regulations that will be made by SEBI and, if necessary, supported by an enabling law;

? promote the flow of investment to the infrastructure sector by permitting mutual funds to launch and operate dedicated infrastructure funds;

? converge the different regulations that allow individuals and Indian mutual funds to invest in overseas securities by permitting individuals to invest through Indian mutual funds;

? allow short selling settled by delivery, and securities lending and borrowing to facilitate delivery, by institutions;

? put in place an enabling mechanism to permit Indian companies to unlock a part of their holdings in group companies for meeting their financing requirements by issue of Exchangeable Bonds.

Innovative Financing for Infrastructure

95. The minimum obligation of States to borrow from the National Small Savings Fund (NSSF) has been brought down to 80 per cent of net collections. Repayments of past NSSF loans by the Central and State Governments have also commenced from 2005-06, making available resources for long-term lending. I therefore propose that these funds may also be borrowed from NSSF by India Infrastructure Finance Company Limited (IIFCL).

96. An initiative that has borne fruit is the launch of the US$5 billion infrastructure financing initiative by Citigroup, Blackstone, IDFC and IIFCL.

97. A committee chaired by Shri Deepak Parekh has made a number of recommendations for financing infrastructure. One of the recommendations is to use a small part of the foreign exchange reserves without the risk of monetary expansion. The Committee has suggested the establishment of two wholly-owned overseas subsidiaries of IIFCL with the following objectives:

(i) to borrow funds from the RBI and lend to Indian companies implementing infrastructure projects in India, or to co-finance their ECBs for such projects, solely for capital expenditure outside India; and
(ii) to borrow funds from the RBI, invest such funds in highly rated collateral securities, and provide 'credit wrap' insurance to infrastructure projects in India for raising resources in international markets.
The loans by RBI to these two subsidiary companies will be guaranteed by the Government of India and the RBI will be assured of a return higher than the average rate of return on its incremental investment. Government proposes to examine the legal and regulatory aspects of the recommendation, in consultation with RBI, in order to find an innovative method of enhancing the financial resources for infrastructure.

X. OTHER PROPOSALS

Defence Expenditure

98. I propose to increase the allocation for Defence to Rs.96,000 crore. This will include Rs.41,922 crore for capital expenditure. Needless to say, any additional requirement for the security of the nation will be provided.

Information Technology

99. Government has launched an ambitious programme for e-governance. The goal is to improve efficiency, convenience, accessibility and transparency in Government functions and take Government services to the common citizen.

I propose to increase the allocation for e-governance from Rs.395 crore in 2006-07 to Rs.719 crore in 2007-08. The Central Government supports e-governance action plans at State levels, and I propose to increase the allocation for such support from Rs.300 crore in 2006-07 to Rs.500 crore in 2007-08. I also propose to provide Rs.33 crore for a new scheme of manpower development for the software export industry.

Backward Regions Grant Fund

100. The Backward Regions Grant Fund received Rs.5,000 crore in 2006-07. I propose to increase the allocation to Rs.5,800 crore in 2007-08. This will finance two components, one pertaining to 250 districts and the other pertaining to the special plan for Bihar. KBK districts of Orissa, which are included in the 250 districts, will continue to receive the same quantum of assistance as they have been receiving in the past.

Mumbai as a Financial Centre

101. The High Powered Expert Committee to make Mumbai a regional financial centre has submitted its report recently. I intend to place the report in the public domain and obtain feedback. It is my hope that we would be able to build a consensus on the key recommendations of the Committee, promote a world class financial centre in Mumbai, and realise the objective of making 'financial services' the next growth engine for India.

Vocational Education Mission

102. To sustain a high level of economic growth, it is essential to have a reservoir of skilled and trained manpower. Shortages have already emerged in a number of sectors. Moreover, we can take advantage of the demographic dividend thrown up by an increase in the working age population only if our young men and women have the required skills. The Prime Minister spoke of a Vocational Education Mission in his Independence Day address in 2006. A taskforce in the Planning Commis

sion is chalking out strategies for vocational education programmes. Alternate models may be adopted, but the approach will be based on public-private partnership. I propose to make an initial provision of Rs.50 crore for beginning work on this mission.

Upgradation of ITIs

103. Honourable Members will recall that Government had taken up a programme for upgradation of 500 ITIs over five years beginning 2005. Revised courses in the first lot of 100 upgraded ITIs were started in August 2005 and in the second lot of 100 upgraded ITIs in August 2006. I expect that another 300 ITIs will be covered by August 2009. That would still leave 1,396 Government ITIs.

104. I propose that the 1,396 ITIs be upgraded into centres of excellence in specific trades and skills under public-private partnership. Under the proposed scheme, the State Government, as the owner of the ITI, will continue to regulate admissions and fees; the new management will be given academic and financial autonomy; and the Central Government will provide financial assistance by way of seed money. ITIs will be encouraged to start a second shift. Once a tripartite MoU is signed among the three stakeholders, I propose to grant an interest free loan up to Rs.2.5 crore to each ITI for upgradation and revision of courses. I seek the cooperation of State Governments in upgrading at least 300 ITIs every year, beginning 2007-08, under the PPP mode. I have kept aside Rs.750 crore for this purpose.

Employment for the Physically Challenged

105. Among the disadvantaged sections of the society are physically challenged persons. They face difficulties in obtaining regular employment. In order to incentivise employers in the organised sector to provide regular employment, I propose a scheme whereunder Government will reward the employer once the physically challenged employee is regularised and is enrolled under the Employees Provident Fund (EPF) and the Employees State Insurance (ESI).

Under the scheme, Government will reimburse the employer's contribution to the EPF and ESI for the first three years. Government is ready to support the creation of about 100,000 jobs every year for physically challenged persons with a salary limit of Rs.25,000 per month. I estimate the cost to Government at Rs.150 crore per annum rising to Rs.450 crore per annum when the scheme is fully rolled out. I have therefore earmarked Rs.1,800 crore.

Debt Management Office

106. World over, debt management is distinct from monetary management. The establishment of a Debt Management Office (DMO) in the Government has been

advocated for quite some time. The fiscal consolidation achieved so far has encou aged us to take the first step. Accordingly, I propose to set up an autonomo DMO and, in the first phase, a Middle Office will be set up to facilitate the transiti to a full-fledged DMO.

Development Cooperation

107. In keeping with India's growing stature in international affairs, we must wi ingly assume greater responsibility in promoting development in other developi countries. At present, India extends development cooperation through a number Ministries and agencies and the total sum is about US$ 1 billion per annum. It is f that all activities relating to development cooperation should be brought under o umbrella. Accordingly, Government proposes to establish the India Internatio Development Cooperation Agency (IIDCA). The Ministries of External Affai Finance and Commerce and other stakeholders will be represented on IIDCA.

Climate change

108. India is not a significant contributor to green house gas (GHG) emissions, r will it be so in the foreseeable future. Nevertheless, in line with the principle "common but differentiated responsibility", India has taken important steps mitigate GHG emissions and adapt to climate change impact. India has also stron promoted the clean development mechanism (CDM) under the Kyoto Protocol a has the world's largest number of CDM projects. Nevertheless, India is among countries more vulnerable to climate change. Hence, Government proposes to point an expert committee to study the impact of climate change on India a identify the measures that we may have to take in the future.

Commonwealth Games

109. India bid for and won for the city of Delhi the Commonwealth Games 2010. T nation was filled with pride when, under the guidance of Shri Rajiv Gandhi, successfully hosted the Asian Games in 1982. We owe it to our people to make Commonwealth Games an equally memorable event. I propose to provide in 2007- Rs.150 crore to the Ministry of Youth Affairs and Sports and Rs.350 crore to Delhi Government for the Games. Similarly, I propose to provide Rs.50 crore for Commonwealth Youth Games 2008 to be held in Pune.

History and Culture

110. As we celebrate the 150th year of the First War of Independence and centenary year of the Satyagraha Movement, our thoughts go to the instituti that continue the work of Gandhiji and other constructive work. I intend to set ap Rs.30 crore for four institutions whose work we gratefully acknowledge. These Sabarmati Ashram, Ahmedabad; Sevagram Ashram, Wardha; Bhandarkar Orie

esearch Institute, Pune; and Rajendra Smriti Sanghrahalaya, Patna. I also intend provide Rs.20 crore to reposition the Nehru Memorial Museum and Library, elhi, as a major centre of intellectual activity.

11. The Ministry of Culture proposes to engage scholars from Indian and foreign stitutions to work on specific projects. The terms of engagement will provide eedom and flexibility to the scholars. I intend to make an initial grant of Rs.5 crore encourage this effort.

stitutions of Excellence

12. As in the last two years, I propose to make a special grant of Rs.100 crore to cognise excellence. Government has selected the Govind Ballabh Pant University Agriculture & Technology, Pantnagar and the Tamil Nadu Agricultural University, Coimbatore, and each will be given Rs.50 crore.

I. PUBLIC FINANCE

13. Thanks to the Fiscal Responsibility legislations, the Central Government and e State Governments have regained lost fiscal ground. Rs. 110,268 crore of States' bt has been consolidated. Twenty States have availed of the benefit of debt aiver to the tune of Rs.8,575 crore.

14. In 2006-07, the Centre will give to the States as their share of taxes and duties s.120,377 crore. In 2007-08, this amount will increase to Rs.142,450 crore. Besides, tal grants and loans, both under Plan and non-Plan, to States and Union Territoes will increase from Rs.90,521 crore in 2006-07 to Rs.106,987 crore in 2007-08.

AT, CST and a Roadmap towards GST

5. VAT has proved to be an unqualified success. VAT revenues of the implementg States increased by 13.8 per cent in 2005-06 and by 24.3 per cent in the first nine onths of 2006-07. The next logical step is to phase out Central Sales Tax (CST). I n glad to report that the Central Government has reached an agreement with State overnments to phase out CST. Consequently, the CST rate will be reduced from 4 r cent to 3 per cent with effect from April 1, 2007. I have provided Rs.5,495 crore r compensation for losses, if any, on account of VAT and also on account of CST.

6. I wish to record my deep appreciation of the spirit of cooperative federalism splayed by State Governments and especially their Finance Ministers. At my quest, the Empowered Committee of State Finance Ministers has agreed to work ith the Central Government to prepare a roadmap for introducing a national level oods and Services Tax (GST) with effect from April 1, 2010.

7. So far as the Central Government is concerned, the fiscal consolidation is

proceeding according to the FRBM Act. Based on Revised Estimates, I am happy to report that the revenue deficit for the current year will be 2.0 per cent (against a BE of 2.1 per cent) and the fiscal deficit will be 3.7 per cent (against a BE of 3.8 per cent).

XII. BUDGET ESTIMATES FOR 2007-08

118. I turn to the Budget Estimates for 2007-08.

Plan Expenditure

119. I estimate Plan expenditure for 2007-08 at Rs.205,100 crore. As a proportion of total expenditure (net of the SBI share acquisition), Plan expenditure will be 32.0 per cent.

Non-Plan Expenditure

120. Non-Plan Expenditure in 2007-08 (net of the SBI share acquisition) is estimated at Rs.435,421. The increase over 2006-07 is only 6.5 per cent.

Revenue Deficit and Fiscal Deficit

121. Mr. Speaker, Sir, in the Budget Estimates for 2007-08, the total expenditure is estimated at Rs.680,521 crore (including Rs.40,000 crore for the SBI share acquisition). The total revenue receipts of the Central Government are projected to be Rs.486,422 crore and the revenue expenditure to be Rs.557,900 crore. Consequently the revenue deficit is estimated at Rs.71,478 crore which is 1.5 per cent of the GDP The fiscal deficit is estimated at Rs.150,948 crore, which is 3.3 per cent of the GDP I am happy to report that we are on course to achieve the FRBMA targets.

Part - B

XIII. TAX PROPOSALS

122. Mr. Speaker, I shall now present my tax proposals.

123. The UPA Government promised that "tax rates will be stable and conducive to growth, compliance and investment". The increase in gross tax revenue is proof of a promise fulfilled. While we have raised more tax revenue, we have also left more money in the hands of the people as savings and for investment.

124. Gross tax revenue has grown by 19.9 per cent, 20.0 per cent and 27.8 per cent in the first three years of this Government. The tax to GDP ratio has increased from 9. per cent in 2003-04 to 11.4 per cent in 2006-07. We intend to keep our tax rates moderate and stable and administer the tax laws in a tax payer-friendly manner.

Indirect Taxes

125. I shall begin with indirect taxes. Firstly, customs duties.

126. In January 2007, Government announced wide ranging reductions in tariffs. Import duties on capital goods, project imports, metals and specified inorganic chemicals were reduced by 2.5 percentage points and, in some cases, by 5 percentage points. Duties on some edible oils were reduced by 10 to 12.5 percentage points.

127. In order to take one more step towards comparable East Asian rates, I propose to reduce the peak rate for non-agricultural products from 12.5 per cent to 10 per cent.

128. I propose to reduce the duties on most chemicals and plastics from 12.5 per cent to 7.5 per cent.

129. The duty on prime steel is 5 per cent. Seconds and defectives augment supply. Keeping in mind the need for a differential, I propose to reduce the duty on seconds and defectives of steel from 20 per cent to 10 per cent.

130. I propose to fully exempt from duty all coking coal irrespective of the ash content.

131. Last year, I reduced the excise duty on all man-made fibres and yarns from 16 per cent to 8 per cent. To further encourage this industry, I propose to reduce the customs duty on polyester fibres and yarns from 10 per cent to 7.5 per cent. Consequently, the customs duty on raw-materials such as DMT, PTA and MEG will also be reduced from 10 per cent to 7.5 per cent.

132. Another industry that is a growth- and employment- driver is gem and jewellery. I propose to bring down the duty on cut and polished diamonds from 5 per cent to 3 per cent; on rough synthetic stones from 12.5 per cent to 5 per cent; and on unworked corals from 30 per cent to 10 per cent.

133. I propose to fully exempt dredgers from import duty.

134. To augment irrigation facilities and processing of agricultural products, I propose to reduce the duty on drip irrigation systems, agricultural sprinklers and food processing machinery from 7.5 per cent to 5 per cent.

135. While specified medical equipment attract a concessional duty of 5 per cent, other equipment are taxed at 12.5 per cent. I propose to bring down the general rate of import duty on medical equipment to 7.5 per cent.

136. In order to make edible oils more affordable, I propose to exempt crude as well as refined edible oils from the additional CV duty of 4 per cent. I also propose to reduce the duty on sunflower oil, both crude and refined, by 15 percentage points.

137. I have good news for cat and dog lovers. I propose to reduce the duty on pet foods from 30 per cent to 20 per cent.

138. I propose to reduce the duty on watch dials and movements as well as umbrella parts from 12.5 per cent to 5 per cent.

139. In order to promote research and development, I propose to extend the concessional rate of 5 per cent duty available to public funded research institutions to all research institutions registered with the Directorate of Scientific and Industrial Research. For the pharmaceutical and biotechnology sector, I propose to reduce the duty on 15 specified machinery from 7.5 per cent to 5 per cent.

140. Import of aircraft, including helicopters, by Government and scheduled airlines is, at present, exempt from all duties, and that position will continue. However, there is no reason to allow the exemption to other private importers. Hence, I propose to levy an import duty of 3 per cent, which is the WTO bound rate, on all private import of aircraft including helicopters. Such import will also attract countervailing duty and additional customs duty.

141. The Hoda Committee has submitted a report on mineral policy. Taking a leaf out of the report, and in order to conserve our natural resources as well as to raise revenue, I propose to impose an export duty of Rs.300 per metric tonne on export of iron ores and concentrates and Rs.2,000 per metric tonne on export of chrome ores and concentrates.

142. I shall now turn to my proposals on excise duties and service tax.

143. There will be no change in the general CENVAT rate or in the service tax rate.

144. On February 15, 2007, Government reduced the price of petrol and diesel by Rs.2 per litre and Re.1 per litre, respectively. I had agreed that the Revenue will bear a part of the burden. Hence, I propose to reduce the ad valorem component of excise duty on petrol and diesel from 8 per cent to 6 per cent.

145. Keeping in mind the special needs of several sectors and the interest of the consumers, I propose to grant relief from excise duty in deserving cases, especially job creating sectors:

? I propose to raise the exemption limit for small scale industry (SSI) from Rs.1 crore to Rs.1.5 crore.

? The food processing sector is poised to achieve high growth. Concessions were extended last year to several items of food. This year, I propose to fully exempt from excise duty biscuits whose retail sale price does not exceed Rs.50 per kilogram. I also propose to fully exempt from excise duty all kinds of food mixes including instant mixes. I can no longer be accused of being partial to idli and dosa mixes.

? I propose to reduce excise duty on umbrellas and parts of footwear from 16 per cent to 8 per cent.

? Plywood helps to save wood. Hence, I propose to reduce excise duty on plywood from 16 per cent to 8 per cent.

? Biodiesel will greatly reduce our dependence on fossil fuels. Hence, I propose to fully exempt biodiesel from excise duty.

146. To provide access to pure drinking water for households and communities, I propose to fully exempt from excise duty water purification devices operating on specified membrane based technologies as well as domestic water filters not using electricity.

147. Pipes used for carrying water from a water supply plant to a storage facility are exempt from excise duty. I propose to extend the exemption to all pipes of diameter exceeding 200 mm used in water supply systems.

148. There has been a significant increase in the retail price of cement. Last year, at this time, a bag of 50 kilogram was sold at a Maximum Retail Price (MRP) of Rs.190 or less which, I understand, is a remunerative price. I propose to reward cement manufacturers who hold the price line and tax those who do not. Accordingly, I propose to reduce the present rate of excise duty of Rs.400 per metric tonne to Rs.350 per metric tonne on cement which is sold in retail at not more than Rs.190 per bag. On cement that has a higher MRP, the excise duty will be Rs.600 per metric tonne.

149. I strongly support the campaign "say no to tobacco". Hence, I propose to increase the specific rates of excise duty on cigarettes by about 5 per cent. Similarly, excise duty (excluding cess) on biris, which was last fixed in 2001, will be raised from Rs.7 to Rs.11 per thousand for non-machine made biris and from Rs.17 to Rs.24 per thousand for machine made biris. There is an exemption from excise duty for un-branded biris up to 20 lakh biris in a year. Complaints have been received of misuse of the exemption. This exemption will henceforth be available subject to fulfilment of the condition of declaration with the Department of Central Excise and regular monitoring.

150. Pan masala containing tobacco will continue to bear an excise duty of 66 per cent. However, in the case of pan masala not containing tobacco, the duty will be

reduced from 66 per cent to 45 per cent. I also propose to withdraw the exemption for pan masala containing tobacco and other tobacco products that is now given to units in the North Eastern States.

151. Based on a comprehensive review of exemptions and having posted them on the website and having invited comments, I propose to remove certain excise duty exemptions which are redundant or have outlived their utility.

152. I propose to raise the exemption limit for small service providers from Rs.400,000 to Rs.800,000. Consequently, 200,000 assessees out of a total of 400,000 assessees will go out of the service tax net. The revenue loss will be Rs.800 crore, but I am happy to give away this sum in the interest of the small service provider and the consumer.

153. While I bid goodbye to 200,000 assessees, I welcome the new assessees who will be brought into the fold. I propose to extend service tax to:

? Services outsourced for mining of mineral, oil or gas;

? Renting of immovable property for use in commerce or business; however, residential properties, vacant land used for agriculture and similar purposes, land for sports, entertainment and parking purposes, and immovable property for educational or religious purposes will be excluded;

? Development and supply of content for use in telecom and advertising purposes;

? Asset management services provided by individuals; and

? Design services.

154. State Governments levy a tax on the transfer of property in goods involved in the execution of a works contract. The value of services in a works contract should attract service tax. Hence, I propose to levy service tax on services involved in the execution of a works contract. However, I also propose an optional composition scheme under which service tax will be levied at only 2 per cent of the total value of the works contract.

155. I propose to exempt service tax on services provided by Resident Welfare Associations to their members who contribute Rs.3000 or less per month for services rendered.

156. In order to encourage innovation, I propose to exempt from service tax all services provided by technology business incubators. Similarly, their incubatees whose annual business turnover does not exceed Rs.50 lakhs will be exempt from service tax for the first three years.

157. To make India a preferred destination for drug testing, I propose to exempt clinical trial of new drugs from service tax.

158. The scope of some services that are currently taxed is being expanded or redefined. However, I shall not burden the House with the details.

159. The telecommunications industry has repeatedly requested that the multifarious taxes, charges and fees applicable to the industry should be unified and a single levy on revenue should be collected. The request merits consideration. Hence, I propose to request the Department of Telecommunications to constitute a committee to study the present structure of levies and make suitable recommendations to Government.

Direct Taxes

160. I shall now move to direct taxes.

161. In the current year, there has been better tax compliance by individuals. I hope this trend will continue.

162. The current slabs and rates of personal income tax (PIT) were introduced only two years ago. They constitute a moderate tax regime. A comprehensive review should await the proposed Income Tax code which will be introduced in Parliament this year. Nevertheless, without altering the rates, I am inclined to consider giving some relief to tax payers, especially in view of the cooperation they have extended to the Department of Revenue. Accordingly, I propose that:

? the threshold limit of exemption in the case of all assessees be increased by Rs.10,000, thus giving every assessee a relief of Rs.1,000;

? consequently, in the case of a woman assessee, the threshold limit be increased from Rs.135,000 to Rs.145,000, giving her a relief of Rs.1,000;

? the threshold limit of exemption in the case of a senior citizen be increased from Rs.185,000 to Rs.195,000, giving him or her a relief of Rs.2,000; and

? the deduction in respect of medical insurance premium under section 80D be increased to a maximum of Rs.15,000 and, in the case of a senior citizen, a maximum of Rs.20,000.

163. On the corporate income tax (CIT) side too, there has been better compliance. Consequently, I propose to keep the same rate of CIT with one important modification. In order to encourage small and medium enterprises to invest and grow, I propose to remove the surcharge on income tax on all firms and companies with a taxable income of Rs.1 crore or less. This will benefit about 1,200,000 firms and

companies.

164. Profit-making cooperative banks, other than primary societies and primary banks (i.e., PACs and PCARDBs), have been brought on par with other banks. However, I have noticed some anomalies and I propose to correct them in the interest of the cooperative banks. Accordingly, the benefit of Section 36(1)(viii) will be available to cooperative banks. Likewise, cooperative banks will also be allowed deduction in respect of provision for bad and doubtful debts under section 36(1)(viia). Amalgamation and de-merger of banking companies is tax neutral and this benefit will be extended to cooperative banks.

165. Section 80IA of the Income Tax Act lists the infrastructure facilities that are entitled to tax concessions. There are some obvious claimants to this benefit. One is cross country natural gas distribution network, including gas pipeline and storage facilities integrated to the network. The second is navigation channel in the sea. I propose to extend the tax concession to these two facilities.

166. In order to facilitate the creation of urban infrastructure, I propose to allow issue of tax-free bonds through State Pooled Finance Entities formed for raising funds for a group of urban local bodies.

167. Last year, I had constituted an expert body to advise the Government on tax policy in respect of the gem and jewellery industry. Taking into account its recommendations, the best international practices and the need for a simple tax regime, I propose to introduce a benign assessment procedure for assessees engaged in diamond manufacturing and trading who declare profits from such activities at 8 per cent or more of the turnover. Instructions in this regard will issue shortly.

168. We will require 20,000 more hotel rooms for the Commonwealth Games. Hence, I propose a five year holiday from income tax for two, three or four star hotels as well as for convention centres with a seating capacity of not less than 3,000. They should be completed and begin operations in the National Capital Territory of Delhi or in the adjacent districts of Faridabad, Gurgaon, Ghaziabad or Gautam Budh Nagar during the period April 1, 2007 to March 31, 2010.

169. Section 35(2AB) allows a weighted deduction of 150 per cent for expenditure relating to in-house research and development. I propose to extend the concession for five more years until March 31, 2012.

170. Undertakings in Jammu & Kashmir presently enjoy a tax holiday that is due to end on March 31, 2007. Considering the importance of promoting further investment in that State, I propose to extend the benefit for another five years up to March 31,2012.

171. E-filing of corporate returns introduced this financial year has been a resounding success. Until January 31, 2007, 301,736 returns were electronically filed by corporates. Our analysis shows that the effective rate of tax paid by all corporates, thanks to numerous tax concessions and exemptions - several of them well-intended - was only 19.2 per cent. In 1996-97, we introduced the Minimum Alternate Tax (MAT) for companies with book profits, and its purpose is to bring about horizontal equity in taxation. MAT should therefore apply, as far as possible, to all corporate incomes. Hence, I propose to extend MAT to income in respect of which deduction is claimed under sections 10A and 10B of the Income Tax Act.

172. I also propose to partially modify a deduction that is available to certain companies. Without altering the overall limit of the special reserve equal to twice the net worth under section 36(1)(viii) of the Income Tax Act, I propose to stretch out the period by restricting the deduction to 20 per cent of the profits each year and limit the benefit to banks and certain financial corporations.

173. Venture capital funds are a useful source of risk capital, especially for start-up ventures in the knowledge-intensive sectors. Since such funds enjoy a pass-through status, it is necessary to limit the tax benefit to investments made in truly deserving sectors. Accordingly, I propose to grant pass-through status to venture capital funds only in respect of investments in venture capital undertakings in biotechnology; information technology relating to hardware and software development; nanotechnology; seed research and development; research and development of new chemical entities in the pharmaceutical sector; dairy industry; poultry industry; and production of bio-fuels. In order to promote business tourism, I also propose to allow this benefit to venture capital funds that invest in hotel-cum-convention centres of a certain description and size.

174. In December 2006, I put a limit of Rs.50 lakh per investor per year with respect to capital gains bonds issued by NHAI and REC under section 54EC of the Income Tax Act. As a result, many small investors could obtain these bonds and save on capital gains. I propose to continue this provision and, accordingly, I propose to amend section 54EC to that effect.

175. I propose to expand the tax base of capital gains to include certain works of art.

176. I believe that my direct tax proposals have brought about more horizontal equity. It is also necessary to improve vertical equity. Having regard to the capacity to pay, I propose to raise the rate of dividend distribution tax from 12.5 per cent to 15 per cent on dividends distributed by companies.

177. Dividends distributed by money market mutual funds and liquid mutual funds enjoy concessional tax rates giving rise to huge arbitrage opportunities. I propose to address this distortion by raising the dividend distribution tax on dividends paid

by such entities to 25 per cent for all investors.

178. Fringe Benefit Tax (FBT) has now stabilized. I have received a few representations regarding some aspects of sales promotion. Hence, I propose to clarify the doubts by excluding expenditure on free samples as well as expenditure on displays from the scope of FBT.

179. A number of companies provide fringe benefits to employees through Employees' Stock Option Plan (ESOP). I propose to bring ESOPs under FBT. The value of the fringe benefit will be determined, in accordance with a prescribed method, on the date of exercise of the option.

180. The Banking Cash Transactions Tax (BCTT) continues to be an extremely useful tool to track unaccounted monies and trace their source and destination. It has led the Income Tax Department to many money laundering and hawala transactions. Having regard to the experience gained, I propose to exclude cash withdrawals by the Central and State Governments from the scope of BCTT. Further, I propose to raise the exemption limit for individuals and HUFs from Rs.25,000 to Rs.50,000. As other instruments become more effective, I think it would be possible to review BCTT next year.

181. I have a proposal regarding the cess for education. While the cess of 2 per cent on all taxes to fund basic education will remain, I propose to levy an additional cess of 1 per cent on all taxes to fund secondary education and higher education and the expansion of capacity by 54 per cent for reservation for socially and educationally backward classes.

182. Finally, there is a small matter which has large beneficial consequences. In 2001, 'Aviation Turbine Fuel sold to turbo-prop aircraft' was included in the list of declared goods under section 14 of the CST Act. Turbo-prop aircraft have been replaced by new generation small aircraft which have taken air services to smaller airports and to the remote parts of the country. Hence, I propose to amend the provision to cover all small aircraft with maximum takeoff mass of less than 40,000 kgs operated by scheduled airlines.

183. Along with tax reforms, the Government has laid great emphasis on tax administration. The cost of collection of taxes in India is among the lowest in the world. A number of administrative goals have been set for 2007-08. These include expanding the coverage of Annual Information Returns, extending the Refund Banker System to more areas, extending the e-payment facility through more banks, making electronic filing of returns mandatory for more categories of assessees and creating new Large Tax Payer Units.

184. My tax proposals on direct taxes are estimated to yield a gain of Rs.3,000 crore.

On the indirect taxes side, the proposals are revenue neutral.

XIV. CONCLUSION

185. Mr. Speaker, Sir, our human and gender development indices are low not because of high growth but because growth is not high enough. Faster economic growth has given us, once again, the opportunity to unfurl the sails and catch the wind. Without growth, I could not have given a new thrust to agriculture. I could not have given relief to the small tax payer, the small service provider and to small scale industry. I could not have promised 100,000 scholarships or 100,000 jobs for the physically challenged. I could not have promised a massive ground water recharge programme or social security for rural landless households.

186. The UPA Government has delivered on the promise of savings and investment, and will deliver on the promise of encouraging more savings and translating the savings into more investment. It has delivered on the promise of growth, and will deliver on the promise of making growth more inclusive. I believe that, given a right mix of policies, the poor will benefit from growth that is driven by savings and investment and that is more inclusive. As Dr. Muhammad Yunus, the Nobel laureate, said, "Faster growth rate is essential for faster reduction in poverty. There is no other trick to it."

187. Sir, with these words, I commend the Budget to the House.

(5)

ENVIRONMENT POLICY 2006

(The National Environment Policy is a response to our national commitment to a clean environment, mandated in the Constitution in Articles 48 A and 51 A (g), strengthened by judicial interpretation of Article 21. It is recognized that maintaining a healthy environment is not the state's responsibility alone, but also that of every citizen. A spirit of partnership should thus be realized throughout the spectrum of environmental management in the country. While the state must galvanize its efforts, there should also be recognition by each individual - natural or institutional, of its responsibility towards maintaining and enhancing the quality of the environment.

The National Environment Policy has been motivated by the above considerations and is intended to mainstream environmental concerns in all development activities. It briefly describes the key environmental challenges currently and prospectively facing the country, the objectives of environment policy, normative principles underlying policy action, strategic themes for intervention, broad indications of the legislative and institutional development , needed to accomplish the strategic themes, and mechanisms for implementation and review. It has been prepared through a process of extensive consultation with experts, as well as diverse stakeholders, and this process is also documented.

The National Environment Policy is intended to be a guide to action: in regulatory reform, programmes and projects for environmental conservation; and review and enactment of legislation, by agencies of the Central, State, and Local Governments.

The policy also seeks to stimulate partnerships of different stakeholders, i.e. public agencies, local communities, academic and scientific institutions, the investment community, and international development partners, in harnessing their respective resources and strengths for environmental management.)

ENVIRONMENT POLICY 2006

1. Environmental Challenges:

Causes and Impacts

The key environmental challenges that the country faces relate to the nexus of environmental degradation with poverty in its many dimensions, and economic growth. These challenges are intrinsically connected with the state of environmental resources, such as land, water, air, and their flora and fauna. The proximate drivers of environmental degradation are population growth, inappropriate technology and consumption choices, and poverty, leading to changes in relations between people and ecosystems, and development activities such as intensive agriculture, polluting industry, and unplanned urbanisation. However, these factors give rise to environmental degradation only through deeper causal linkages, in particular, institutional failures, resulting in lack of clarity or enforcement of rights of access and use of environmental resources, policies which provide disincentives for environmental conservation (and which may have origins in the fiscal regime), market failures (which may be linked to shortcomings in the regulatory regimes), and governance constraints.

Environmental degradation is a major causal factor in enhancing and perpetuating poverty, particularly among the rural poor, when such degradation impacts soil fertility, quantity and quality of water, air quality, forests, wildlife and fisheries. The dependence of the rural poor, in particular,tribal societies, on their natural resources, especially biodiversity, is self-evident. Women in particular face greater adverse impacts of degradation of natural resources, being directly responsible for their collection and use, but rarely for their management. The commitment of time and effort in collection of these resources has a direct impact on the capacity of rural women to devote time to raising and educating children, enhancing their earning skills, or participating in gainful livelihoods.

The poor are also more vulnerable to loss of resilience in ecosystems . Large reductions in resilience maymean that the ecosystems, on which livelihoods are based, break down, causing distress. The loss of the environmental resource base can result in certain groups of people being made destitute, even if overall, the economy shows strong growth. Further, urban environmental degradation, through lack of (or inappropriate) waste treatment and sanitation, industry and transport related pollution, adversely impacts air, water, and soil quality, and differentially impacts the health of the urban poor. This, in turn, affects their capability to seek and retain employment, attend school, and enhances gender inequalities , all of which perpetuate poverty.

Poverty itself can accentuate environmental degradation, given that institutional failures persist. For the poor, several environmental resources are complementary in production and consumption to other commodities (e.g. water in relation to agricultural production, fuel wood in relation to consumption of food), while a number of environmental resources are a source of income or food (e.g. fisheries, non-timber forest produce). This is frequently a source of cumulative causation, where poverty, gender inequalities, and environmental degradation mutually reinforce each other. Poverty and environmental degradation are also reinforced by, and linked to population growth, which in turn, depends on a complex interaction of diverse causal factors and stages of development. The social and economic context of population growth has been detailed in the National Population Policy 2000, which recognizes stabilization of population as a necessary condition for sustainable development.

Economic growth, in its turn, bears a dichotomous relationship to environmental degradation. On the one hand, growth may result in "excessive" environmental degradation through use of natural resources and generation of pollution aggravated by institutional failures. If impacts on the environmental resource base are neglected, an incorrect picture is obtained from conventional monetary estimates of national income. On the other hand, economic growth permits improvement in environmental quality by making available the necessary resources for environmental investments, and generating societal pressures for improved environmental behaviour, and institutional and policy change. Unsustainable consumption patterns, particularly in industrialized countries also have serious adverse impacts on the environment, both local, and global. The global impacts are largely manifest in developing countries, and further accentuate poverty.

It is increasingly evident that poor environmental quality has adversely affected human health. Environmental factors are estimated as being responsible in some cases for nearly 20 percent of the burden of disease in India, and a number of environment-health factors are closely linked with dimensions of poverty (e.g. malnutrition, lack of access to clean energy and water). It has been shown that interventions such as reducing indoor air pollution, protecting sources of safe drinking water, protecting soil from contamination, improved sanitation measures, and better public health governance, offer tremendous opportunities in reducing the incidence of a number of critical health problems. It is also evident that these environmental protection measures would be difficult to accomplish without extensive awareness raising and education, on good practices with respect to public and private behaviour. Institutional failures, referring to unclear or insufficiently enforced rights of access to, and use of, environmental resources, result in environmental degradation because third parties primarily experience impacts of suchdegradation, without cost to the persons responsible for the damage. Such rights, both community based and individual, are critical institutions mediating the relationships between humans and the use of the environment. Traditionally, village commons water sources, grazing grounds, local forests,fisheries, etc., have been protected by local communities from overexploitation through various norms, which may include penalties for disallowed behaviour. These norms, may, however, be degraded through the very process of development, including urbanization, and population growth resulting from sharp reduction in mortality, and also through state actions which may create conditions for the strengthening of individual over communitarian rights, and in doing so allow market forces to press for change that has adverse environmental implications. If such access to the community resources under weakened norms continues, the resources would be degraded, and the livelihoods of the community would suffer.

Policy failures can emerge from various sources, including the use of fiscal instruments, such as explicit and implicit subsidies for the use of various resources, which provide incentives for excessive use of natural resources. Inappropriate policy can also lead to changes in commonly managed systems, with adverse environmental outcomes.

Another major set of challenges arises from emerging global environmental concerns such as climate change, stratospheric ozone depletion, and biodiversity loss. The key is to operationalize the principle of common but differentiated responsibility of countries in relation to these problems. Multilateral regimes and programmes responding to these global environmental issues must not adversely impact the development opportunities of developing countries. Further, the sharing of global natural resources must proceed only on the basis of equal sharing per-capita across all countries.

2. Objectives of the National Environment Policy

The principal Objectives of this policy are enumerated below. These Objectives relate to current perceptions of key environmental challenges. They may, accordingly, evolve over time:

i. Conservation of Critical Environmental Resources:

To protect and conserve critical ecological systems and resources, and invaluable natural and man-made heritage, which are essential for lifesupport, livelihoods, economic growth, and a broad conception of human well-being.

ii. Intra-generational Equity: Livelihood Security for the Poor:

To ensure equitable access to environmental resources and quality for all sections of society, and in particular, to ensure that poor communities, which are most dependent on environmental resources for their livelihoods, are assured secure access to these resources.

iii. Inter-generational Equity:

To ensure judicious use of environmental resources to meet the needs and aspirations of the present and future generations.

iv. Integration of Environmental Concerns in Economic and Social Development:

To integrate environmental concerns into policies, plans, programmes, and projects for economic and social development.

v. Efficiency in Environmental Resource use:

To ensure efficient use of environmental resources in the sense of reduction in their use per unit of economic output, to minimize adverse environmental impacts.

vi. Environmental Governance:

To apply the principles of good governance (transparency, rationality, accountability, reduction in time and costs, participation, and regulatory independence) to the management and regulation of use of environmental resources.

vii. Enhancement of Resources for Environmental Conservation:

To ensure higher resource flows, comprising finance, technology, management skills, traditional knowledge, and social capital, for environmental conservation through mutually beneficial multistakeholder partnerships between local communities, public agencies, the academic and research community, investors, and multilateral and bilateral development partners.

3. Principles

This policy has evolved from the recognition that only such development is sustainable, which respects ecological constraints, and the imperatives of justice. The Objectives stated above are to be realized through various strategic interventions by different public authorities at Central, State, and Local Government levels. They would also be the basis of diverse partnerships. These strategic interventions, besides legislation and the evolution of legal doctrines for realization of the Objectives, may be premised on a set of unambiguously stated Principles depending upon their relevance, feasibility in relation to costs, and technical and administrative aspects of their application. The following Principles, may accordingly, guide the activities of different actors in relation to this policy. Each of these Principles has an established genealogy in policy pronouncements, jurisprudence, international environmental law, orinternational State practice:

i. Human Beings are at the Centre of Sustainable Development Concerns:

Human beings are at the centre of concerns for sustainable development. They are entitled to a healthy and productive life in harmony with nature.

ii. The Right to Development:

The right to development must be fulfilled so as to equitably meet developmental and environmental needs of present and future generations.

iii. Environmental Protection is an Integral part of the Development Process:

In order to achieve sustainable development, environmental protection shall constitute an integral part of the development process and cannot be considered in isolation from it.

iv. The Precautionary Approach:

Where there are credible threats of serious or irreversible damage to key environmental resources, lack of full scientific certainty shall not be used as a reason for postponing cost-effective measures to prevent environmental degradation.

v. Economic Efficiency:

In various public actions for environmental conservation, economic efficiency would be sought to be realized .This Principle requires that the services of environmental resources be given economic value, and such value to count equally with the economic values of other goods and services, in analysis of alternative courses of action. Further implications of this Principle are as follows:

a) Polluter Pays :

Impacts of acts of production and consumption of one party may be visited on third parties who do not have a direct economic nexus with the original act. Such impacts are termed "externalities". If the costs (or benefits) of the externalities are not re-visited on the party responsible for the original act, the resulting level of the entire sequence of production or consumption, and externality, is inefficient. In such a situation, economic efficiency may be restored by making the perpetrator of the externality bear the cost (or benefit) of the same.

The policy will, accordingly, promote the internalization of environmental costs, including through the use of incentives based policy instruments, taking into account the approach that the polluter should, in principle, bear the cost of pollution, with due regard to the public interest, and without distorting international trade and investment.

b) Cost Minimization:

Where the environmental benefits of a course of action cannot, for methodological or conceptual reasons, be imputed economic value (as in the case of "Incomparable Entities" [see below]), in any event the economic costs of realizing the benefits should be minimized.

Efficiency of resource use may also be accomplished by the use of policy instruments that create incentives to minimize wasteful use and consumption of natural resources. The principle of efficiency also applies to issues of environmental governance by streamlining processes and procedures in order to minimize costs and delays.

vi Entities with "Incomparable" Values:

Significant risks to human health, life, and environmental life-support systems, besides certain other unique natural and man-made entities, which may impact the well-being, broadly conceived, of large numbers of persons, may be considered as "Incomparable" in that individuals or societies would not accept these risks for compensation in money or conventional goods and services. A conventional economic cost-benefit calculus would not, accordingly, apply in their case, and such entities would have priority in allocation of societal resources for their conservation without consideration of direct or immediate economic benefit .

vii. Equity:

The cardinal principle of equity or justice requires that human beings cannot be treated differently based on irrelevant differences between them. Equity norms must be distinguished according to context, i.e. "procedural equity", relating to fair rules for allocation of entitlements and obligations, and "end-result equity", relating to fair outcomes in terms of distribution of entitlements and obligations. Each context, in addition, must be distinguished in terms of "intra-generational equity", relating to justice within societies, and in particular, providing space for the participation of the underprivileged, and "inter-generational equity", relating to justice between generations.Equity, in the context of this policy refers to both equity in entitlements to, and participation of, the relevant publics, in processes of decision-making over use of environmental resources.

viii. Legal Liability:

The present environmental redressal mechanism is predominantly based on doctrines of criminal liability, which have not proved sufficiently effective, and need to be supplemented.

Civil liability for environmental damage would deter environmentally harmful actions, and compensate the victims of environmental damage. Conceptually, the principle of legal liability may be viewed as anembodiment in legal doctrine of the "polluter pays" approach, itself deriving from the principle of economic efficiency.The following alternative approaches to civil liability may apply:

a) Fault Based Liability

In a fault based liability regime a party is held liable if it breaches a preexisting legal duty, for example, an environmental standard.

b) Strict Liability

Strict liability imposes an obligation to compensate the victim for harm resulting from actions or failure to take action, which may not necessarily constitute a breach of any law or duty of care .

ix. Public Trust Doctrine:

The State is not an absolute owner, but a trustee of all natural resources, which are by nature meant for public use and enjoyment, subject to reasonable conditions, necessary to protect the legitimate interest of a large number of people, or for matters of strategic national interest.

x. Decentralization:

Decentralization involves ceding or transfer of power from a Central Authority to State and Local Authorities, in order to empower public authorities having jurisdiction at the spatial level at which particular environmental issues are salient, to address these issues.

xi. Integration:

Integration refers to the inclusion of environmental considerations in sectoral policymaking, the integration of the social and natural sciences in environment related policy research, and the strengthening of relevant linkages among various agencies at the Central, State, and Local Self- Government levels, charged with the implementation of environmental policies.

xii. Environmental Standard Setting:

Environmental standards must reflect the economic and social development situation in which they apply. Standards adopted in one society or context may have unacceptable economic and social costs if applied without discrimination in another society or context.

Setting environmental standards would involve several considerations, i.e. risks to human health, risks to other environmental entities, technical feasibility, costs of compliance, and strategic considerations.

xiii. Preventive Action:

It is preferable to prevent environmental damage from occurring in the first place, rather than attempting to restore degraded environmental resources after the fact.

xiv. Environmental Offsetting:

There is a general obligation to protect threatened or endangered species and natural systems that are of special importance to sustaining life, providing livelihoods, or general well-being. If for exceptional reasons of overriding public interest such protection cannot be provided in particular cases, cost-effective offsetting measures must be undertaken by the proponents of the activity, to restore as nearly as may be feasible, the lost environmental services to the same publics.

4. Strategies and Actions

The foregoing statement of policy Objectives and Principles are to be realized by concrete actions in different areas relating to key environmental challenges. A large number of such actions are currently under way, and have been for several years, in some cases, for many decades. In some aspects new themes would need to be pursued to realize the Principles and Objectives. Action plans would need to be prepared on identified themes by the concerned agencies at all levels of Government Central, State/UT, and Local. In particular, the State and Local Governments would be encouraged to formulate their own strategies or action plans consistent with the National Environment Policy. Empowerment of Panchayats and the Urban Local Bodies, particularly, in terms of functions, functionaries, funds, and corresponding capacities, will require greater attention for operationalising some of the major provisions of this policy.

Integration of environmental concerns in all relevant development processes is among the Objectives of this policy. Further, inclusion of environmental considerations in sectoral policy making has also been recognized as among the Principles underpinning the policy. In order to operationalize these, a mechanism for ensuring necessary due diligence at all levels of government, will be institutionalized.

The following Strategic Themes, and outlines of actions to be taken in each, focus on both ongoing activities, functions, and roles, as well as new initiatives that are necessary. However, they are not necessarily a complete enumeration in each case.

5. Regulatory Reforms:

The regulatory regimes for environmental conservation comprise a legislative framework, and a set of regulatory institutions. Inadequacies in each have resulted in accelerated environmental degradation on the one hand, and long delays and high transactions costs in development projects on the other. Apart from legislation which is categorically premised on environmental conservation, a host of sectoral and cross-sectoral laws and policies, including fiscal regimes, also impact environmental quality (some of these are discussed in the succeeding sections).

5.1.1 Revisiting the Policy and LegislativeFramework:

The present legislative framework is broadly contained in the umbrella *Environment Protection Act 1986 Water (Prevention and Control of Pollution) Act, 1974 Water Cess Act, 1977 Air (Prevention and Control of Pollution) Act, 1981 Indian Forest Act, 1927 Forest (Conservation) Act 1980 Wild Life (Protection) Act, 1972 Biodiversity Act, 2002*.. There are several other enactments, which complement the provisions of these basic enactments.

The following specific actions would be taken:

a) Institutionalize a holistic and integrated approach to the management of environmental and natural resources, explicitly identifying and integrating environmental concerns in relevant sectoral and cross-sectoral policies, through review and consultation, in line with the National Environment Policy

b) Identify emerging areas for new legislation, due to better scientific understanding, economic and social development, and development of multilateral environmental regimes, in line with the National Environment Policy.

c) Review the body of existing legislation in order to develop synergies among relevant statutes and regulations,eliminate obsolescence, and amalgamate provisions with similar objectives, in line with the National Environment Policy. Further, encourage and facilitate review of legislation at the level of State and Local Governments with a view to ensuring their consistency with this policy.

d) Take steps to adopt and institutionalize techniques for environmental assessment of sector policies and programmes to address any potential adverse impacts, and enhance potential favourable impacts.

e) Ensure accountability of the concerned levels of Government (Centre, State, Local) in undertaking the necessary legislative changes in a defined time-frame, with due regard to the Objectives and Principles of

National Environment Policy, in particular, ensuring the livelihoods and well-being of the poor by ensuring improved access to the necessary environmental resources.

5.1.2 Process Related Reforms:

(i) Approach:

The recommendations of the *Committee on Reforming Investment Approval and Implementation Procedures* (The Govindarajan Committee) which identified delays in environment and forest clearances as the largest source of delays in development projects, will be followed for reviewing the existing procedures for granting clearances and other approvals under various statutes and rules. These include the *Environment Protection Act,Forest Conservation Act, the Water (Prevention and Control of Pollution)Act, the Air (Prevention and Control of Pollution) Act, the Wildlife (Protection) Act, and Genetic Engineering Approval Committee (GEAC) Rules under the Environment Protection Act.* The objective is to reduce delays and levels of decision-making, realize decentralization of environmental functions, and ensure greater transparency and accountability.

In addition, the following actions will be taken:

a) In order to ensure faster decision making with greater transparency, and access to information, use of information technology based tools will be promoted, together with necessary capacity-building, under all action plans.

b) In order to realize greater decentralization, State level agencies may be given greater responsibility for environmental regulation and management. Such empowerment must, however, be premised on increased transparency, accountability, scientific and managerial capacity, and independence in regulatory decision making and enforcement action. Accordingly, States would be encouraged to set up Environment Protection Authorities on this basis.

c) Mechanisms and processes would be set up to identify entities of "Incomparable Value" in different regions. It would be ensured that all regulatory mechanisms are legally empowered to follow the principles of good Governance.

(ii) Framework for Legal Action:

The present approach to dealing with environmentally unacceptable behaviour in India has been largely based on criminal processes and sanctions. Although criminal sanctions, if successful, may create a deterrent impact, in reality they are rarely fruitful for a number of reasons. On the other hand, giving unfettered powers to enforcement authorities may lead to rent-seeking. Civil law, on the other hand, offers flexibility, and its sanctions can be more effectively tailored to particular situations. The evidentiary burdens of civil proceedings are less daunting than those of criminal law. It also allows for preventive policing through orders and injunctions.

Accordingly, a judicious mix of civil and criminal processes and sanctions will be employed in the legal regime for enforcement, through a review of the existing legislation. Civil liability law, civil sanctions, and processes, would governmost situations of non-compliance. Criminal processes and sanctions would be available for serious, and potentially provable, infringements of environmental law, and their initiation would be vested in responsible authorities. Recourse may also be had to the relevant provisions in the Indian Penal Code, and the Criminal Procedure Code. Both civil and criminal penalties would be graded according to the severity of the infraction.

5.1.3 Substantive Reforms:

(i) Environment and Forests Clearances:

Environmental Impact Assessment (EIA) will continue to be the principal methodology for appraising and reviewing new projects. The assessment processes are under major revision in line with the Govindarajan Committee recommendations. Under the new arrangements, there would be significant devolution of powers to the State/UT level. However, such devolution, to be effective, needs to be accompanied by adequate development of human and institutional capacities.

Further, in order to make the clearance processes more effective, the following actions will be taken: a) Encourage regulatory authorities, Central and State, to institutionalize regional and cumulative environmental impact assessments (R/CEIAs) to ensure that environmental concerns are identified and addressed at the planning stage itself.

b) Specifically assess the potential for chemical accidents of relevant projects as part of the environmental appraisal process

c) Give due consideration, to the quality and productivity of lands which are proposed to be converted for development activities, as part of the environmental clearance process. Projects involving large-scale diversion of prime agricultural land would require environmental appraisal.

d) Encourage clustering of industries and other development activities to facilitate setting up of environmental management infrastructure, as well as monitoring and enforcing environmental compliance. Emphasize postproject monitoring and implementation of environmental management plans through participatory processes, involving adequately empowered relevant levels of government, industry, and the potentially impacted community.

e) Restrict the diversion of dense natural forests and areas of high endemism of genetic resources, to non-forest purposes, only to site-specific cases of vital national interest. No further regularisation of encroachment on forests should be permitted.

f) Ensure that in all cases of diversion of forest, the essential minimum needed for the project or activity is diverted. The diverted area must not be cleared until the actual construction starts.

g) Ensure provision for environmental restoration after decommissioning of industries, in particular mine closure in all approvals of mining plans, and institutionalise a system of post-monitoring of such projects.

h) Formulate, and periodically update, codes of "good practices" for environmental management for different categories of regulated activities.

(ii) Coastal Areas:

Development activities in the coastal areas are regulated by means of the Coastal Regulation Zone notifications and Integrated Coastal Zone Management (ICZM) plans made under them. However, there is need to ensure that the regulations are firmly founded on scientific principles, including the physical, natural, and social sciences. This is necessary to ensure effective protection to valuable coastal environmental resources, without unnecessarily impeding livelihoods, or legitimate coastal economic activity, or settlements, or infrastructure development. Islands offer unique ecosystems and coastal planning and regulation in their case needs to take into account features such as their geological nature, settlement patterns, volcanic or coral nature of the island, size of the habitations, unique cultures, livelihood patterns, etc. Adequate environmental safeguards should be built into development projects in the islands, in particular those relating to tourism, high value agriculture, deep sea fishing, prospecting for oil and natural gas, etc. It is recognized that states will require both technical and financial resources for preparation of ICZM plans.

The following actions will be taken:

a) Revisit the Coastal Regulation Zone (CRZ) notifications to make the approach to coastal environmental regulation more holistic, and thereby ensure protection to coastal ecological systems, coastal waters, and the vulnerability of some coastal areas to extreme natural events and potential sea level rise. The Integrated Coastal Zone Management (ICZM) plans need to be comprehensive, and prepared on strong scientific basis by experts with the participation of the local communities both in formulation and implementation. The ICZM plans should be reviewed at pre-determined intervals to take account of changes in geomorphology, economic activities, settlement patterns, and coastal and marine environmental conditions.

b) Decentralize, to the extent feasible, the clearance of specific projects to State level environmental authorities, exempting activities, which do not cause significant environmental impacts, and are consistent with approved ICZM plans.

(iii) Living Modified Organisms (LMOs):

Biotechnology has immense potential to enhance livelihoods and contribute to the economic development of the country. On the other hand, LMOs may pose significant risks to ecological resources, and perhaps, human and animal health. In order to ensure that development of biotechnology does not lead to unforeseen adverse impacts, the following actions will be taken:

a) Review the regulatory processes for LMOs so that all relevant scientific knowledge is taken into account, and ecological, health, and economic concerns are adequately addressed.

b) Periodically review the National Bio-safety Guidelines, and Bio-safety Operations Manual to ensure that these are based on current scientific knowledge.

c} Ensure the conservation of bio-diversity and human health when dealing with LMOs in transboundary movement in amanner consistent with the multilateral Bio-safety Protocol.

(iv) Environmentally Sensitive Zones:

Environmentally Sensitive Zones may be defined as areas with identified environmental resources having "Incomparable Values" which require special attention for their conservation.

In order to conserve and enhance these resources, without impeding legitimate socio-economic development of these areas, the following actions will be taken:

a) Identify and give legal status to Environmentally Sensitive Zones in the country having environmental entities with "Incomparable values" requiring special conservation efforts.

b) Formulate area development plans for these zones on a scientific basis, with adequate participation by the local communities.

c) Create local institutions with adequate participation for the environmental management of such areas, to ensure adherence to the approved area development plans, which should be prepared in consultation with the local communities.

(v) Monitoring of Compliance:

Weak enforcement of environmental compliance is attributed to inadequate technical capacities, monitoring infrastructure, and trained staff in enforcement institutions. In addition, there is insufficient involvement of the potentially impacted local communities in the monitoring of compliance, and absence of institutionalized public-private partnerships in enhancement of monitoring infrastructure.

The following actions will be taken:

a) Take measures, including capacity development initiatives to enable Panchayati Raj Institutions and urban local bodies to undertake monitoring of compliance with environmental management plans. Measures will also be taken to encourage municipalities to annually report their environmental performance to their governing bodies.

b) Develop feasible models of public-private partnerships to leverage financial, technical, and management resources of the private sector in setting up and operating infrastructure for monitoring of environmental compliance, with ironclad safeguards against possible conflict of interest or collusion with the monitored entities.

(vi) Use of Economic Principles in Environmental Decision-making:

It is necessary that the costs associated with the degradation and depletion of natural resources be incorporated into the decisions of economic actors at various levels, to reverse the tendency to treat these resources as "free goods" and to pass the costs of degradation to other sections of society, or to future generations of the country.

At the macro-level, a system of natural resource accounting is required to assess whether in the course of economic growth we are drawing down, or enhancing, the natural resource base of production, including relevant depletable assets. In addition, the environmental costs and benefits associated with various activities, including sectoral policies, should be evaluated to ensure that these factors are duly taken into account in decision-making.

The current near exclusive reliance on fiats based instruments for environmental regulation do not permit individual actors to minimize their own costs of compliance. This leads, on the one hand, to noncompliance in many cases, and on the other,unnecessary diversion of societal resources from other pressing needs. Economic instruments, of which a large, feasible suite, has emerged through practical experience in several developed and developing countries, work by aligning the interests of economic actors with environmental compliance, primarily through application of "polluter pays". This may ensure that for any given level of environmental quality desired, the society-wide costs of meeting the standard are minimized. However, in some cases, use of economic instruments may require intensive monitoring, which too may entail significant societal costs. On the other hand, use of existing policy instruments, such as the fiscal regime, may significantly reduce or eliminate the need for enhanced institutional capacities to administer the incentive based instruments. In future, accordingly, a judicious mix of incentives and fiats based regulatory instruments would be considered for each specific regulatory situation.

The following actions will be taken:

a) Strengthen, including through capacity building, the initiatives, taken by the Central Statistical Organization in the area of natural resource accounting, with a view to its adoption in the system of national income accounts. Further strengthen in all respects, the system of collection, collation and analysis of all significant and relevant environmental monitoring data.

b) Develop and promote the use of standardized environmental accounting practices and norms in preparation of statutory financial statements for large industrial enterprises, in order to encourage greater environmental responsibility in investment decision-making, management practices, and public scrutiny.

c) Encourage financial institutions to adopt appropriate appraisal practices, so that environmental risks are adequately considered in the financing of projects.

d) Facilitate the integration of environmental values into cost-benefit analysis, to encourage more efficient allocation of resources while making public investment decisions.

e) Prepare and implement an action plan on the use of economic instruments for environmental regulation in specified contexts, including those relating to unsustainable production and consumption.

f) Consider creation of a National Environment Restoration Fund from the net proceeds of economic instruments, user fees for access to specified natural resources, and voluntary contributions. The Fund may be used for restoration of environmental resources, including clean-up of toxic and hazardous waste legacies.

5.2. Enhancing and Conserving Environmental Resources:

Perverse production and consumption practices are the immediate causes of environmental degradation, but an exclusive focus on these aspects alone is insufficient to prevent environmental harm. The causes of degradation of environmental resources lie ultimately in a broad range of policy, and institutional, including regulatory shortcomings, leading to the direct causes. However, the range of policies, and legal and institutional regimes, which impact the proximate factors, is extremely wide, comprising fiscal and pricing regimes, and sectoral and cross-sectoral policies, laws, and institutions. Accordingly, apart from programmatic approaches, review and reform of these regimes to account for their environmental consequences is essential. In addition, there is lack of awareness of the causes and effects of environmental degradation, and how they may be prevented, among both specialized practitioners of the relevant professions, including policymakers, as well as the general public, which needs to be redressed. In this subsection, in respect of major categories of environmental resources, the proximate and deeper causes of their degradation, and specific initiatives for addressing them are outlined.

5.2.1 Land Degradation:

The degradation of land, through soil erosion, alkali-salinization, water logging, pollution, and reduction in organic matter content has several proximate and underlying causes. The proximate causes include loss of forest and tree cover (leading to erosion by surface water run-off and winds), unsustainable grazing, excessive use of irrigation (in many cases without proper drainage, leading to leaching of sodium and potassium salts), improper use of agricultural chemicals (leading to accumulation of toxic chemicals in the soil), diversion of animal wastes for domestic fuel (leading to reduction in soil nitrogen and organic matter), and disposal of industrial and domestic wastes on productive land.

These proximate causes of land degradation in turn, are driven by implicit and explicit subsidies for water, power, fertilizer and pesticides. Grazing lands are usually common property resources, and insufficient empowerment of local institutions for their management leads to overexploitation of the biomass base. The absence of conducive policies and persistence of certain regulatory practices reduces people's incentives for afforestation, and leads to reduced levels of green cover.

It is essential that the relevant fiscal, tariffs, and sectoral policies take explicit account of their unintentional impacts on land degradation, if the fundamental basis of livelihoods for the vast majority of our people is not to be irreparably damaged.

In addition, to such policy review, the following specific initiatives would be taken:

a) Encourage adoption of science-based, and traditional sustainable land use practices, through research and development, extension of knowledge, pilot scale demonstrations, and large scale dissemination, including farmer's training, and where necessary, access to institutional finance.

b) Promote reclamation of wasteland and degraded forestland, through formulation and adoption of multistakeholder partnerships, involving the land owning agency, local communities, and investors.

c) Prepare and implement thematic action plans incorporating watershed management strategies, for arresting and reversing desertification, and expanding green cover.

d) Promote sustainable alternatives to shifting cultivation where it is no longer ecologically viable, ensuring that the culture and social organisation of the local people are not disrupted.

e) Encourage agro-forestry, organic farming, environmentally sustainable cropping patterns, and adoption of efficient irrigation techniques.

5.2.2 Desert Ecosystems:

The arid and semi-arid region of India covers 127.3 mha (38.8%) of India's geographical area and spreads over 10 states. The Indian desert fauna is extremely rich in species diversity of mammals and winter migratory birds. However the pressures of a rapidly increasing population on the natural resource base necessitate adoption of innovative and integrated measures for conservation of desert ecosystems. These pressures are enhanced by practices which lead to land degradation, as described above.

The needed measures include:

a) Intensive water and moisture conservation through practices based on traditional and science based knowledge, and relying on traditional infrastructure.

b) Enhancing and expanding green cover based on local species.

c) Reviewing the agronomic practices in these areas, and promoting agricultural practices and varieties, which arewell adapted to the desert ecosystem.

5.2.3 Forests and Wildlife:

(i) Forests:

Forests provide a multiplicity of environmental services. Foremost among these is the recharging of mountain aquifers, which sustain our rivers. They also conserve the soil, and prevent floods and drought. They provide habitat for wildlife and the ecological conditions for maintenance and natural evolution of genetic diversity of flora and fauna. They are the homes of traditional forest dependent communities. They yield timber, fuel wood, and other forest produce, and possess immense potential for economic benefits, in particular for local communities, from sustainable eco-tourism.

On the other hand, in recent decades, there has been significant loss of forest cover, although there are now clear signs of reversal of this trend. The principal direct cause of forest loss has been the conversion of forests to agriculture, settlements, infrastructure, and industry. In addition, commercial extraction of fuelwood, illegal felling, and grazing of cattle, has degraded forests. These causes, however, have their origins in the fact that the environmental values provided by forests are not realized as direct financial benefits by various parties, at least to the extent of exceeding the monetary incomes from alternative uses, including those arising from illegal use. Moreover, while since antiquity forest dwelling communities had generally recognized traditional community entitlements over the forests, on account of which they had strong incentives to use the forests sustainably and to protect them from encroachers, following the commencement of formal forest laws and institutions in 1865, these entitlements were effectively extinguished in many parts of the country. Such disempowerment has led to the forests becoming open access in nature, leading to their gradual degradation in a classic manifestation of the "*Tragedy of the Commons*". It has also led to perennial conflict between the forest dependent communities and the Forest Department, constituting a major denial of justice. The *Panchayats(Extension to the Scheduled Areas) Act, 1996*; and the relevant provisions of *Part IX of the Constitution* may provide a framework for restoration of the key traditional entitlements.

It is essential that women play a greater role in the management of natural resources. While they have to bear the burden of natural resource degradation, they have little control over the management of these resources. Relevant provisions of the National Policy for the Empowerment of Women provide a framework for incorporating elements of proposed actions.

It is possible that some site-specific non-forest activities may yield overall societal benefits significantly exceeding that from the environmental services provided by the particular tract of forest. However, large scale forest loss would lead to catastrophic, permanent change in the country's ecology, leading to major stress on water resources and soil erosion, with consequent loss of agricultural productivity, industrial potential, living conditions,and the onset of natural disasters, including drought and floods. In any event, the environmental values of converted forests must be restored, as nearly as may be feasible, to the same publics.

The *National Forest Policy, 1988* ; and the *Indian Forest Act, 1927*; as well as the regulations under it, provide a comprehensive basis for forest conservation. The *National Forest Commission* , set up in 2003, is reviewing the policy, legislative and institutional basis of forest management. Nevertheless, it is necessary, looking to some of the underlying causes of forest loss, to take some further steps. These include:

a) Give legal recognition of the traditional entitlements of forest dependant communities taking into consideration the provisions of the *Panchayats (Extension to the Scheduled Areas) Act, 1996* (PESA). This would remedy a serious historical injustice, secure their livelihoods, reduce possibilities of conflict with the Forest Departments, and provide long-termincentives to these communities to conserve the forests.

b) Formulate an innovative strategy for increase of forest and tree cover from the 2003 level of 23.69 percent of the country's land area, to 33 percent in 2012, through afforestation of degraded forest land, wastelands, and tree cover on private or revenue lands. Key elements of the strategy would include: (i) the implementation of multistakeholder partnerships involving the Forest Department, land owning agencies, local communities, and investors, with clearly defined obligations and entitlements for each partner, following good governance principles, to derive environmental, livelihood, and financial benefits; (ii) rationalization of restrictions on cultivation of forest species outside notified forests, to enable farmers to undertake social and farm forestry where their risk-return-termprofiles are more favourable than cropping, (iii) universal adoption of community based practices such as Joint Forest Management, Van Panchayats and their variants, in forest management, with assured participation of women, throughout the country, (iv) focus public investments on enhancing the density of natural forests, mangroves conservation, and universalization of community based practices.

c) Formulate an appropriate methodology for reckoning and restoring the environmental values of forests, which are unavoidably diverted to other uses.

d) Formulate and implement a "Code of Best Management Practices" for dense natural forests, to realize the Objectives and Principles of National Environment Policy. Forests of high indigenous genetic diversity should be treated as entities with Incomparable Value.

e) Denotify Bamboo and similar other species as 'Forest Species' under the *Fores Conservation Act* , to facilitate their cultivation outside notified forests, and encourage their productive utilisation in economic activities.

f) Promote plantation of only such species as are conducive to the conservatior and sustainability of given ecosystems.

(ii) Wildlife:

The status of wildlife in a region is an accurate index of the state of ecologica resources, and thus of the natural resource base of human well-being. This i because of the interdependent nature of ecological entities *("the web of life")*, i which wildlife is a vital link . Moreover, several charismatic species of wildlif embody "Incomparable Values", and at the same time, comprise a major resourc base for sustainable eco-tourism.

Conservation of wildlife, accordingly, involves the protection of entire ecosystems However, in several cases, delineation of and restricting access to such Protecte Areas (PAs), as well as disturbance by humans on these areas has led to man animal conflicts. While physical barriers and better policing may temporarily reduc such conflict, it is also necessary to address their underlying causes. These ma largely arise from the non-involvement of relevant stakeholders in identificatio and delineation of PAs, as well as the loss of traditional entitlements of local peopl especially tribals, over the PAs. There is also a strong need for creation of corrido to ensure proper genetic flows across habitats. Since wildlife does not remai confined to particular areas, there is also need to ensure greater protection, an habitat enhancement outside the PAs.

In respect of **Wildlife Conservation**, the following actions will be pursued:

a) Expand the Protected Area (PA) network of the country, including Conservatic and Community Reserves, to give fair representation to all bio-geographic zones the country. In doing so, develop norms for delineation of PAs in terms of t Objectives and Principles of the National Environment Policy, in particular, partic pation of local communities, concerned public agencies, and other stakeholde who have a direct and tangible stake in protection and conservation of wildlife, harmonize ecological and physical features with needs of socio-economic develo ment.

b) Revisit the norms, criteria and needs of data for placing particular species different schedules of the Wildlife Protection Act.

c) Formulate and implement programs for conservation of endangered species o side protected areas, while reducing the scope for man-animal conflict.

d) Empower, build capacities, and facilitate access to finance and technology, for local people, in particular tribals, who are relocated from PAs, or live in the fringe areas, for provision of ecotourism services in the PAs.

e) Paralleling multistakeholder partnerships for afforestation, formulate and implement similar partnerships for enhancement of wildlife habitat in Conservation Reserves and Community Reserves, to derive both environmental and eco-tourism benefits.

f) Promote site-specific eco-development programmes in fringe areas of PAs, to restore livelihoods and access to forest produce by local communities, owing to access restrictions in PAs.

g) Strengthen capacities and implement measures for captive breeding and release into the wild, identified endangered species.

h) Review and tighten the provisions of relevant legislation to enhance their deterrence. Further, strengthen institutional measures and capacities of enforcement authorities, with respect to intelligence collection, investigation, and prosecution, to deal with wild life crime.

i) Ensure that human activities on the fringe areas of PAs do not degrade the habitat or otherwise significantly disturb wildlife.

5.2.4 Biodiversity, Traditional Knowledge, and Natural Heritage:

Conservation of genetic diversity, is crucial for development of improved crop varieties resistant to particular stresses, new pharma products, etc., apart from ensuring the resilience of ecosystems. Traditional Knowledge (TK), referring to ethno-biology knowledge possessed by local communities, is the basis of their livelihoods, and also a potent means of unlocking the value of genetic diversity through reduction in search costs.

Natural heritage sites, including endemic "biodiversity hotspots", sacred groves and landscapes, are repositories of significant genetic and eco-system diversity, and the latter are also an important basis for eco-tourism. They are nature's laboratories for evolution of wild species in response to change in environmental conditions.

India is fortunate in having, through the efforts of dedicated scientists over many decades, developed vast inventories of floral and faunal resources, as well as ethno-biology knowledge. India is, thus well-placed to tap this enormous resource base for benefits for the country as a whole, and local communities in particular, provided that the genetic resources are conserved, and appropriate Intellectual Property Rights (IPRs) conferred on local communities in respect of their ethno-biology knowledge.

A large-scale exercise has been completed for providing inputs towards a National Biodiversity Strategy and Action Plan. These inputs would be reviewed in terms of the Objectives and Principles of National Environment Policy, scientific validity, financial and administrative feasibility, and legal aspects. In any event, the following measures would be taken:

a) Strengthen the protection of areas of high endemism of genetic resources ("biodiversity hot spots"), while providing alternative livelihoods and access to resources to local communities who may be affected thereby.

b) Pay explicit attention to the potential impacts of development projects on biodiversity resources and natural heritage. In appraisal of such projects by cost-benefit analysis, assign values to biodiversity resources at or near the upper end of the range of uncertainty. In particular, ancient sacred groves and "biodiversity hotspots" should be treated as possessing "Incomparable Values".

c) Enhance conservation of genetic resources in designated gene banks across the country. Genetic

material of threatened species of flora and fauna must be conserved on priority.

d) The Patents Act, 1970 addresses several aspects of the issue of disclosure. The Act mandatorily requires disclosure of source and geographical origin of biological material used in an invention while applying for patents. Failure to disclose and wrongful disclosure are allowed as grounds for opposition to the grant of patent and patent may be revoked on these grounds. The Patent Act also requires the applicant to furnish a declaration with regard to having obtained necessary permission of the competent authority to use the biological material from India. There is need to harmonize these provisions with the Biodiversity Conservation Act, in particular to enable local communities holding traditional knowledge of use of such biological material to benefit from providing access to such knowledge.

e) There is need to formulate an appropriate system for Prior Informed Consent and Fair and Equitable Benefit sharing in respect of biological material and traditional knowledge of use of such biological material to enable the country and local communities respectively to derive economic benefits from providing access. These issues are complex and therefore, modalities for their implementation need to be carefully worked out. Towards this end, attempt would be made to attain greater congruence between these Trade Related Aspects of Intellectual Property Rights.

5.2.5 Freshwater Resources:

India's freshwater resources comprise the single most important class of natural endowments enabling its economy and its human settlement patterns. The fresh-water resources comprise the river systems, groundwater, and wetlands. Each of these has a unique role, and characteristic linkages to other environmental entities.

(i) River Systems:

India's river systems typically originate in its mountain eco-systems, and deliver the major part of their water resources to the populations in the plains. According to the Third Assessment Report of the Intergovernmental Panel on Climate Change (IPCC, 2001) almost 67% of the glaciers in the Himalayan mountain range have retreated in the past decade. Available records suggest that the Gangotri glacier is retreating by about 30 meters per year. Elevated global mean temperature may increase net melting rates resulting in glacial retreat and consequent adverse impact on flows in major rivers.

Rivers are also subject to siltation from sediment loads due to soil loss, itself linked to loss of forest and tree cover. They are also subject to significant net water withdrawals along their course, due to agricultural, industrial, and municipal use; as well as pollution from human and animal waste, agricultural run-offs, and industrial effluents. Although the rivers possess significant natural capacity to assimilate and render harmless many pollutants, the existing pollution inflows in many cases substantially exceed such natural capacities. This fact, together with progressive reductions in stream flows, ensures that the river water quality in the vast majority of cases declines as one goes downstream. The results include loss of aquatic flora and fauna, leading to loss of livelihoods for river fisherfolk, significant impacts on human health from polluted water, increased drudgery for poor, rural women in collecting drinking water from distant water bodies, loss of habitat for many bird species, and loss of inland navigation potential. Apart from these, India's rivers are inextricably linked with the history and religious beliefs of its peoples, and the degradation of important river systems accordingly offends their spiritual, aesthetic, and cultural sensibilities. The direct causes of river degradation are, in turn, linked to several policies and regulatory regimes. These include tariff policies for irrigation systems and industrial use, which, through inadequate costrecovery, provide incentives for overuse near the headworks' of irrigation systems, and drying up of irrigation systems at the tail-ends. This results in excessive cultivation of water intensive crops near the headworks, which may lead to inefficient water use, water logging and soil salinity and alkalinity. The irrigation tariffs also do not yield resources for proper maintenance of irrigation systems, leading to loss in their potential. In particular, resources are generally not available for lining irrigation canals to prevent seepage loss. These factors result in reduced flows in the rivers. Pollution loads are similarly linked to pricing policies leading to inefficient use of agricultural chemicals, and municipal and industrial water use. In particular, revenue yields for the latter two are insufficient to install and maintain sewage and effluent treatment plants, respectively. Pollution regulation for industries is typically not based on formal spatial planning to facilitate clustering of industries to realize scale economies in effluent treatment, resulting in relatively high costs of effluent treatment, and consequent increased incentives for non-compliance. There is, accordingly need to review the relevant pricing policy regimes and regulatory mechanisms, in terms of their likely adverse environmental impacts.

The following comprise elements of an **action plan for river systems**:

a) Promote research in glaciology to evaluate the impacts of climate change on glaciers and river flows.

b) Promote integrated approaches to management of river basins by the concerned river authorities, considering upstream and downstream inflows and withdrawals by season, interface between land and water, pollution loads and natural regeneration capacities, to ensure maintenance of adequate flows, in particular for maintenance of in-stream ecological values, and adherence to water quality standards throughout their course in all seasons.

c) Consider and mitigate the impacts on river and estuarine flora and fauna, and the resulting change in the resource base for livelihoods, of multipurpose river valley projects, power plants, and industries.

d) Consider mandating the installation of water saving closets and taps in the building bye-laws of urban centres, and other available regulatorymechanisms.

e) Integrate conservation and wise use of wetlands into river basin management involving all relevant stakeholders, in particular local communities, to ensure maintenance of hydrological regimes and conservation of biodiversity.

f) Incorporate a special component in afforestation programmes for afforestation on the banks and catchments of rivers and reservoirs to prevent soil erosion and improve green cover.

(ii) Groundwater:

Groundwater is present in underground aquifers in many parts of the country. Aquifers near the surface are subject to annual recharge from precipitation, but the rate of recharge is impacted by human interference. Deep aquifers, on the other hand, occur below a substratum of hard rock. The deep aquifers generally contain very pure water, but since they are recharged only over many millennia, must be conserved for use only in periods of calamitous drought, such as may happen only once in several hundred years. The boundaries of groundwater aquifers do not generally correspond to the spatial jurisdiction of any local public authorities or private holdings, nor are they easily discernable, nor can withdrawals be easily monitored, leading to the unavoidable situation of groundwater being an open access resource.

The water table has been falling rapidly in many areas of the country in recent decades. This is largely due to withdrawal for agricultural, industrial, and urban use, in excess of annual recharge. In urban areas, apart from withdrawals for domestic and industrial use, housing and infrastructure such as roads, prevent sufficient recharge. In addition, some pollution of groundwater occurs due to leaching of stored hazardous waste and use of agricultural chemicals, in particular, pesticides. Contamination of groundwater is also due to geogenic causes, such as leaching of arsenic and fluoride from natural deposits. Since groundwater is frequently a source of drinking water, its pollution and contamination leads to serious health impacts.

The direct causes of groundwater depletion have their origin in the pricing policies for electricity and diesel. In the case of electricity, wherever individual metering is not practiced, a flat charge for electricity connections makes the marginal cost of electricity effectively zero. Subsidies for diesel also reduce the marginal cost of extraction to well below the efficient level. Given the fact that groundwater is an open access resource, the user then "rationally" (i.e. in terms of his individual perspective), extracts groundwater until the marginal value to him equals his now very low marginal cost of extraction. The result is inefficient withdrawals of groundwater by all users, leading to the situation of falling water tables. Support prices for several water intensive crops with implicit price subsidies aggravate this outcome by strengthening incentives to take up these crops rather than less water intensive ones. In coastal areas this overexploitation and inadequate recharge of ground water may also cause serious problem of saline ingress, leading to adverse health impacts and loss of land productivity.

Falling water tables have several perverse social impacts, apart from the likelihood of mining of deep aquifers, "*the drinking water source of last resort*". The capital costs of pump sets and bore wells for groundwater extraction when water tables are very deep may be relatively high, with no assurance that water would actually be found. In such a situation, a user who may be a marginal farmer able to borrow the money only at usurious rates of interest, may, in case water is not found, find it impossible to repay his debts. This may lead to destitution, or worse. Even if the impacts were not so dire, there would be excessive use of electricity and diesel.

The efficient use of groundwater would, accordingly, require that the practice of non-metering of electric supply to farmers be discontinued in their own enlightened self-interest. It would also be essential to progressively ensure that the environmental impacts are taken into account in setting electricity tariffs, and diesel pricing.

Increased run-off of precipitation in urban areas due to impermeable structures and infrastructure prevents natural groundwater recharge. This is an additional cause of falling water tables in urban areas as large quantities of ground water are pumped out for urban use. In rural areas several cost-effective rainwater harvesting and artificial recharge techniques have been proven to enhance groundwater recharge. A number of effective traditional water management techniques to recharge ground-water have been discontinued by the local communities due to the onset of pump sets extraction, and need to be revived. Finally, increase in tree cover, is also effective in enhancing soil moisture retention and preventing soil erosion.

Pollution of groundwater from agricultural chemicals is also linked to their improper use, once again due to pricing policies, especially for chemical pesticides, as well as agronomic practices, which do not take the potential environmental impacts into account. While transiting through soil layers may considerably eliminate organic pollution loads in groundwater, this is not true of several chemical pesticides. The pesticides themselves may become a source of pollution when it leaches into the ground water.

The following actions will be taken:

a) Take explicit account of impacts on groundwater tables of electricity tariffs and pricing of diesel.

b) Promote efficient water use techniques, such as sprinkler or drip irrigation, among farmers. Provide necessary pricing, inputs, and extension support to feasible and remunerative alternative crops which may be raised by efficient water use.

c) Ensure availability of ground water potential maps through a designated institution.

d) Support practices of rain water harvesting and artificial recharge and revival of traditional methods for enhancing groundwater recharge.

e) Mandate water harvesting and artificial recharge in all new constructions in relevant urban areas, as well as design techniques for road surfaces and infrastructure to enhance groundwater recharge. Promote capacity development of relevant stakeholders and provide web based information on water harvesting techniques.

f) Prepare and implement a comprehensive strategy for regulating use of ground water by large industrial and commercial establishments on the basis of a careful evaluation of aquifer capacity and annual recharge.

g) Support R&D in cost effective techniques suitable for rural drinking water projects for remedial measures and removal of arsenic fluoride, and other toxic substances and mainstream their adoption in rural drinking water schemes in relevant areas.

h) Improve productivity per unit of water consumed in industrial processes, by making water assessments and water audits mandatory in identified industries and utilities.

(i) Suitable sites for dumping the toxic waste material may be identified and remedial measures may be taken to prevent the movement of the toxic waste in the ground water.

(j) Excessive use of fertilizers, pesticides and insecticides are the main non point source of the pollution. These pollutants contribute to the pollution of the ground water as well as surface water. The optional utilization of fertilizers, pesticides and insecticides should be encouraged for improving the water quality.

(iii)Wetlands:

Wetlands , natural and manmade, freshwater or brackish, provide numerous ecological services. They provide habitat to aquatic flora and fauna, as well as numerous species of birds, including migratory species. The density of birds, in particular, is an accurate indication of the ecological health of a particular wetland. Several wetlands have sufficiently unique ecological character as to merit international recognition as Ramsar Sites.

Wetlands also provide freshwater for agriculture, animal husbandry, and domestic use, drainage services, and provide livelihoods to fisherfolk. Larger wetlands may also comprise an important resource for sustainable tourism and recreation.

They may be employed as an alternative to power, technology, and capital intensive municipal sewage plants; however, if used for this purpose without proper reckoning of their assimilative capacity, or for dumping of solid and hazardous waste, they may become severely polluted, leading to adverse health impacts. The inadvertent introduction of some alien species of flora in wetlands have also degraded their ecology.

Wetlands are under threat from drainage and conversion for agriculture and human settlements, besides pollution. This happens because public authorities or individuals having jurisdiction over wetlands derive little revenues from them, while the alternative use may result in windfall financial gains to them.However, in many cases, the economic values of wetlands' environmental services may significantly exceed the value from alternative use. On the other hand, the reduction in economic value of their environmental services due to pollution, as well as the health costs of the pollution itself, are not taken into account while using them as a waste dump. There also does not yet exist a formal system of wetland regulation outside the international commitments made in respect of Ramsar sites. A holistic view of wetlands is necessary, which looks at each identified wetland in terms of its causal linkages with other natural entities, human needs, and its own attributes.

The following actions will be taken:

a) Set up a legally enforceable regulatory mechanism for identified valuable wetlands, to prevent their degradation and enhance their conservation. Develop a national inventory of such wetlands.

b) Formulate conservation and prudent use strategies for each significant catalogued wetland, with participation of local communities, and other relevant stakeholders.

c) Formulate and implement eco-tourism strategies for identified wetlands through multistakeholder partnerships involving public agencies, local communities, and investors.

d) Take explicit account of impacts on wetlands of significant development projects during the environmental appraisal of such projects; in particular, the reduction in economic value of wetland environmental services should be explicitly factored into cost-benefit analyses.

e) Consider particular unique wetlands as entities with "Incomparable Values", in developing strategies for their protection.

f) Integrate wetland conservation, including conservation of village ponds and tanks, into sectoral development plans for poverty alleviation and livelihood improvement, and link efforts for conservation and sustainable use of wetlands with the ongoing rural infrastructure development and employment generation programmes. Promote traditional techniques and practices for conserving village ponds.

5.2.6 Mountain Ecosystems:

Mountain ecosystems play a key role in providing forest cover, feeding perennial river systems, conserving genetic diversity, and providing an immense resource base for livelihoods through sustainable tourism. At the same time, they are among the most fragile of ecosystems in terms of susceptibility to anthropogenic shocks. There has been significant adverse impact on mountain ecosystems by way of deforestation, submergence of river valleys, pollution of freshwater sources, despoliation of landscapes, degradation of human habitat, loss of genetic diversity, plantation of species not conducive to conservation of the mountain environment, retreat of glaciers, and pollution. The most significant proximate causes of these are illegal logging and commercial fuel wood collection, besides faulty construction of infrastructure, unplanned urbanization and lack of enforcement of building byelaws, absence or disrepair of sanitation systems, setting up of polluting industries, large scale mining of low unit value minerals, climate change, and excessive use of agricultural chemicals. The underlying causes relate to absence of conducive policies to enable local communities to derive adequate financial returns from afforestation and non-consumptive use of forest resources, pricing policies for agricultural chemicals, inadequate enforcement of pollution standards, poor institutional capacities for urban and regional planning and municipal regulatory functions, and preparation of environmental impact assessments of infrastructure; besides absence of consensus on means of financing municipal infrastructure. Clearly, there is need to address these shortcomings through review of the relevant sectoral and crosssectoral policies, and institutional capacity building.

Additionally, the following elements of an Action Plan will be taken up:

a) Adopt appropriate land use planning and watershed management practices for sustainable development of mountain ecosystems.

b) Adopt "best practice" norms for infrastructure construction in mountain regions to avoid or minimize damage to sensitive ecosystems and despoiling of landscapes.

c) Encourage cultivation of traditional varieties of crops and horticulture by promotion of organic farming, enabling farmers to realize a price premium.

d) Promote sustainable tourism through adoption of "best practice" norms for tourism facilities and access to ecological resources, and multistakeholder partnerships to enable local communities to gain better livelihoods, while leveraging financial, technical, and managerial capacities of investors.

e) Take measures to regulate tourist inflows into mountain regions to ensure that these remain within the carrying capacity of the mountain ecology.

f) Consider particular unique mountain scapes as entities with "Incomparable Values", in developing strategies for their protection.

5.2.7 Coastal Resources:

Coastal environmental resources comprise a diverse set of natural and manmade assets, including mangroves, coral reefs, estuaries, coastal forests, genetic diversity, sand dunes, geomorphologies, sand beaches, land for agriculture and human settlements, coastal infrastructure, and heritage sites. These provide habitats for marine species, which, in turn comprise the resource base for large numbers of fisherfolk, protection from extreme weather events, a resource base for sustainable tourism, and agricultural and urban livelihoods. In recent years there has been significant degradation of coastal resources, for which the proximate causes include poorly planned human settlements, improper location of industries and infrastructure, pollution from industries and settlements, and overexploitation of living natural resources. In the future, sea level rise due to climate change may have major adverse impacts on the coastal environment. The deeper causes of these proximate factors lie in inadequate institutional capacities for, and participation of local communities in, formulation and implementation of coastal management plans, the open access nature of many coastal resources, and lack of consensus on means of provision of sanitation and waste treatment.

The following further actions will be taken up:

a) Mainstream the sustainable management of mangroves into the forestry sector regulatory regime, ensuring that they continue to provide livelihoods to local communities.

b) Disseminate available techniques for regeneration of coral reefs, and support activities based on application of such techniques.

c) Explicitly consider sea-level rise and vulnerability of coastal areas to climate change and geological events, in coastal management plans, as well as infrastructure planning and construction norms.

d) Adopt a comprehensive approach to Integrated Coastal Management by addressing linkages between coastal areas, wetlands, and river systems, in relevant policies, regulation, and programs.

e) Develop a strategy for strengthening regulation, and addressing impacts, of ship-breaking activities on human health, and coastal and near marine resources.

5.2.8 Pollution Abatement:

Pollution is the inevitable generation of waste streams from the production and consumption of anything. Pollution directly impacts the quality of the receiving medium, i.e. air, water, soil, or electromagnetic spectrum, and when this impaired medium acts upon a receptor, say, a living being, also impacts the receptor. In general, the impacts on the receptor are adverse, but not always. Typically, ecosystems have some natural capacities to assimilate pollution; however, these vary considerably with the nature of the pollutant and the ecosystem. In general, it is cheaper to reduce the emissions of pollution, than to mitigate it after generation, or to treat the receiving medium or receptor. The impacts of pollution may differentially impact the poor, or women, or children, or developing regions, who may also have relatively low contributions to its generation, and accordingly the costs and benefits of abatement may have important implications for equity.

(i) Air Pollution:

Air pollution may have adverse impacts on human health, as well the health of other living entities, manmade heritage, and life-support systems, such as global climate. Depending upon the lifetime of the pollutants, the location of the source, and the prevailing air currents, the receptors may be located at homestead, local, regional, or global levels, at time intervals from near instantaneous, to several decades.

The direct causes of air pollution are emissions from the use of fossil energy, and other industrial processes, and some consumption activities. The deeper causes arise in a multiplicity of policy, and institutional, including regulatory shortcomings, in particular, inefficient pricing of fossil fuel based energy. Indoor air pollution, a special case, arises from the low societal status of women, leading to continued use of polluting, inefficient biomass stoves, besides pricing policies for agricultural chemicals which lead to substitution of biomass based fertilizer by chemicals, the biomass then being used inefficiently as fuel. These deeper causes need to be addressed through policies and programmes for redressing women's status, and dialogue aimed at consideration of the environmental impacts of pricing policies for agricultural chemicals.

In addition, the following specific actions will be taken:

a) Take an integrated approach to energy conservation and adoption of renewable energy technologies, including hydropower, by appropriately linking efforts to improve conversion, transmission, distribution, and end-use efficiency, and R&D in, and dissemination of renewable energy technologies. Remove policy, legal, and regulatory barriers to setting up decentralized generation and distribution systems for power and other secondary energy forms, based on local primary energy resources.

b) Accelerate the national programmes of dissemination of improved fuelwood stoves, and solar cookers, suited to local cooking practices and biomass resources.

c) Strengthen the monitoring and enforcement of emission standards for both point and non-point sources.

d) Prepare and implement action plans for major cities for addressing air pollution for both point and non-point sources, relying on a judicious combination of fiats and incentive based instruments.

e) Formulate a national strategy for urban transport to ensure adequate investment, public and private, in low pollution mass transport systems.

f) Promote reclamation of wastelands by energy plantations for rural energy through multistakeholder partnerships involving the land owning agencies, local communities, and investors.

g) Strengthen efforts for partial substitution of fossil fuels by bio-fuels, through promotion of biofuels plantations, promoting relevant research and development, and streamlining regulatory certification of the new technologies.

(ii)Water Pollution:

The direct and indirect causes of pollution of surface (river, wetlands) water sources, groundwater, and coastal areas have been discussed above.

The following comprise further elements of an action plan:

a) Develop and implement, initially on a pilot scale, public-private partnership models for setting up and operating effluent and sewage treatment plants. Once the models are validated, progressively use public resources, including external assistance, to catalyze such partnerships. Enhance the capacities of municipalities for recovery of user charges for water and sewage systems.

b) Prepare and implement action plans for major cities for addressing water pollution, comprising regulatory systems relying on a appropriate combination of fiats and incentive based instruments, projects implemented through public agencies as well as public-private partnerships for treatment, reuse, and recycle where applicable, of sewage and wastewater from municipal and industrial sources, before final discharge to water bodies.

c) Take measures to prevent pollution of water bodies from other sources, especially waste disposal on lands.

d) Enhance capacities for spatial planning among the State and Local Governments, with adequate participation by local communities, to ensure clustering of polluting industries to facilitate setting up of common effluent treatment plants, to be operated on cost recovery basis. Ensure that legal entity status is available for common effluent treatment plants to facilitate investments, and enable enforcement of standards.

e) Promote R&D in development of low cost technologies for sewage treatment at different scales, in particular, replication of the East Kolkata wetlands and other bio-processing based models for sewage treatment, to yield multiple benefits.

f) Take explicit account of groundwater pollution in pricing policies of agricultural inputs, especially pesticides, and dissemination of agronomy practices. Encourage Integrated Pest Management (IPM) and use of biodegradable pesticides.

(iii) Soil Pollution:

Similarly, the immediate and deeper causes of soil pollution have been considered above. Management of industrial and municipal waste is the major cause of soil pollution and is a serious challenge in terms of magnitude and required resources.

An Action Plan will comprise:

a) Develop and implement viable models of public-private partnerships for setting up and operating secure landfills, incinerators, and other appropriate techniques for the treatment and disposal of toxic and hazardous waste, both industrial and biomedical, on payment by users, taking the concerns of local communities into account. The concerned local communities and State Governments must have clear entitlements to specified benefits from hosting such sites, if access is given to non-local users. Develop and implement strategies for clean up of toxic and hazardous waste dump legacies, in particular in industrial areas, and abandoned mines, and reclamation of such lands for future, sustainable use.

b) Survey and develop a national inventory of toxic and hazardous waste dumps, and an online monitoring system for movement of hazardous wastes. Strengthen capacities of institutions responsible for monitoring and enforcement in respect of toxic and hazardous wastes.

c) Strengthen the legal arrangements and response measures for addressing emergencies arising out of transportation, handling, and disposal of hazardous wastes, as part of the chemical accidents regime.

d) Strengthen the capacities of local bodies for segregation, recycling, and reuse of municipal solid wastes- recognizing inter-alia the positive impacts it may have on the welfare of safai-karamcharis, and setting up and operating sanitary landfills, in particular through competitive outsourcing of solid waste management services.

e) Give legal recognition to, and strengthen the informal sector systems of collection and recycling of various materials. In particular enhance their access to institutional finance and relevant technologies.

f) Promote organic farming of traditional crop varieties through research in and dissemination of techniques for reclamation of land with prior exposure to agricultural chemicals, facilitating marketing of organic produce in India and abroad, including by development of transparent, voluntary, science-based labelling schemes.

g) Promote biodegradable and recyclable substitutes for non-biodegradable materials, and develop and implement strategies for their recycle, reuse, and final environmentally benign disposal, including through promotion of relevant technologies, and use of incentive based instruments.

h) Develop and enforce regulations and guidelines for management of e-waste, as part of the hazardous waste regime.

i) Promote, through incentives, removal of barriers, and regulation, the beneficial utilisation of generally nonhazardous waste streams such as fly ash, bottom ash, red mud, and slag, including in cement and brick making, and building railway and highway embankments.

(iv) Noise Pollution:

Persistent exposure to elevated noise levels has been established to result in significant adverse health impacts. While in many instances, the identification of a particular sound as "noise" is unambiguous, in the case of others, such as "music" or "chanting" or "fireworks displays", it is inherently subjective. In all such cases, societal well-being would require that exposure levels to third parties be maintained below levels at which significant adverse health impacts may occur. At the same time, it needs to be understood that certain environments in which people choose to live and work necessarily involve a certain level of noise.

The following will comprise elements of an Action Plan on abatement of noise pollution:

a) Make appropriate distinctions between different environments in terms of setting ambient noise standards, e.g. rural versus urban; educational and medical establishments versus other areas, night-time versus daytime in residential areas, areas in the vicinity of road, rail, airport infrastructure, and protected areas, etc.

b) Distinguish between noise standards in the context of occupational exposure (with protection measures), and environmental exposure to third parties.

c) Formulate noise emissions norms (e.g. loudspeaker, automobile horns, fireworks ratings) appropriate to various activities to ensure that exposure levels to third parties who are not participants in the activity do not exceed prescribed ambient standards.

d) Include ambient noise as among the environmental quality parameters to be routinely monitored in specified urban areas.

e) Encourage dialogue between State/Local Authorities and religious/community representatives on the adoption of enforceable durations, timings, and use of loudspeakers/fireworks, etc, in case temporary exceedance of prescribed ambient noise standards for observance of traditional religious/cultural/social events cannot be avoided.

5.2.9 Conservation of Manmade Heritage:

Manmade heritage reflects the prehistory, history, ways of living, and culture, of a people. In the case of India, such heritage is at the core of our national identity. At the same time, considerable economic value, and livelihoods may be derived from conservation of manmade heritage and their sustainable use, through realization of their tourism potential.

The criteria for, and processes of identification of heritage sites, besides legislation and fiscal measures to ensure that they are not damaged or converted by direct human interference, are outside the scope of the National Environment Policy. However, the impact of environmental quality on their conservation is an environmental policy concern. Heritage sites may be impacted by pollution, or they may face threats of inundation or conversion by development projects. Several prominent heritage sites may be held to possess "IncomparableValues".

The following action points will be pursued:

a) In setting ambient environmental standards, especially for air quality, the potential impacts on designated heritage sites must be taken into account.

b) Heritage sites considered to have "Incomparable Values" would merit stricter standards than otherwise comparable situations, and particular attention should be paid to monitoring and enforcement of environmental standards in their case. Integrated regional development plans should be drawn up, with participation of the local community, to shift polluting activities or render them much less polluting, to treat waste streams, to review transportation options, and adopt building norms which maintain the overall heritage ambience of the area.

c) Impacts on designated heritage sites must be considered at the stage of developing the terms of reference for environmental impact assessments of projects, and consideration given to the potential impacts during appraisal, in terms of the Objectives and Principles of the National Environment Policy.

5.2.10 Climate Change:

Climate change, resulting from anthropogenic emissions of a suite of gases (called "greenhouse gases" or GHGs) due to fossil fuel use, certain agricultural and industrial activities, and deforestation, leading to their increasing concentrations in the atmosphere, has the potential, over the next few generations, to significantly alter global climate. This would result in large changes in ecosystems, leading to possibly catastrophic disruptions of livelihoods, economic activity, living conditions, and human health. On the other hand, abatement of GHGs,would involve significant economic costs.

While climate change is a global environmental issue, different countries bear different levels of responsibility for increase in atmospheric GHGs concentrations. Further, the adverse impacts of climate change will fall disproportionately on those who have the least responsibility for causing the problem, in particular, developing countries, including India.

India's GHG emissions in 1994 were 1228 million ton (Mt) CO equivalent, which is below 3% of global GHG emissions. In per-capita terms, it is 23 per cent of the global average, and 4 per cent of USA, 8 per cent of Germany, 9 per cent of UK, and 10 per cent of Japan, per capita emissions in 1994. In terms of the GHG intensity of the economy, in Purchasing Power Parity terms, India emitted a little above 0.4 ton CO equivalent per 1000 US dollars in 2002, which is lower than the global average. In terms of primary energy use, India's share of renewable energy (being a nonGHG emitting energy form) at 36 per cent is far higher than industrialized countries can hope to reach in many decades. Since GHG emissions are directly linked to economic activity, India's economic growth will necessarily involve increase in GHG emissions from the current extremely low levels. Any constraints on the emissions of GHG by India, whether direct, by way of emissions targets, or indirect, will reduce growth rates.

On the other hand, India's policies for sustainable development, by way of promotion of energy efficiency, appropriate mix of fuels and primary energy sources including nuclear, hydro and renewable sources, energy pricing, pollution abatement, afforestation, mass transport, besides differentially higher growth rates of less energy intensive services sectors as compared to manufacturing, results in a relatively GHGs benign growth path.

Anthropogenic climate change, significant responsibility for which clearly does not lie with India or other developing countries, may, on the other hand, have likely adverse impacts on India's precipitation patterns, ecosystems, agricultural potential, forests, water resources, coastal and marine resources, besides increase in range of several disease vectors. Large-scale resources would clearly be required for adaptation measures for climate change impacts, if catastrophic human misery is to be avoided. Accordingly, the following will comprise essential elements of India's response to climate change:

a) Adherence to the principle of common but differentiated responsibilities and respective capabilities of different countries in respect of both mitigation of GHGs, and adaptation measures.

b) Reliance on multilateral approaches, as opposed to bilateral or plurilateral or unilateral measures.

c) Equal per-capita entitlements of global environmental resources to all countries.

d) Over-riding priority of the right to development.

e) Identify key vulnerabilities of India to climate change, in particular impacts on water resources, forests, coastal areas, agriculture, and health.

f) Assess the need for adaptation to future climate change, and the scope for incorporating these in relevant programmes, including watershed management, coastal zone planning and regulation, forestry management, agricultural technologies and practices, and health programmes.

g) Encourage Indian Industry to participate in the Clean Development Mechanism (CDM) through capacity building for identifying and preparing CDM projects, including in the financial sector.

h) Participate in voluntary partnerships with other countries both developed and developing, to address the challenges of sustainable development and climate change, consistent with the provisions of the UN Framework Convention on Climate Change.

5.3 Environmental Standards,Management Systems, Certification, and Indicators:

5.3.1 Environmental Standards:

Environmental Standards refer both to the acceptable levels of specified environmental quality parameters at different categories of locations ("ambient standards"), aswell as permissible levels of discharges of specified waste streams by different classes of activities ("emission standards").

It is now well understood that environmental standards cannot be universal, and each country should set standards in terms of its national priorities, policy objectives, and resources. These standards, may, of course, vary (in general, become more stringent) as a country develops, and has greater access to technologies and financial resources for environmental management. While within the country different states, UTs and local bodies may adopt stricter standards, based on local considerations, they would require concurrence of the Central Government to ensure adherence to the provisions of this policy. Environmental standards also need to relate to other measures for risk mitigation in the country, so that a given societal commitment of resources for achieving overall risk reduction yields the maximum aggregate reduction in risk.

Specific considerations for setting ambient standards in each category of location (residential, industrial, environmentally sensitive zones, etc.) include the reductions in potential aggregate health risks (morbidity and mortality combined in a single measure) to the exposed population; the risk to sensitive, valuable ecosystems and manmade assets; and the likely societal costs, of achieving the proposed ambient standard.

Similarly, emissions standards for each class of activity need to be set on the basis of general availability of the required technologies, the feasibility of achieving the applicable environmental quality standards at the location (specific or category) concerned with the proposed emissions standards, and the likely unit costs of meeting the proposed standard. It is also important that the standard is specified in terms of quantities of pollutants that may be emitted, and not only by concentration levels, since the latter can often be easily met through dilution, with no actual improvement in ambient quality. The tendency to prescribe specific abatement technologies should also be eschewed, since these may unnecessarily increase the unit and societal costs of achieving the ambient environmental quality, and in any case because a technology that is considered ideal for meeting a given emission standard may not be acceptable on other relevant parameters, including possibly other sources of societal risk.

The following specific actions will be taken:

a) Set up a permanent machinery comprising experts in all relevant disciplines to review notified ambient and emissions standards in the light of new scientific and technological information as they become available, and changing national circumstances, ensuring adequate participation by potentially impacted communities, and industry associations.

b) Strengthen the testing infrastructure and network for monitoring ambient environmental quality, including through participation by local communities, and public-private partnerships. Progressively ensure real-time, and on-line availability of the monitoring data.

5.3.2 Environmental Management Systems, Ecolabeling and Certification

Environmental Management Systems (EMS), such as ISO 14000, by requiring the adoption of standardized environmental management practices, documenting their actual use, and credible third party verification of the fact, may significantly ease the public burden of monitoring and enforcement of prescribed emissions standards. On the other hand, their adoption may involve transaction costs, which, for small and medium enterprises may be significant in relation to their total investment. Global harmonization of EMS , however, is a safeguard against adoption of arbitrary national EMS regimes to serve as non-tariff barriers.

Ecolabeling (and other voluntary certification mechanisms) differ from the EMS in that they address the preferences of environmentally conscious consumers, rather than ensuring adherence to national environmental standards. They may involve review of the entire product cycle, from sourcing raw materials, to final disposal of the product after use, and since they are concerned primarily with consumer preferences, may relate to external or ad-hoc, rather than national environmental standards. Further, at present, nonpublic bodies have established several labeling schemes in India's export destinations, with no satisfactory evidence of being based on scientific knowledge, or participation by the potentially affected producers. Moreover, they may be based on prescriptions of production processes, and not only of the product characteristics, and for this reason, their mandatory application is inconsistent with provisions of theWTO regime.

Ecolabels, etc., clearly have the potential to be employed as trade barriers, at least by competing firms in the export destinations, if not directly by their Governments. The obtaining of an ecolabel, especially one granted by an agency located in a developed country, may involve large transactions costs. However, ecolabeled products may command significant price premia, as well as ease of entry to markets. On the other hand, the fact of a large, rapidly growing, environmentally conscious consumer base in India itself, may provide the required leverage to realize significant advantages from mutual recognition of ecolabeling schemes.

The following actions will be taken:

a) Encourage industry associations to promote the adoption of ISO 14000 among their members, through provision of technical and training support. Mainstream promotion of ISO 14000 in the small-scale sector in the various promotion schemes for the sector.

b) Encourage adoption of EMS through purchase preference for ISO 14000 goods and services for Government procurement, except for items reserved for the small-scale sector at any given time. Mandate ISO 14000 when a sufficient number of domestic suppliers for each good or service have ISO 14000 certification.

c) Formulate "Good Practice Guidelines" for ecolabels to enhance their scientific basis, transparency, and requirements of participation. Promote the mutual recognition of Indian and foreign ecolabels, which adhere to the Good Practice Guidelines, to ensure that Indian exporters enhance their market access at lower costs.

d) Promote "good practices" norms in all relevant sectors to conserve natural resources and reduce adverse environmental impacts, covering siting, choice of materials, use of appropriate energy efficiency and renewable energy options, and addressing solid wastes generation, effluents and sewage handling, gaseous emissions, and noise.

5.4 Clean Technologies and Innovation:

Clean technologies, as distinct from "end-of-pipe" abatement technologies minimize the generation of waste streams in the production processes and utilize waste from other consumption goods and production processes, rather than treating the waste after generation. In general, clean technologies are less intensive in use of raw materials and energy, than conventional technologies, which rely on pollution abatement after generation. For this reason, they may also offer significant cost advantages to the producer.

Barriers to the adoption of clean technologies are, first, the fact that many of them are proprietary, and protected by strong patent regimes held abroad. The vendors, accordingly, would be able to extract large premiums in the absence of competitive substitutes. In such cases a project specific approach will be adopted in respect of enhancing market access. Second, lack of capacity in development financial institutions for appraisal of proposals for switching existing production facilities to clean technologies. Third, the lack of coordination in R&D efforts in India aimed at developing a shelf of commercially viable clean technologies. The last should also be viewed against the fact that in future, almost all commercial transfers of production technology worldwide may be for clean technologies.

The following will comprise elements of an Action Plan:

a) Encourage capacity building in the financial sector for appraising clean technology switchover project proposals.

b) Set up a mechanism to network technology research institutions in the country, public and private, for cooperation in technology research and development and adaptation, information, and evaluation of clean technologies. Create a database of such technologies, and promote dissemination of new technologies developed both in India and abroad.

c) Consider use of revenue enhancing fiscal instruments to promote shifts to clean technologies in both existing and new units.

d) Promote adoption of clean technologies by industry, in particular in the small and medium sector, through regulatory and fiscal measures, and standards setting.

5.5 Environmental Awareness, Education,

and Information:

Enhancing environmental awareness is essential to harmonize patterns of individual behaviour with the requirements of environmental conservation. This would minimize the demands placed on the monitoring and enforcement regimes; in fact, largescale non-compliance would simply overwhelm any feasible regulatory machinery. Awareness relates to the general public, as well as specific sections, e.g.the youth, adolescents, urban dwellers, industrial and construction workers, municipal and other public employees, etc. Awareness involves not only internalization of environmentally responsible behaviour, but also enhanced understanding of the impacts of irresponsible actions, including to public health, living conditions, sanitation, and livelihood prospects.

Environmental education is the principal means of enhancing such awareness, both among the public at large, and among focused groups. Such education may be formal, or informal, or a combination of both. It may rely on educational institutions at different levels; the print, electronic, or live media; and various other formal and informal settings. Several steps to expand and enrich the content of the environment awareness and education programmes have been taken. The Supreme Court has also mandated that environmental education must be imparted at all levels, including higher education in the formal system. However, there is need for further strengthening the existing programmes and making them more inclusive and participatory.

Access to environmental information is the principal means by which environmentally conscious stakeholders may evaluate compliance by the concerned parties with environmental standards, legal requirements, and covenants. They would thereby be enabled to stimulate necessary enforcement actions, and through censure, motivate compliance. Access to information is also necessary to ensure effective, informed participation by potentially impacted publics in various consultation processes, such as for preparation of environmental impact assessments, and environment management plans of development projects.

The National Natural Resources Management System (NNRMS) was set up in 1983 for optimally managing the natural resources and environment of the country using an optimal mix of remote sensing and conventional techniques. Remote Sensing and data, both satellite and aerial, is being used extensively in the country for mapping and managing the natural resources and environment, over the past three decades.

The following actions will be taken:

a) Develop and operate an online, real time, publicly accessible environmental information system to provide all relevant information on key environmental resources and parameters, including ambient quality, aswell as major point sources of pollution, and make archival data available in convenient format.

b) Further promote the use of Remote Sensing data to provide valuable inputs on the extent and quality of forests, wildlife habitats, biodiversity, wastelands, wetlands, groundwater, deserts, rivers, etc., and monitor pollution and its impacts.

c) Mainstream scientifically valid environment content in the curricula of formal education, at primary, secondary, tertiary, and professional levels, focusing on the content appropriate at each stage, and without increasing the course load overall, besides non-formal programmes, such as adult education. Special midcareer training programmes may be conducted for groups with special responsibilities, e.g. the judiciary, policy makers, legislators, industrial managers, city and regional planners, and voluntary and community based organizations.

d) Prepare and implement a strategy for enhancing environmental awareness among the general public, and special groups, by professional production and airing of information products through diverse media catering to the different target groups. The media products should, as far as possible, eschew focusing on the achievements of public agencies, but instead document real world events of human interest. The production, as well as dissemination may involve public, private, and voluntary agencies. Ensure that adequate financial resources are available for the purpose.

5.6 Partnerships and Stakeholder Involvement:

Conservation of the environment requires the participation of multiple stakeholders, who may bring to bear their respective resources, competencies, and perspectives, so that the outcomes of partnerships are superior to those of each acting alone. Implementing and policy making agencies of the Government, at Central, State, Municipal, and Panchayat levels; the legislatures and judiciary; the public and private corporate sectors; financial institutions; industry associations; academic and research institutions; independent professionals and experts; the media; youth clubs; community based organizations; voluntary organizations; and multilateral and bilateral development partners, may each play important roles in partnerships for the formulation, implementation, and promotion of measures for environmental conservation.

Institutions of local self-government have an important role in management of the environment and natural resources. The 73 and 74 Constitutional amendments provide the framework for their empowerment. Further policy and legislative changes are necessary to enable them to actually realize such a role, and participate in various partnerships in this context.

A number of specific themes for partnerships have been identified above. A generic classification of some, not exhaustive, possible partnerships is as follows:

a) Public-Community Partnerships, by which public agencies and local communities cooperate in the management of a given environmental resource, each partner bringing agreed resources, assuming specified responsibilities, and with defined entitlements, e.g. Joint Forestry Management.

b) Public-Private Partnerships, by which specified public functions with respect to environmental management are contracted out competitively to private providers, e.g. monitoring of environmental quality.

c) Public-Community-Private Partnerships, in terms of which the partners assume joint responsibility for a particular environmental function, with defined obligations and entitlements for each, with competitive selection of the private sector partner, e.g. afforestation of degraded forests.

d) Public-Voluntary Organization Partnerships, similar to public-private partnerships, in respect of functions in which voluntary organizations may have a comparative advantage over others, the voluntary organizations, in turn, being selected competitively, e.g. environmental awareness raising.

e) Public-Private-Voluntary Organization Partnerships, in which the provision of specified public responsibilities is accomplished on competitive basis by the private sector, and the provision is monitored by competitively selected voluntary organizations, e.g. "Build, Own, Operate" sewage and effluent treatment plants.

f) It is also essential that all partnerships are realized through, and are carried out in terms of the principles of good governance, in particular, transparency, accountability, cost effectiveness, and efficiency.

g) Youth constitute the most vibrant segment of the country's population. Their strength needs to be harnessed and channelised in protection and conservation of environment. They also need to be involved in relevant stakeholder participation.

5.7 Capacity Building:

The multi-stakeholder character of environmental issues and continuous developments in the field of environment, make it necessary to have a continuing focus on capacity building in all concerned institutions: public, private, voluntary, academic, research, and the media.

The following actions are necessary:

a) Review the present institutional capacities at the Central and State levels, in respect of enforcement of environmental laws and regulations. Prepare and implement suitable programs for enhancement of the capacities, as required.

b) Incorporate in all environmental programmes a capacity development component, with sufficient earmarked funds.

c) Ensure continuous upgradation of knowledge and skills of the scientific and technical personnel involved in environmental management in public institutions at all levels: Central, State, and Local, through dedicated capacity building programs.

5.8 Research and Development:

In order to rapidly advance scientific understanding of environmental issues, it is necessary to promote properly focussed research by competent institutions. A continuous engagement with the scientific community, in government, academic, and private institutions, will provide important insights for policy making and regulation, including in the field of multilateral negotiations, and help realize deeper and broader skills in the scientific community.

Key areas of research are as follows (not in order of priority, which is changeable over time):

.Taxonomies of living natural resources.

.Research leading to better understanding of ecological processes and pathways.

.Research which provides direct inputs to policy making.

.R&Din technologies for environmental management and clean production.

The following actions would be taken:

a) Periodically identify and prioritize areas for research.

b) Establish a research programme in priority areas within the Government, with expected outputs clearly specified.

c) Encourage research in priority areas outside theGovernment,with necessary financial and institutional support.

5.9 International Cooperation:

India has participated in major international events on the environment, since 1972. The country has contributed to, and ratified several key multilateral agreements on environmental issues in recognition of the transboundary nature of several environmental problems, and has complied with its commitments. It has also participated in numerous regional and bilateral programs for environmental cooperation. Given the need to enhance our own capacities to comply with our commitments, and ensure sustained flows of resources for environmental management, the following steps would be taken:

a) Avail of multilateral and bilateral cooperation programs, for capacity building for environmental management, particularly in relation to commitments under multilateral instruments.

b) Participate in mechanisms and arrangements under multilateral agreements for enhancing flows of resources for sustainable development.

c) Provide assistance to other developing countries, in particular for scientific and technical capacity building for environmental management.

5.10 Review of the Policy:

We live in a rapidly changing global community, in a rapidly developing, highly diverse country. The environmental issues that are salient as of now may evolve over time, and new ones may take their place. Scientific understanding of environmental matters would advance rapidly. Changes in economic structure, technologies, resource availability, in each case nationally as well as globally, are likely, as are evolution of global environmental regimes, and norms arising from jurisprudence.

To set forth an immutable National Environment Policy in this dynamic situation would be unwise. A prudent course would be to provide for updating every few years in light of new knowledge and developments, and a comprehensive review in about a decade.

The following provisions are, accordingly made for **review, updating, and renewal of theNational Environment Policy:**

a) Undertake consultations every three years with groups of diverse stakeholders, i.e. researchers and experts, community based organizations, industry associations, and voluntary organizations, and update the National Environment Policy.

b) In the third of the three-year reviews, undertake a more comprehensive examination of the scientific and policy understanding of environmental issues, redefine the Objectives and Principles, and recast the Strategic Themes for Action. A new National Environment Policy should be the outcome.

5.11 Review of Implementation:

Any policy is only as good as its implementation. The National Environment Policy outlines a significant number of new and continuing initiatives for enhancing environmental conservation. These require the coordinated actions of diverse actors, for the major part organized and stimulated by one or more public agencies.

While coordination and review mechanisms are necessary in respect of the individual action plans under each of the strategic themes at relevant operational levels, a formal, periodic high level review of implementation of the different elements of the National Environment Policy is essential. This would enhance accountability of the different public agencies responsible for implementation. It would also reveal practical issues in implementation, including absence of political will at concerned levels, or official indifference.

Accordingly, the Cabinet or a nominated Committee of the Cabinet may be requested to review the implementation of the National Environment Policy, once a year, within three months from the close of the previous fiscal year. The findings of the review should be publicly disclosed, so that stakeholders are assured of the seriousness of the Government in ensuring implementation of the Policy.